Who Is John Galt?

A Navigational Guide to Ayn Rand's *Atlas Shrugged*

by
Timothy Curry
Anthony Trifiletti

For Jim Robinson

Foreword

This book began as a discussion thread on the website freerepublic.com, during which it quickly became apparent that a formal consideration of the merits of the novel had become subordinated to contemporary politics, and that its readers had split into two camps: those for whom its literary sins provided an easy excuse for avoiding serious consideration of its underlying philosophy, and those True Believers whose emotional connections with that philosophy conferred an overly forgiving approach toward its literary sins.

The authors attempt to forge a middle ground that is surprisingly little occupied at the present time. We would like to thank the patient readers of that thread for their forbearance, and specifically thank contributors Stephen Darrow and John Jordan, whose criticisms of the authors' approach have made their way into the present volume.

There will be the inevitable misapprehensions and outright mistakes, for which the authors take full responsibility. The principal failing of contemporary literary criticism is that it arrogates to itself an Olympian view that is immune from the inadequacies of the creative work under consideration. The authors make no claim to that arid ground. If in fact we draw down the outraged curses of both camps on our heads, we will consider our work happily done.

Timothy Curry and Anthony Trifiletti

Table of Contents   Page

Introduction

Ayn Rand's 1957 classic, *Atlas Shrugged*, has suddenly been thrust into the public eye by events eerily similar to those chronicled within its 1100 pages. It is, by most literary standards, a unique piece – a broad, sweeping narrative of the breaking of the country's industrial sinews overlaid on a body of radical individualist philosophy unprecedented in its time and scarcely matched since. It is an angry book, lashing out against the oppression of a class that most of its author's contemporaries were reluctant to consider oppressed at all. It is a cry against sexual repression, against the oppression of women, against the stifling of entrepreneurial and pioneering spirit, against the slow smothering of every achievement its author believed made her adopted country great.

As such it deserves the place in the modern literary canon that recent reconsideration is belatedly conferring upon it. The reasons for the delay may be summed up in a single phrase: the novel is, by most cultural standards before it and since, astonishingly politically incorrect.

Any novel of this size and written with the intent to overthrow conventional thought in philosophy, morality and culture must inevitably contain flaws. Whether those flaws invalidate the overall message will be the topic under consideration in the following pages.

The Strange World of *Atlas Shrugged*

Rand's book was written between 1945 and 1956 and published in 1957. During the postwar years, America saw massive changes in society and technology, and the shape of world politics underwent a major sea change. For the purposes of fiction the real-world narrative was frozen somewhere before the Second World War, and Rand allowed it to grow in a different direction, isolating the real-world political continuum to the confines of a

1

single country, the United States. This fictional America was intended to resemble the real one enough to contain a warning of what might yet be. In brief, it contained the following:

- There was no Cold War. Nation after nation accepted some form of socialism without argument and took the title of *"People's State"*. America drifted more slowly into socialism, and the book can be viewed as the story of how a group of brave entrepreneurs fought the final plunge into the abyss.

- America was frozen in time with respect to culture and technology. Television did not replace radio as an influential popular medium. Live classical music was still played on network radio.

- The Interstate Highway System, proposed by Eisenhower in 1956, was never built. In the book, America was connected by a network of decaying two-lane roads and a network of vital railways.

- Commercial air travel did not come to fruition. There is a hint that airlines were operating their own separate airports just as railroads operated their own separate stations before the concept of "union stations" came along in the Twenties. An executive who needed to fly elsewhere got a pilot's license and flew his own private plane.

- Railroads were still the primary form of transportation, and passenger rail was thriving. The conversion from steam to diesel locomotives, a major event in railroading in the Fifties in our time line, went much more slowly in the book. Coal and even wood fired steam locomotives still plied the rails. Radio was not used in communication, instead relying on the older technology of telegraphs and phone boxes.

- Outside the cities, it was difficult to find a place to make a long distance telephone call.

- American heavy industry did not flee the country to escape high labor costs because the rest of the world had preceded it into communism.

- Good industrialists branded their companies with their own names, such as Wyatt Oil, Rearden Steel, d'Anconia Copper and Mulligan Bank. Bad industrialists hid behind corporate names such as Associated Steel.

- Congress was now called the National Legislature, and the President was now called the Head of State. The Takings Clause of the Fifth Amendment was even less operative than in our own time. The Constitution is scarcely mentioned in the novel, and its provisions that we still take for granted had apparently been discarded. All real power was vested in bureaucrats.

- The can-do spirit of America was being deliberately and systematically crushed. The ubiquitous cry of frustration was, *"Who is John Galt?"* To nearly everyone using it, it was a nonsense question with no answer, an acceptance of futility.

How might this scenario might have resulted from what Rand saw before her in 1945 makes for interesting speculation. Here is one possible alternate timeline:

The Alternate History of *Atlas Shrugged*

One might start with the four way election of 1948. In this alternate universe, Henry Wallace won the race, defeating Truman, Dewey and Thurmond, and established a Labor government on the British model in America. The warning voices of Martin Dies, John Bricker, Joseph McCarthy and Richard Nixon were stilled.

3

Wallace wanted no cold war with the Soviets, and with the quick withdrawal of American forces from Europe, Germany was reunified under a communist People's State government. The Soviet Union, now the People's State of Russia, never geared up for war, settling instead for passive mediocrity. Britain never rejected Clement Atlee, and with the abolition of the monarchy and the establishment of a written constitution on the German model, the People's State of England replaced the United Kingdom. In France, De Gaulle never came to power, and the Fourth Republic morphed into the People's State of France.

In the Western Hemisphere, figures similar to Fidel Castro established the People's State of Mexico and other communist countries in Central and South America.

America did not go all the way to People's State status, however, although intellectuals worked hard toward that end, their final efforts comprising the bulk of *Atlas Shrugged*. Americans accepted that things were hopeless and that nothing could be done, settling into a gray, decaying society that dimmed slowly, irresistibly, until at last it went dark altogether. Feelings replaced facts. The very nature of reality was questioned. Rand describes the decade of economic stasis, misguided politics and cultural pollution that served the final descent into hell.

Reading This Book

Rand divided *Atlas Shrugged* into three sections with ten chapters each. Each of these chapters will be examined through a synopsis, identification of certain key issues within, one or more explanatory essays to give the proper background for those issues, and questions to stimulate debate. The authors offer no firm conclusions on any of these issues – that would be entirely contrary to the spirit of the novel and an insult to the intellect of the serious student. One must, as Rand would insist, check one's own premises.

Read on.

Part I: Non-Contradiction

Chapter I: The Theme

Synopsis

"Who is John Galt?" The words come from the mouth of a bum to Eddie Willers, as he walks down the streets of a decaying New York, gold leaf peeling from exteriors that are no longer maintained. Something has left the city that Eddie misses: its pride.

Eddie enters the office of Jim Taggart, president of the Taggart Transcontinental Railroad *("From ocean to ocean!")* to inform him that there has been another wreck on the Rio Norte Line. The track is shot, and he points out that Orren Boyle of Associated Steel has failed to deliver rail for the past thirteen months. Jim forbids Eddie to approach Boyle's competitor Rearden Steel. Taggart's own competitor, the Phoenix-Durango Railroad, is threatening to take over Taggart's exclusive relationship with Wyatt Oil, an enterprising new firm that has brought the Colorado oil fields back to life. Jim complains that all Ellis Wyatt cares about is money, and that his growing oil business has *"...dislocated the economy of the entire country..."*

"How can we have any security or plan anything if everything changes all the time?"

As Eddie leaves Jim's office, he notes that Pop Harper's typewriter is broken and has not been fixed. Pop won't requisition a new typewriter because the new ones are all substandard, and he recites a litany of bankruptcies and mechanical failures in New York. The city's inhabitants, as well as its maintenance crews, have lost their pride.

We first meet Dagny Taggart in the coach section of the *Taggart Comet*. Dagny hears a brakeman whistling a tune that she recognizes immediately as something by the composer Richard Halley, but a piece she hasn't heard before. The brakeman mentions that it's Halley Fifth Concerto. Dagny, who is a passionate Halley fan, informs him that Halley has only written *four* concertos. But it certainly sounds like Halley.

After dozing restlessly, Dagny awakes to discover that the train has been shunted onto a siding at a red block signal for about an hour. The *Comet* has never been late before, but the crew doesn't care so much about that as it does avoiding blame, and they want to wait for somebody else to take responsibility for the decision that will resolve the situation. They will not move until Dagny, their Vice President of Operations, takes personal responsibility.

Arriving in New York, Dagny, with Eddie in attendance, tells Jim that she has ordered rail from Rearden, not Boyle, to rebuild the Rio Norte Line. Jim is furious but will not take responsibility for canceling the Rearden order. He whines that it's unfair to give all of the railroad's business to Rearden just because he produces on schedule. He is horrified when Dagny tells him that the order is not for conventional steel but for a new material called "Rearden Metal" that nobody has ever used before. She then further infuriates her brother by informing him that his pet project, the San Sebastian Line, is to be nationalized shortly by People's State of Mexico.

Dagny interviews a vigorous and effective subordinate named Owen Kellogg in order to give him the top spot at the Ohio Division, replacing an incompetent who is a personal friend of Jim's. But Kellogg won't take the job, resigns from Taggart Transcontinental, and leaves Dagny with the apparently aimless phrase, *"Who is John Galt?"*

The Villainy of James Taggart

James Taggart is the most finely drawn of Rand's villains, all of whom seem to have leapt from the pages of recent newspapers. These are precise and devastating character studies, eclipsing those of her heroes with only two exceptions: Dagny herself and the steel magnate Hank Rearden, whom we are soon to meet. In Rearden she captures the conflict that will occur in real people if Atlas does shrug, the factors that urge him to continue a futile effort in pursuit of the dreams of excellence, and the ones that will, at the last, challenge his very beliefs in the system that he is maintaining.

6

But James Taggart is very special – first chapter to last, the reader always knows exactly what motivates him and wonders how such an individual could possibly manage to keep the fingers of those closest to him from his throat. Rand shows us that he is the sort that thrives in that pathological environment, and why. He's infuriating, despicable – and delicious.

He is not alone. Typical of Rand, these characters drip banality and evil years before Hannah Arendt joined those words in her essay about Adolf Eichmann. More will join their ranks in future chapters.

Indifference and Responsibility

Early in the novel Rand describes a working population paralyzed both by its members fearing to take responsibility for their actions and by the indifference that results. It is a combination familiar to employees of many contemporary corporations, one consequence of the dictum that risk is something to be managed, to be evaluated on a cost/benefit basis by persons paid to do so. That is management's job. The reason initiative occasionally tends to be discouraged is that it has a cost when the inherent risk doesn't work out. A poorly managed corporation cannot afford to absorb that cost, discourages risk, and kills initiative.

In the case of Taggart Transcontinental, one has to sympathize a little with the listless employees. They'll be paid anyway, so why take the risk? Out of pride? Pride is a commodity that is becoming scarce. Dagny's own pride in it is at least in part because her name is on it. It will become clear that other Taggart employees share this pride, but that poor management is slowly killing it.

Jim's poor management, surely, is the main factor. But Dagny's astonishment at the stoppage of the *Comet* does not reflect well on her own management abilities. She is, after all, Taggart's Vice President of Operations, and if her employees' deteriorating morale is news to her, why? If her employees are risk-averse and intimidated, what has she done about it? It is not a comfortable question, and Rand does not examine it in any great detail.

New York and the Railroads

New York was a railroader's nightmare in the 19th Century because the Hudson River was an insurmountable barrier. Approaching from the west, railroads terminated at Jersey City or Hoboken, and each railroad operated its own private navy to get people across the Hudson to downtown Manhattan. Only the New York Central and its partners had direct access to New York into midtown's Grand Central Depot, a wooden structure built in 1871 and rebuilt as Grand Central Station in 1900.

After the Civil War, the Pennsylvania Railroad made two attempts to bridge the Hudson, one killed by the Army Corps of Engineers and the other by its exorbitant cost. A tunnel project was deemed impossible using the technology available at the time.

In 1899, Pennsylvania Railroad president Alexander Cassatt visited Paris to see his sister, the famous impressionist artist Mary Cassatt, and while there he dropped by the newly opened Gare du Quai Dorsai. This station had been built for electric railroading with an approach via a tunnel under the Seine. Cassatt saw the solution to his Hudson River problem.

In 1906, Cassatt announced that the Pennsylvania Railroad would build two tubes suspended in the Hudson River silt. These tunnels would carry electric trains powered by third rail direct current, which would run from a location in the New Jersey meadowlands, Manhattan Transfer, into the new Pennsylvania Station in midtown Manhattan. This station would be designed by the architectural firm of McKim, Mead and White and be modeled on the Basilica of Constantine and the Baths of Caracalla in Rome, creating a true temple of the American railroad. This architectural monument opened in 1910 and was one of America's great railroad stations until its demolition in 1963.

Upset by the presence of a greater temple of railroading, the New York Central built a new station to replace the 1900 structure. Atop two levels of underground tracks would stand the New York Central's temple of railroading, Grand Central Terminal, which opened in 1913.

In Rand's novel there is only one great railroad station in New York, Taggart Terminal, which has characteristics of both Pennsylvania and Grand Central.

America and the Railroads

Today there are seven Class I railroads in North America, all of which were created by a series of mergers and acquisitions spanning nearly 150 years; only one is transcontinental. At the time of Rand's book there were a vast number of Class I railroads, but none were transcontinental.

In *Atlas Shrugged*, there are two transcontinental railroads: Taggart Transcontinental dominates the northern half of the US and Atlantic Southern dominates the south.

Railroad baron Nat Taggart founded his railroad in the 19th Century, and it was transcontinental in scope from the very beginning, not achieving that status by a process of slow merger and acquisition. This is a serious departure from actual railroad history. Taggart did not rely on Lincoln's government land grants for financing but did it the hard way, which makes his model the real life James Jerome Hill, the man who built the Great Northern. Like Hill, Taggart worked his way from the bottom in railroading and was not a financial operator.

Dagny Taggart and Richard Halley

In the book, there is no indication that Dagny Taggart had ever taken music lessons or that her interest in classical music extended beyond contemporary composer Richard Halley. Yet a brakeman on a train whistles a melody, and Dagny immediately recognizes it not only as Halley, but *unpublished* Halley. Is this possible?

Classical musicians and people who are heavily involved in classical music occasionally amuse themselves by "dittersdorfing", where they hear a piece with which they are unfamiliar and guess the composer from their knowledge of the classical repertoire. It is named after Karl von Dittersdorf, a contemporary of Franz Joseph Haydn, whose music sounds a lot like Haydn, but lacks Haydn's facility with musical architecture.

Possible, yes. A stretch, certainly. Later in the novel we will find Dagny displaying several unlikely talents including aeronautics and marksmanship; she is, after all, Rand's ideal woman, and even her appearance, dwelt on frequently and possibly an idealized version of Rand herself, displays the perfection found seldom outside the boundaries of fiction.

Discussion Topics

- Eddie Willers remembers a tree at the Taggart estate that had been struck by lightning, revealing a hollow core destroyed by dry rot. He connects this with the unrepaired spire, the brake failure in the New York subway and Doc's typewriter. But what about moral rot? What behavior in this chapter, and by whom, exemplifies moral failure?

- Jim Taggart obsesses about stability, planning and maintaining an atmosphere of stasis. Change is to be avoided, even if it improves conditions. What parallels can be drawn to current events?

- Jim believes that priority of corporate effort should be determined by need, putting emphasis on helping the disadvantaged people of Mexico. Is there an echo of this in American foreign policy today? If so, where?

- What is disturbing about the Mayor of New York, not the owner of the building, wanting the current date displayed on a large calendar mounted on a skyscraper? What are the implications of this?

Chapter II: The Chain

Synopsis

Hank Rearden watches the first heat of steel for Rearden Metal poured at his mill. It is an epochal moment for him, the consummation of a lifetime's effort of labor and invention. He walks home, fingering a chain of Rearden Metal in his pocket.

At home he is greeted by his mother, his wife Lillian, his brother Philip and his friend Paul Larkin. The group makes fun of the fact that his mind is back at the steel mill and complains that all he cares about is money. Hank tries to tell them about the big event at the mill, but they neither understand what it means to him nor do they care. He gives Lillian the chain, a bracelet, which is the very first thing made from Rearden Metal. She accepts it as a mother might accept the drawing of a kindergartener.

Larkin takes Hank aside and tells him what a fine product he has but hints that there might be trouble brewing. Hank has a bad press, is only interested in his steel and mills, and doesn't care about public opinion. Larkin hints that there may be a problem with Hank's lobbyist in Washington but doesn't go into detail.

Philip Rearden says he is spending his time raising money for the Friends of Global Progress, and he complains that rich people – meaning his brother Hank – have no social conscience. Hank tells Philip to go down to the mill tomorrow and pick up a check for ten thousand dollars. He doesn't care about the press and is only giving the money to Philip to make him happy. Philip says that he has no selfish interest in the money – but that he wants the money in cash so that Hank Rearden's tainted name cannot be attached to it.

Larkin tells Hank that he shouldn't have given the money to Philip, and Lillian sees the act as a display of Hank's vanity, not an act of charity. She likens the bracelet of Rearden Metal to a chain of bondage.

The Bracelet

It is, of course, a chain, and as a symbol of bondage it cuts two ways: first, the bondage of the individual wearing it to Rearden, and second, the reverse of the same, the bonds of his own feelings for family, however unmerited by any real return of love.

But we are a little impatient with Lillian's failure to understand at least the outward significance of the gift – it's a bracelet. What else would one expect him to make for his wife of a small batch of prototypical metal that is, after all, his life's work? At what point does her insistence on thinking of it purely as a symbol of bondage make her appreciation of the other nuances impossible?

It is in this clash of the symbols of the bracelet that we most clearly see the divergence in the values of the persons involved. To Lillian the thing is coarse, unattractive, and quite impossible to match within a modern wardrobe. To Hank it's the achievement of a lifetime. It must be profoundly lonely not to have those whom one loves understand one's greatest achievement. They are too unlike Hank for that. Someone more like him will understand, will appreciate, will acknowledge, should Hank ever meet him – or her. And that's going to present a problem for those who don't.

Philip Rearden's Sense of Entitlement

Something makes Philip Rearden feel entitled to the fruits of his brother's labor, and this turns into one of the overarching themes of *Atlas Shrugged*. It is simply this: what Philip feels is a sense of moral superiority – and intellectual superiority as well. All this stems from the idea that those in the room have succeeded in making a living off Rearden by doing things Hank could not or did not: marketing, on the more innocent hand, and bribery and corruption, on the less innocent. Even an upright man like Rearden has his still unnamed agent in Washington. And those activities really are necessary. It is the necessity of those activities that Rand regards as corruption, and the wealth that results from them derivative and invalid. Rand will insist that Rearden's family and people like them have no right to this wealth because they had no role in its creation; Rearden's relatives, on the other hand, consider that they have a right to wealth because they have fulfilled the functions necessary to extract it from a corrupt system. Whether that is so or not, they have certainly extracted it from Rearden himself.

His family's sense of superiority is that felt by a thief toward his victims. They are rule-setters, keepers of the terms under which Rearden is permitted to engage in his creative activity. But their power to do so depends on their victim's acceptance of it, his sanction. Rand will develop the significance of that sanction as the novel proceeds, and when, at last, he accedes no longer, Atlas will shrug.

Discussion Topics

- It's Rearden Steel, Rearden Metal, Rearden Ore, Rearden Coal and Rearden Limestone. Like all the heroic characters in the book, Hank Rearden puts his brand on everything that matters. Even Lillian Rearden makes it plain that she is Rearden's Wife. Lillian's remark about the bracelet being a chain, the symbol of the family's bondage to Hank, is rather egregious. Is this just another case of familiarity breeding contempt, or is there something more pernicious at work?

- A professor of economics: *"Of what importance is an individual in the titanic collective achievements of our industrial age?"* A journalist sitting next to him: *"Hank Rearden is the kind of man who sticks his name on everything he touches. You may from this, form your own opinion of Hank Rearden."* What is the difference between what those critics evidently mean and the impression we are beginning to form of Hank Rearden?

Chapter III: The Top and the Bottom

Synopsis

The bar is the most expensive in New York. Located on the 60th floor of a skyscraper, it looks like a cellar, even forcing its patrons to stoop to get across the room. Orren Boyle of Associated Steel, James Taggart, Paul Larkin and Wesley Mouch, now identified as Hank Rearden's lobbyist, meet to discuss the order of Rearden Metal from the railroad.

Boyle explains to Jim that the delay in supplying steel is due to his inability to obtain iron ore, thanks to played out mines, worn out equipment and general transportation problems. He wants others to help shoulder his burdens. He believes that Rearden Metal is dangerous because of its lightness; the National Council of Metal Industries has created a commission to study it.

Boyle continues that while monopolies are bad, so is unbridled, destructive competition. Rearden's ability and success are destroying everyone else in the steel business; therefore, there should be a national industrial policy aimed at giving everybody a fair shot at the iron ore that Rearden seems to obtain so easily and that Boyle cannot. And he wants Taggart's help in Washington.

Jim wants something for himself, similar to Boyle's own demand, and anti-competitive in nature. Newcomers are squeezing his old, established lines. Boyle bargains – he agrees that his friends at the National Alliance of Railroads might weigh in on this in Jim's favor.

Larkin, who apparently has some pull in Washington, is uncomfortable about betraying his friend Hank Rearden, but he will, and so will the man Rearden has employed to protect his interests there, Wesley Mouch. The deals are sealed.

Boyle says he has visited the San Sebastian mines in the People's State of Mexico, the last piece of private property left in that benighted country. Taggart asks about the rumors of imminent nationalization, and Boyle labels them as malicious slander.

We learn, in a flashback, the relationship between Dagny and Jim and their friendship with Francisco d'Anconia. And as we have already seen, Dagny runs the railroad while Jim works Washington for favors and influence. Jim had built the line to Francisco's mines at San Sebastian. The line had never shown a profit; the overt rationale for building the line was to help the people of Mexico, the ulterior one currying favor with the communist government which they believed was the wave of the future.

This misallocation of resources is causing the more important Rio Norte Line to crumble, prompting Ellis Wyatt to move his oil by the competing Phoenix-Durango Railroad.

The San Sebastian Line isn't producing because the mines aren't producing, but Francisco had explained that his mines were still in development. Dagny knows that Francisco has become utterly worthless over the past decade, but she does not understand why; Jim still believes he can deliver. Dagny has been putting the worst assets of the railroad into service in Mexico because she believes the line is about to be nationalized, and Jim, outraged, orders her to run better service in Mexico. She calls his bluff, demanding that he allocate their resources if he thinks she is doing so inappropriately. Jim buckles, and Dagny continues to do precisely as she pleases.

Eddie Willers dines in the corporate cafeteria with an old friend we shall name the Anonymous Rail Worker. He tells the Worker that the Rio Norte Line is the last hope for Taggart Transcontinental. There have been more accidents on the system; diesel locomotives are being lost, and United Locomotive Works is two years behind schedule in delivering new equipment. McNamara of Cleveland will lay the new rail on the Rio Norte Line once Rearden delivers. Eddie also tells the Worker of Dagny's love for the music of Richard Halley.

The Amazing Wesley Mouch

We meet at last Rearden's man in Washington. Wesley Mouch is another of Rand's finely-drawn villains, Rearden's turncoat lobbyist who, as we shall see, hopes to leverage the betrayal of that trust into greater things. It is evident that Mouch produces nothing of his own but is adept at peddling influence.

15

That is currency in this new society, that is power, and Mouch intends to ride it as far as it will take him. That may be farther than we think.

Fairness and Its Ambiguities

This chapter brings us to a recurrent topic in *Atlas Shrugged*, that of "fairness" and how that ambiguous word is used to cover a grand rhetorical confidence game. One hears it from the mouths of both sides, the bad guys somewhat more often than the good, but what they mean by it are two very different things. Just as no two cultures agree on the definition of the term "justice", they don't agree on "fair" either. The novel is, on multiple levels, the story of the clash of two cultures on a moral basis.

In the mouths of Rand's protagonists the term "fair" might be considered interchangeable with "merited" or "earned"; that is, one's desserts being a function of one's actions. In the mouths of such as Jim Taggart, it represents an equitable division of material possessions regardless of one's actions: meritless. Rand considers the latter immoral.

This is the fundamental philosophical conflict between the two sides. The notion that material possessions are somehow evenly distributed "naturally" is central to such systems as Marxism, that state of nature existing nowhere other than the theoretician's fantasy. It is a premise central to collectivist approaches at building a society, and its corollaries are: (1) that inequities of such distribution are undesirable and constitute theft by the individual from the collective, and (2) that it is the proper function of authority to remediate them.

This sort of "fairness" is a perfect metaphor for the socialist view of private property in general, to be held in the name of the collective and doled out to its individual members as deemed desirable by those entrusted to lead – the cadre, the ruling class. "Fair" here is to be taken however that authority chooses to define it. It never turns out to be particularly equitable, as commentators from George Orwell to Milovan Djilas have shown, and they've shown why. Those calling most for this sort of "fairness" tend not to be the disadvantaged, but the advantaged, and the reason isn't

16

that they want more material possessions themselves, but that they want the power to distribute them. That sort of "fairness" is always arbitrary, and the power of arbitration is the power to rule.

Contrasted to this is Rand's view that "fairness" in the distribution of material goods is a function of creative activity and that those who manage it by jobbing the system are the thieves – "moochers and looters," as she puts it. It is easy to envisage Mouch and James Taggart as moochers – Mouch's name even resembles it – useless parasites on a system that heretofore could muster the surplus necessary to support them. The death of the host is in the interest of no competent parasite.

But competent these parasites are not. To Rand they truly are looters, and the death of the host is inconsequential to these parasites so long as the system may be maintained, because there will always be other hosts. It is the system, and not the looters themselves, that the host Atlas must shrug from his shoulders.

The roots of economic value within this system are the creative activity of such individuals as Dagny and Hank Rearden, the likes of Jim Taggart adding little value to the product but a great deal of cost.

That is invalid in Rand's capitalistic framework – at first glance this resembles the Labor Theory of Value of Ricardo and Marx, although Marx insisted it was a definition, not a theory, and refused to debate it as the latter. But even under the strict *laissez-faire* capitalism that is the root of Rand's system, a commodity is worth what it takes to acquire it and nothing more. There is, in fact, room for mooching and looting there, which is probably why all economic systems tend to display them. It is unclear that they necessarily would be absent from the post-Shrug world.

Substitute the phrase "social justice" for "fairness" and we may read precisely this case in our own newspapers. Inequities in the distribution of material goods are presented as the results of systemic theft, "institutional racism," and a host of other neologisms, and it is the putative responsibility of authority to remediate them. Authority, in the form of the State, merely *distributes*, a position of considerable advantage to those holding its reins, but is incapable of the actual production of wealth. Those who do produce, own, but ownership is declared injustice in the face of others who do not own because they do not produce. The next step, to the idea that the product of a few is rightfully the property of all, is a very small one.

Railroads and Government Transportation Policy

From the earliest days of railroading, government at all levels was involved. States would grant corporate charters to one group to build a railroad in order to prevent another group favored by competing interests from building a different railroad. Favoritism and influence peddling were part of the game from the very beginning. Abraham Lincoln, a railroad lawyer by trade, gave away vast tracts of the American West to railroads to raise the capital necessary to build across the continent and link the country together. This was a product of grand vision – and even grander influence peddling.

Because railroads are so capital-intensive, most rail entrepreneurs were financiers first, people who built rail lines with equal parts blarney and other people's money. It was a rare man, like the real life James Hill and the fictional Nat Taggart, who did it the hard way, raising money outside of Wall Street. Most rail entrepreneurs had some facet of government policy on their side.

One of the possible sources of *Atlas Shrugged* was a 1922 novel by Garet Garrett titled *The Driver*, a novel whose hero's name, Henry Galt, appears in a recurring question, "Who is Henry Galt?" The similarity to Rand's signature question is obvious, as is the fact that he is a financier deeply involved in the ownership of a railroad. The likeness between the two novels ends at that point, but it is revealing that Henry Galt's principal challenge was precisely this toxic amalgam of government finance and private entrepreneurialism that constituted the life stories of such real-world tycoons as Jim Hill and Edward Harriman.

Rand's image of the lone entrepreneur building a railroad is both noble and rare, but it does exist. Government was always a key player, now friend, and as we shall see, occasionally foe.

Discussion Topics

- Orren Boyle started his company with $100 thousand of his own money – plus a $200 million government loan. Contrast this with how Hank Rearden started and what that implies, both in terms of personal character and government policy.

- *"The only justification of private property is public service."* This sounds rather inflammatory coming from Orren Boyle, but it is very close to a quote from Theodore Roosevelt in his 1912 presidential campaign on the Progressive ("Bull Moose") ticket. On occasion TR would work himself into a state of high dudgeon and say things he regretted in more sober moments, but this statement was never retracted by the former president. Its roots are in the proto-anarchist Pierre-Joseph Proudhon ("Property is theft") by way of Karl Marx. Explore this statement and what it implies, not only on the part of the speaker, but the listeners at the meeting.

- Shortages have become so endemic that there is now a stark choice between running the Rio Norte Line and running the San Sebastian Line. This implies major failures, not just in the supply chain, but in the financial system itself. What may have happened before the book opened to create this problem?

- The most expensive bar in New York is on the upper floor of a skyscraper and is designed to look like a cellar, not taking advantage of the view from its height. Discuss the multiple symbolisms in this peculiar décor.

Chapter IV: The Immovable Movers

Synopsis

Dagny needs locomotives and she can't get them. She fails to get a straight answer from the president of the United Locomotive Works as to when she will get her diesel engines and what is the source of the delay. He regards the very questions as impolite. Upon returning to the office, Eddie Willers tells her that her preferred rail construction firm, McNamara of Cleveland, has gone out of business, and owner Dick McNamara has mysteriously disappeared.

Dagny walks home through the streets of New York, and along the way she encounters symptoms of decadence that are signs of the times: a shop where a radio speaker is broadcasting a classical music concert with a piece that is both atonal and pointless, a book store whose best seller is a novel advertised as *"the penetrating study of a businessman's greed,"* and an advertisement for a movie that is trivial and contemptible. A couple leaves a nightclub, drunk and staggering.

Arriving at her midtown apartment, Dagny puts on a recording of Richard Halley's Fourth Concerto, which leads to a flashback on the life and career of the composer and his curious disappearance eight years earlier after the triumph of his opera "Phaeton". Reading the newspaper, she stumbles upon a picture of Francisco d'Anconia, in town at his suite at the Wayne-Falkland Hotel for the purpose of dating a hat check girl and eating at a famous deli. Dagny drops the newspaper and silently sobs at the degradation of her former friend.

Jim Taggart awakens past noon and boasts to his paramour, Betty Pope, that at this afternoon's board meeting he will put Dagny in her place. He is interrupted by a hysterical phone call from Mexico. The People's State of Mexico has not only nationalized Francisco's San Sebastian mines but Taggart Transcontinental's San Sebastian Line as well.

Jim puts the best face possible on this development at the board meeting. He takes credit for running substandard service – actually Dagny's ploy – with old equipment so that the Mexican government could not confiscate any useful assets of the railroad. Delegating blame, he asks the board to request the resignations of the consultant who recommended building the line and the railroad's Mexican agent.

Upon returning to his office, Jim finds Orren Boyle waiting for him. Francisco has lost $15 million in the nationalization, and Jim and Orren want to find out how he plans to recoup their own investments. Jim asks for a meeting with Francisco only to be told that Francisco does not deign to meet with him because Jim bores him.

The National Alliance of Railroads passes the amusingly named *"Anti-dog-eat-dog Rule,"* aimed at curbing *"vicious competition".* Railroads defined as newcomers to an area serviced by a senior railroad must shut down within nine months. They can instead build in *"blighted areas"* where there is no market because *"the prime purpose of a railroad was public service, not profit."* Major railroads, however, are entitled to public support to help survive. Dan Conway of the Phoenix-Durango Railroad, the intended victim of the rule, shuffles out of the meeting chamber a stunned and beaten man.

Jim brags to Dagny that he has taken Conway out of the game, but Dagny is furious. She goes to Conway and offers to help him against the looters, but he demurs, pointing out that the majority has made its decision and he doesn't have the right to buck it considering the tenor of the times. *"Who is John Galt?"* he asks. Conway tells Dagny that she needs to get the Rio Norte Line fixed up because it's the only lifeline keeping Ellis Wyatt and the businessmen of Colorado going. And they are all that is keeping the country going.

Returning to her office, she finds oilman Ellis Wyatt crashing in on her. He gives Dagny an ultimatum: in nine months time, either the railroad gives him the service he requires, or he will take it down with him when its failure destroys him. He sees Dagny as one of the looters in view of the decision of the board. Dagny tells him, *"You will get the transportation you need, Mr. Wyatt."*

Dagny meets with Hank Rearden at his mill, asking him for a nine month delivery schedule for Rearden Metal rather than twelve, and Rearden agrees. He enjoys charging Dagny more for the rail,

21

but Dagny has no problem with that. This is business, and she is not a moocher. The intention was for Colorado to save the railroad, but now the railroad must save Colorado, and Colorado, the country. Hank insists that this lunacy just *has* to be temporary. They understand each other:

"We haven't any spiritual goals or qualities. All we're after is material things."

And Dagny knows that to be a lie.

Risk and Reward

What James Taggart and Orren Boyle accomplish through the auspices of the National Alliance of Railroads is a restraint of trade that is nominally illegal in the United States since the 1890 Sherman Antitrust Act. It is a textbook example of a cartel, an illustration of how and why this sort of anti-competitive behavior takes place. Competition isn't crushed, it isn't beaten; it is merely outlawed.

Meanwhile Jim Taggart deftly takes credit for his sister's actions in moving railroad assets out of Mexico before the nationalization. It's caddish, perfectly in character and Jim's specialty: a reward without risk, the height of the looters' art. This is actually the main premise of the entire novel in miniature. In view of the later real-world historical nationalization by Mexico of her privately held oil industry, one has to tip one's hat to Rand for prescience. Whether she saw that instance coming or not, she knew her villains well.

Rand, Aristotle and Nietzsche

It is time to lay the groundwork for the consideration of *Atlas Shrugged* not simply as a story, but as a novel of ideas, Rand's vehicle for the presentation of her new philosophy she termed Objectivism. It concerns the relationship of man to the universe and of man toward man. A radical individualist and a fiercely independent woman, Rand attempted nothing less than the

22

reconsideration of all philosophy from first principles. Her intention is no more audacious than any first-year Philosophy undergraduate, which at one point Rand was, as Alisa Rosenbaum, a student in pre-Communist Petrograd of the philosopher N. O. Lossky. Unlike an ordinary undergraduate, however, Rand actually managed to achieve it.

We leave the gritty circumstances of industry for the contemplation of the relentlessly abstract, and Rand will spend the rest of the novel convincing us that the two are related and showing us how. The Greek philosopher Aristotle has not simply dropped in for a visit, he belongs here. Rand informs us of that in the chapter title, the "immovable mover", a term quoted from Aristotle's *Metaphysics*.

And further, Rand titled the three sections of *Atlas Shrugged* after the three axioms of Aristotlean logic: non-contradiction, either/or, and identity. This is the framework on which both the novel and her philosophy of Objectivism will be constructed.

We're also going to encounter a heavy dose of Friedrich Nietzsche. Rand studied both Aristotle and Nietzsche before emigrating to the United States, and Chris Sciabarra (*Ayn Rand: The Russian Radical*) informs us that Nietzsche's *Thus Spake Zarathustra* was the first book she purchased upon arriving in her adopted land.

To Aristotle the "immovable mover" of the chapter title is God, both for him and his subsequent interpreters, the brilliant rabbi Maimonides with respect to Judaism, the philosopher Averroes with respect to Islam and Christianity, and St. Thomas Aquinas with respect to Christianity. Here the existence of God is not so much "proven" by Aristotle's system of logic, but appears as a necessary consequence; you can't have the system without the implication. Students of medieval philosophy will immediately recognize it in the roots of St. Anselm's ontological argument for the existence of God. He is one of a number of early Church fathers collectively known as the Medieval Schoolmen who dealt with these fundamental issues.

And yet Rand herself was an atheist. How are we to reconcile the two positions? Enter Nietzsche. Far from denying it, Rand embraces Aristotle's conclusion, moving not God Himself, but the functions of godhead, into men and women, Dagny and Rearden to be specific, at the end of this chapter. This manifestation of an immovable mover is what she meant by her statement in the first paragraph that the skyscraper was dependent on motion for its existence. The building – the society – is not in her view the immovable mover; certain creative, productive people within it are. Atlas shrugs when at last they decline to move it.

Nietzsche is most famous for his assertion that God is dead, meaning that God, being in Nietzsche's view an imaginary collective construct, ceases to exist when His reality is rejected – as Nietzsche felt that it was in Europe at the time – and that when that happens, God ceases to be a source of values and morals, not to mention spiritual comfort. Further, this deficiency in the basis of morals needed to be addressed lest humanity slide into nihilism, which as a working philosopher Nietzsche found abhorrent.

Jews, Christians and Muslims may believe that the notion of God needing to be believed in to exist is itself a misplacement of primacy. It is certainly contrary to Aristotle's system. It is also, in Nietzsche's, quite unproven, as it turns out to be in Rand's.

But in Nietzsche's defense, he may have been right about nihilism. It is, after all, the root of the multiculturalism that is gripping the cultural leadership of Europe at the present time, and one cause of that, just as Nietzsche predicted, is the popular rejection of religion as a cultural anchor. God may or may not be dead, but if He is ignored, that is sufficient.

Nietzsche's answer to all this was the advent of an *übermensch*, imperfectly translated as "superman" and carrying with it the unfortunate connotations of a fellow with a cape flying through the air. "Overman" is as good. The basic idea was that this creature transcended humanity, being a more perfect version of its progenitor, exempt from the moral strictures that originally were necessary to circumscribe the latter's behavior. And that once expressed, this new creature would be not only a paragon of a new morality but its very source and origin. One hears echoes of this in both those golems of the 20th Century's tragic history, the Blond Beast of Nazism and the New Soviet Man. One hears less malevolent echoes of it in Rand's heroes and heroines, because as an eyewitness to its excesses, she knew enough not to take the

24

whole thing more seriously than it warrants. One major topic of discussion surrounding *Atlas Shrugged* is just how seriously she did take it.

The reason Rand's overmen and -women are less malevolent is something Rand commented on herself. She stated that Nietzsche's "epistemology subordinates reason to 'will', or feeling or instance of blood or innate virtues of character." (Introduction to *The Fountainhead*). Hers celebrates the subordination of man only to reason. Aristotle hasn't left us after all.

But before we put Nietzsche back on the shelf, a few comments. First, that his Zarathustra has so little to do with the historical character of that name that real Zoroastrians – there are quite a few – must be scratching their heads wondering how the old fellow could have come up with this stuff. Second, that Nietzsche places his statement that "God is dead" in the mouth of a madman, which is ironic inasmuch as Nietzsche himself later wound up involuntarily confined in a psychiatric clinic in Basel. But disturbed or not, it was Nietzsche who brought to reluctant attention the difficulties encountered in rejecting God as a source of morality. And here we see the divergence of the cultures in *Atlas Shrugged*: Rand proposes to replace God with reason; her critics and villains, with politics.

And it was Nietzsche, after all, who expressed what might represent the mission of *Atlas Shrugged*:

"The future task of the philosopher…is to solve the problem of value, to determine the true hierarchy of values." *(Beyond Good and Evil)*

Aristotle and Nietzsche. *Atlas Shrugged* seems to circle the two in an irregular orbit like a planet circling a binary star system. It is an impressive philosophical lineage. What Rand will make of it remains to be seen.

Railroads, Regulation and Competition

The early years of railroading saw vicious competition, railroad men fighting not only one another, but seeking the aid of government in their battles. As soon as an operator of sufficient size built, operated and stabilized a line, he either acquired rights over the line of a competitor, making him an ally, or acquired the competitor outright. This is how networks were built and America's major railroads emerged.

The railroads' dealings with their customers verged on the predatory. This was standard behavior in the era after the Civil War, a war in which American industry had defeated American plantation agriculture. And both in the novel and the real world, the customer resented this predation. Ellis Wyatt exclaims:

"You expect to feed off me while you can and to find another carcass to pick dry after you have finished mine."

He is describing the world of *Atlas Shrugged*, but he could just as easily have been describing America in the second half of the 19th Century.

This behavior led to resistance in the form of the Grange Movement, which favored nationalization of the railroads. Outrage reached sufficient levels during the Cleveland Administration that Congress created the Interstate Commerce Commission to regulate the railroads.

A pattern developed which we see in other industries in contemporary America. In two decades the regulated gained enough influence to become the regulators, through a revolving door that circulated executives from regulated industries, lawyers, lobbyists, politicians and regulators themselves. On occasion it also involved the passing of cash. Over time the ICC became the tool by which major railroads excluded competitors by building a bureaucratic structure impossible for any but the best legal minds to penetrate. As long as railroads were the key mover of people and goods, this structure provided stability. But it failed as soon as real competition emerged.

By the early 20th Century, the internal combustion engine prompted states and counties to build roads to make space for all the cars pouring out of Henry Ford's plant. After World War I, this began in earnest and increased exponentially during the

Depression when the federal government created make-work jobs building bridges and highways.

The building of highway infrastructure created space for trucks to compete with trains. At first, America's highway network was a collection of two-lane roads, and trucks were not able to compete well for long distance hauling. But the Interstate Highway System changed all that. On the railroads' part, antiquated work rules, featherbedding and deferred maintenance led to America's railroads tearing out much of their physical plant in the Sixties. Wall Street believed it might even be in the best interest of investors to shut down the railroads and move everything by truck over the new subsidized freeway network. Railroads not only didn't earn the cost of their capital, they were operating at a loss.

It was the Penn Central bankruptcy of 1970 that dashed the public's face with a cold splash of reality. The Penn Central, created in 1968 by the merger of the Pennsylvania and New York Central railroads, crashed so catastrophically that it took down all the railroads in the northeastern US.

In 1980, Rep. Harley Staggers (D-WV) wrote a bill that would replace the ICC with the Surface Transportation Board and finally deregulate the railroads. Following its enactment, by the end of 1980 all major railroads were profitable again. This set off a wave of mergers that is still ongoing. Competition is stiff, and each railroad feels a need to chivy its competitors out of every last available scrap of cargo – while the trucking industry continues to carry the lion's share.

Today there is the Association of American Railroads, which lobbies before Congress. It has none of the monolithic power of Rand's National Alliance of Railroads, but there is a sentence in the book that refers to laws enacted by the National Legislature that the Alliance appears to be enforcing. Much like the old ICC, its practical goal is to protect current operators against upstarts, but it's a voluntary association. Dan Conway was a signatory, and he believes that he must, if necessary, sacrifice himself for the greater good.

Discussion Topics

- Had the diesel locomotives come from the Richards Locomotive Works, run by the tall, dark and handsome Matt Richards, we would have had a different turn of the plot. But hiding behind the corporate name United Locomotive Works we see more of what we've seen from Associated Steel. Why does the owner believe that Dagny is being impolite in asking where her locomotives are?

- Rand is expert at using metaphors and symbols. So far, we've seen a rotted out tree, a bar on the upper floor of a skyscraper that is decked out like a cellar, and now a precision machine rusting away on the property of the United Locomotive Works. Of what significance is this symbol? How does it relate to its predecessors?

- Dagny's walk through Manhattan to her apartment reads like a tour of one of the circles of Dante's hell. It opens a window onto the society of America's greatest city and its influence over the rest of the country. What can we learn from the imagery in that walk?

- We are developing a body count. Richard Halley disappeared eight years ago. Owen Kellogg left the railroad to vanish earlier in the novel. Now Dick McNamara, the Cleveland rail contractor, has gone out of business and disappeared. Build a list and watch it grow.

- Woody Allen once said, "Sex without love is a meaningless experience – but as meaningless experiences go, it's one of the best." Why can't Jim Taggart enjoy his meaningless experience?

- The threat of the railroad's Mexican property being nationalized was foremost in Dagny's mind, which is why she left the railroad's worst assets available for the looters to confiscate. Orren Boyle insisted it would never happen and Jim believed him. When nationalization occurred, Jim took credit for Dagny's quick thinking and then delegated the blame for his own failures to two fall guys who were summarily fired. Is this any different from what happens today in the offices of America's largest corporations? Can we find examples?

- Dan Conway echoes Jim Taggart's statement that it's not right to buck the will of the majority. In his case, however, Conway is the victim of that will. What are the holes in Conway's logic?

- We've seen Dagny interact with Owen Kellogg, Eddie Willers and Jim Taggart. But her interaction with Dan Conway is different; we see her emotions on display. Her interaction with Hank Rearden is of a different nature entirely; they are of like mind and joust not just as competitors, but as friends. How is this different?

- *"All that lunacy is temporary. It can't last. It's demented, so it has to defeat itself."* Hank believes that he, Dagny and other like minded people will save the country from itself. But just how long can such lunacy last? And what might end it?

Chapter V: The Climax of the d'Anconias

Synopsis

Eddie hands a newspaper to Dagny; it has a most interesting story. The People's State of Mexico, upon inspecting the expropriated San Sebastian mines, discovers that they are devoid of copper and utterly worthless. Dagny asks Eddie to call Francisco at the Wayne-Falkland Hotel for an appointment.

What follows is an extended flashback into the childhood of Dagny, Eddie, Francisco and Jim at the Taggart estate on the Hudson.

The teenaged Francisco got a job at Taggart Transcontinental before Dagny, working illegally – even then, they had child labor laws – as a call boy at a station on the Hudson Line. Each of them intended eventually to run the family business. Unlike those d'Anconias who had increased the family holdings by a mere 10%, Francisco's goal was to double them.

Francisco went to Patrick Henry University of Cleveland, the most distinguished institution of learning left in the world, but Francisco did not find all the courses interesting. He learned more than course material there – by playing the stock market he amassed enough money to buy the copper foundry where he had been working secretly at night. He made only two close friends at college. Following college, Francisco worked for his father. One night, meeting Dagny in New York, he said, *"There's something wrong with the world."*

Dagny began the competition with Francisco by taking a job as night operator on the railroad at a nearby station while only sixteen. She went through life without male admirers, and her idea of a good time was working on the railroad. After a formal ball, she noted that she could have squashed any ten of the men she had met. In her freshman year at college Dagny and Francisco became lovers.

And yet in real time, when the chapter begins, Francisco appears to be a worthless playboy squandering the d'Anconia fortune. He had warned her that the next time they met, she wouldn't want to see him. The reader seems more curious than Dagny at whatever could have happened to him.

Returning to the present, Dagny goes to Francisco's room at the hotel and finds him playing with marbles on the floor like a child. Dagny has figured out part of what Francisco intended with the San Sebastian mines swindle – he has hurt the looters' government of Mexico as well as his American investors, but why he should wish to do so is not yet apparent to her.

Dagny prods Francisco when she brings up the Fifth Concerto of Richard Halley, which surprisingly, he seems to know something about. Francisco avoids a direct answer and says only that Halley has stopped composing, although how he knows that is yet another mystery in this most mysterious man.

Francisco lays out the reaction of the Mexican government, which had made promises to its people to be funded by the confiscation of the mines. Now the government blames the greedy capitalists for those promises being broken. The miners' town he built was made of shoddy material and will be gone within a year. He has cost the railroad and his investors millions. Taggart Transcontinental will likely fail, and Ellis Wyatt will be the next to go under. Dagny is, as the reader might expect, horrified. He tells Dagny as she is leaving that she is not ready to hear the reasons behind what he is doing.

Rand and Sexuality

Here the first hints arise of Rand's approach to human sexuality, which was not only ground-breaking at the time, but remains highly controversial to this day. Certain feminists curse Rand for this disquisition; others celebrate her for her independence and even daring in bringing it up.

First, some context. *Atlas Shrugged* was published in 1957, three years before the controversy that the execrable and nearly unreadable *Lady Chatterly's Lover* brought to the publishing world. The entire genre of bodice-ripping romance novels was yet a twinkle in its authors' eyes. This was very hot stuff for the mid-Fifties. Rand has been consigned by certain feminist thinkers as superficial in politics, philosophy and psychology, which is as far from the truth as anyone who has taken the trouble actually to read her can imagine. Noted feminist Susan Brownmiller went so far as to publish the essay titled "Ayn Rand: Traitor to Her Own Sex," (1975), an epithet which, given its source, any sane author would wear as a badge of honor, and Rand probably did so.

Other feminists – ones with a bit more respect for their fellow females – have come to a rather different conclusion. Camille Paglia has touched on the topic in several places, a *Reason* magazine interview for one, wherein she gives us this uncompromising conclusion:

"One would think that women's studies, if it really obeyed its mission, would make her [Rand] part of the agenda. But no, of course not! Women's studies has been oriented toward rediscovering the mediocre thinker, or the writer who talks about her victimization, rather than someone who preaches individualism and independence as Ayn Rand does." *["Interview with the Vamp" Reason Magazine, August/September 1995]*

Just so. Let's discuss Dagny's sexuality, which is the most interesting thing about her. She is in every sense a Superwoman, fit to compete on even terms with any male in the novel and prevail. And yet we see her in her schoolgirl days consorting with her childhood friend Francisco d'Anconia in a deliberate and gleefully subordinate role.

"You haven't any pride at all," [says James Taggart], "The way you run when he whistles and wait on him. Why don't you shine his shoes?"

"Because he hasn't told me to," she answered.

She and Francisco were sixteen at the time, to be sure, and hence certain exaggerations in character were forgivable that would be impermissible to their adult personae. Less forgivable is his reaction to her playful suggestion that she deliberately get D's in school in order to be more popular, which was an outraged

32

slap in the face.   It is the first indication we get that Francisco can also be a bit of a cad.

But what is revealing is Dagny's reaction to her bleeding lip:

He turned abruptly, took out his handkerchief and dipped it into the water of the river.   "Come here," he ordered.

She laughed, stepping back.   "Oh, no.   I want to keep it as it is.   I hope it swells terribly.   I like it."

Does Rand think, then, that masochism is an integral part of female sexuality?   Actually, yes, she does.   From Part 7 of the *Journals of Ayn Rand*, referring to Dominique and her lover Roark in *The Fountainhead:*

"Like most women, and to a greater degree than most, she is a masochist and she wishes for the happiness of suffering at Roark's hands.   Sexually, Roark has a great deal of the sadist, and he finds pleasure in breaking her will and her defiance.   Yet he loves her…"

There is more to it than that, of course.   This aspect of sex is by definition a manifestation of power transfer, one reason it appeals frequently to the powerful in real life.   The excitement in it is a case of release, of vulnerability, of letting go.   It is not in the least restricted to female sexuality, although *Atlas Shrugged* mercifully declines to explore those turbid waters any further than Dagny's case.   But the novel simply drips with this aspect of male/female psychological discourse.   We see this, for example, in the scene where Dagny has determined to beat Francisco in tennis at last: he toys with her, he makes her suffer, and in a climactic moment, she prevails.   And yet, when the two finally do get around to enjoying one another sexually, it is no act of sadomasochism at all, but one of tenderness, respect and learning.   It is then and only then that we can regard either character as remotely adult.

The Sin of Francisco d'Anconia

Francisco has not fallen from a state of grace, he has leapt. This is an unavoidably religious image, a result of Rand's transference of godhead to her human characters. Francisco has sinned, is sinning, and what could possibly offer him redemption? We shall see.

Here we encounter a difficulty in Rand's moral exposition, one that Paglia pointed out in her *Reason* interview: Rand is occasionally quite cruel to her less-than-superhuman characters. And so are her supermen and -women. Francisco has come to see *"the farce,"* by which he does not mean the divorce of the woman he is being falsely blamed for romancing. His farce is the discovery by the Mexican authorities that the d'Anconia property that they nationalized – stole – is in fact worthless. Such a thing must take considerable effort and expense – some $15 million of Francisco's money – to ruin, but it has taken far more of the looters' money with it when it went – Jim Taggart's for one. That was, of course, Francisco's object.

He has sinned. On his properties are d'Anconia employees for whom he has constructed roads, bridges and dwellings out of substandard materials due to the system's corruption. He laughs about this. It is in his view the just desserts of those who participate in that corrupt system to be despoiled by it. And yet we must ask if they are all so worthless that his obligation to return to them his own best effort in recompense for theirs is no longer operative? It is not clear that he appreciates this point, nor is it clear that Dagny does either. We will discuss this at greater length when we come to consider her own treatment of her subordinates, when we attempt to address the question "are there, then, no innocent victims?"

Patrick Henry University

We should not confuse this fictional school with the very real Patrick Henry College of Purcellville, Virginia. Rand's Patrick Henry University was situated in Cleveland, Ohio. It would appear that even during the Forties and Fifties, Rand held a low enough opinion of the Ivy League to locate her ideal university in Cleveland, an industrial city not known as a great seat of learning. In fact, the principal business of Cleveland was manufacturing.

Naming a university dedicated to reason to Patrick Henry, however, is just as problematic as naming a fundamentalist Christian college after the same man, which is the case in Purcellville. Henry does not fit the stereotype of either a man of objective reason or of religious faith. His life and legacy are far more complicated.

The historical Patrick Henry belongs to the same group as Thomas Paine and Samuel Adams, revolutionaries who lit the flame that George Washington kept from being extinguished. Like Adams, Henry had failed in business many times, but while Adams became a wizard at the art of political propaganda, Henry turned instead to the law, standing for home rule and economic self-determination, advocating in favor of the ancient British tradition of being taxed by one's own legislators. He further argued that colonial legislatures could not assign that right to Parliament. Because Parliament had long exercised a general right to tax the colonies, Henry's assertion was considered treasonous.

In addition to the above principles, Henry's intellectual justification for separation from Britain revolved around corruption. For Henry, gold and silver were too important to be diverted into the pockets of looters and moochers, which is why he became the scourge of corruption in Virginia politics. He could personally fight corruption in Williamsburg, but the corruption in London was so entrenched it could only be fought by separation. His appeal to Ayn Rand will become more explicable as the novel carries on.

Discussion Topics

- The philosophical conversations among Dagny, Francisco and Jim at the Taggart estate reveal much about their characters and hold a lot of material for discussion. Example #1 – Francisco: *"So I want to be prepared to claim the greatest virtue of all – that I was a man who made money."* Jim: *"Virtue is the price of admission."* Example #2 – Jim's lecture to Francisco about selfish greed and social responsibilities. Example #3 – Dagny: *"Francisco, what's the most depraved type of human being?"* Francisco: *"The man without a purpose."* Example #4 – Francisco: *"The code of competence is the only system of morality that's on a gold standard."* These snippets are better at conveying information than the long set pieces to come. Discuss the differences between these people and how the differences determine their characters.

- Compare the meaning of sexual relations between the two couples described in the text so far: Dagny Taggart with Francisco d'Anconia, and James Taggart with Betty Pope. What does this tell us about their respective characters?

- *"The government of the People's State of Mexico has issued a proclamation...asking the people to be patient and put up with hardships just a little longer... Now the planners are asking their people not to blame the government, but to blame the depravity of the rich..."* The expropriation of the d'Anconia mines did not work out as the thieves expected. Find contemporary examples.

Chapter VI: The Non-Commercial

Synopsis

This chapter is a set-piece at which some of the foundational ideas of both looter and immovable mover are trotted out in conversation. At first reading it sounds as if it might be rather contrived until over the course of time one hears many of these cases made in earnest by real people. Rand didn't make any of it up; she didn't have to.

Hank Rearden, forgetting about his anniversary party, is sent home by his secretary and dresses for the party. He reads an editorial about the Equalization of Opportunity Bill, which will forbid any businessman from owning more than one business. He has paid Wesley Mouch a lot of money to stop this bill and cannot believe it is about to pass the National Legislature.

Hank goes downstairs in time to hear Dr. Simon Pritchett grandly philosophize that man is nothing but chemicals with delusions of grandeur, there aren't any objective standards, and the purpose of philosophy is to prove that there isn't any meaning to life.

Balph Eubank pontificates on the state of literature, which, in his view, should be to show that the essence of life is suffering and defeat. He suggests an Equalization of Opportunity bill for authors, meaning that no book should be allowed to sell more than ten thousand copies, thus forcing people to buy better books because there will no longer be any best sellers. Only those who are not motivated by making money should be allowed to write.

Bertram Scudder speaks in favor of the Equalization of Opportunity Bill to Philip Rearden and Betty Pope, who both support it. Philip has no problem with the government trimming Hank's fortune.

Dagny Taggart walks in and captures every eye in the room. She tells Hank that this is a celebration of the first sixty miles of Rearden Metal track. Hank is disturbingly formal, as if he and Dagny have never met.

Eubank and Jim Taggart speak about Dagny, whom Eubank sees as a perversion caused by the age of machines; Dagny should be home weaving cloth and having babies.   Hank is enraged to see that Bertram Scudder is drinking in his house, but he is even more upset when Francisco d'Anconia walks in.

Jim takes Francisco aside to discuss the San Sebastian debacle, about which Francisco intends to do nothing.   He tells Jim that the mines and rail line have been seized by the will of the people, and how dare anyone go against the will of the majority?   Everything Francisco did in Mexico was intended to follow the dominant precepts of the age.   The mining engineer was chosen because of his need, workers received wages for producing nothing, and not a penny of profit was made.   It is the perfect manifestation of Jim Taggart's philosophy.

Francisco takes Hank aside and explains to him that he is carrying all the freeloaders in the room, and they have but one weapon against him.   Hank berates him over the Mexican business, and Dagny cannot believe that Francisco is taking it without fighting back.   Francisco leaves, telling Hank he has learned what he needed to learn about him.

Dagny draws Hank into conversation.   Hank is still coldly rigid, but he can't keep his eyes off her bare shoulder.   She offers to slap Bertram Scudder's face.

Dagny overhears a conversation among some elderly people about their fear that the darkness will never leave.   One old woman speaks about detonations heard in Delaware Bay.   The official explanation is Coast Guard target practice, but everyone knows it is the pirate Ragnar Danneskjøld evading the Coast Guard. Several European people's states have put a price on his head. The government has asked the newspapers to enforce a blackout on reporting about him.   An old woman tells Dagny of the legend of John Galt, a variation of the legend of Atlantis.   Dagny doesn't believe it, but Francisco tells Dagny that the story is true.

For Dagny, the last straw comes when she hears Mort Liddy's bastardization of Halley's Fourth Concerto on the radio.   As she prepares to leave, she hears Lillian Rearden speak disparagingly about the bracelet of Rearden Metal she is wearing.   In a fury, Dagny offers to exchange her diamond bracelet for Lillian's Rearden Metal bracelet.   Lillian takes the offer, and Hank suddenly turns solicitous to his wife – and bitterly cold to Dagny.

Hank, in his wife's bedroom, asks that she not invite these people to the house again.

The Party

Hank Rearden is a failure as a husband, which is not as reprehensible as it might be because Lillian is a failure as a wife. This marriage is headed straight for the rocks, slowly and inevitably. *Atlas Shrugged* here shows itself a product of the Fifties, the days before the advent of vending machine divorces wherein a man can be gutted, skinned and hung out to dry in the course of a single morning and still have time for a cup of coffee he can no longer afford. For Hank it is likely to take much longer. Score one for modern efficiency.

To celebrate the eighth anniversary of this shipwreck of a marriage we have The Party. For Dagny, such affairs are misplaced – she says that they should be a celebration, peopled by deserving celebrants. Clearly there is something epochal to celebrate – Rearden Metal. And just as clearly there are very few people there who have earned the right to celebrate it or who are even aware of its significance.

One who is aware is Francisco d'Anconia, who plays here the role of a satyr before the proscenium, commenting mockingly on the earnest posturing of the other partygoers. The only time he is serious is when he is occupied in his principal purpose for attending, which is taking the measure of the industrialist Rearden.

Let us stroll through The Party and examine Rand's menagerie.

The creature in the first cage is one Dr. Simon Pritchett, a philosopher by trade, the successor to Professor Hugh Akston at Patrick Henry University. Observe this specimen.

"Man? What is man? He's just a collection of chemicals with delusions of grandeur," said Dr. Pritchett...

The only chemical that might help here is ethanol, in which neither Dagny nor Hank indulge this evening. It might have helped. Nihilism can be depressing.

"But which concepts are not ugly or mean, Professor?" asked an earnest matron...

"None," said Dr. Pritchett. "None within the range of man's capacity."

A young man asked hesitantly, "But if we haven't any good concepts, how do we know the ones we've got are ugly? By what standard?"

"There are no standards."

Here the Professor has departed the bounds of reason – literally. One can't judge by standards that don't exist, and Pritchett has judged. Nietzsche stated that in the absence of God there is an inescapable trend toward nihilism, which is in this case Pritchett's claim that there are no standards. Rand is stating that in the absence of reason one gets the same result.

Aristotle, here and elsewhere, is her bulwark against nihilism. "Things are not what they seem" is a perfectly permissible proposition both to Rand and to Aristotle. Pritchett's "Things are not what they are," is not. That is what "A is A" means.

But this is the way Rand saw academia decaying, Akston to Pritchett, Aristotle to Sartre, whom she loathed.

"The purpose of philosophy is not to seek knowledge, but to prove that knowledge is impossible to man."

This is a rather weak case – it is knowledge, after all, that enables one to load the rifle when the tiger is coming, and unlike nihilist abstractions, tigers are real.

"A free economy cannot exist without competition. Therefore, men must be forced to compete. Therefore, we must control men in order to allow them to be free."

We may be tempted to laugh at this patent silliness from Pritchett, supposing it an exaggeration on Rand's part – if we hadn't heard it coming from the television so much of late. The underlying theme of much of the economic "stimulus" legislation and its associated regulation is the notion that markets are only truly free under coercion. It is a notion that would merit laughter were it not taken so terribly seriously.

The creature in the next cage is one Bertram Scudder, an author and polemicist by trade. Observe this specimen.

"Property rights are a superstition. One holds property only by the courtesy of those who do not seize it. The people can seize it at any moment. If they can, why shouldn't they?"

"They should," said Claude Slagenhop. "They need it. Need is the only consideration."

"To each according to his need" is of course Marx, whose doctrines Rand would have seen in application first hand before she fled the madness of her native Russia. It didn't work well even then. That formulation was, as Trotsky pointed out in *The Revolution Betrayed*, quite impossible to achieve at that stage of his imagined historical progression. Not, he believed, in the unattainable world of "high" communism, when Party fairies riding proletarian unicorns would run a fairyland State. Stalin found it necessary to re-codify the proposition to "To each according to his *work*," a rather different concept.

But it does prove convenient depending on what one means by "work." Rand's elite is mirrored in the real world, the "brainworkers," who offer a value to society that is quite out of proportion to their actual sweat equity – just ask them – and must be offered a commensurate reward.

He [Rearden] saw the article, "The Octopus," by Bertram Scudder, which was not an expression of ideas but a bucket of slime emptied in public – an article that did not contain a single fact, not even an invented one, but poured a string of sneers and adjectives in which nothing was clear except the filthy malice of denouncing without considering proof necessary.

41

The title "The Octopus" is a reference to Frank Norris' 1901 novel by that name, a bit of populist, anti-railroad propaganda that was far more romantic than accurate, inspired by the events of the Mussel Slough tragedy in California. Here Rand, like Ambrose Bierce before her, wasn't buying into the inflammatory mythology that turned Norris and the Muckrakers into celebrities. Theodore "The Trustbuster" Roosevelt did. It was not one of his better moments.

Finally, as The Party reaches its climax of inanity, there is the bracelet, a recurring symbol of merit, bondage, and Dagny's sexual inclinations. Of those we already had a clue, which Rand reinforces at Dagny's entrance to the party:

The diamond band on the wrist of her naked arm gave her the most feminine of all aspects: the look of being chained.

It's hard to imagine a diamond bracelet in quite that kinky a vein, but symbolic it certainly is, as both Hank and Lillian Rearden grasp fully when Dagny calls Lillian's bluff and exchanges it for the genuine chain of Rearden Metal. She has, in effect, laid claim to Hank. This affront to domesticity is extremely interesting in view of Rand's real-world affair with the much younger Nathaniel Branden, an early Objectivist follower whose name appears in "Nat" Taggart, Dagny's heroic forbear. Rand was writing *Atlas Shrugged* during that affair, which although nominally approved of was reportedly highly distressing to the spouses of both parties. Life and art turned out to be imitating one another.

And so we move from an uncelebratory party to end the chapter in Rearden's painfully uncelebratory marriage bed. Lillian is as cold a fish physically as she is mentally, and clearly Rearden is punishing himself for being with her, by being with her. The arrangement is simply too toxic to continue. Something has to give.

The New York Intellectuals

Intellectuals in general held differing but strong opinions of Ayn Rand.

- William F. Buckley: "Ayn Rand is dead. So, incidentally, is the philosophy she sought to launch; it was, in fact, stillborn."

- Noam Chomsky: "One of the most evil figures of modern intellectual history."

- Chris Sciabarra: "The left was infuriated by her anti-communist, pro-capitalist politics, whereas the right was disgusted with her atheism and civil libertarianism."

After her Hollywood years, Rand came to New York and settled there for the rest of her long life. She had her own group of followers, whom she dubbed "The Collective" as a joke aimed at Marxism. Alan Greenspan was one of them.

Rand no doubt rubbed shoulders with New York's intellectuals of the Left, and the dominant group at that time dubbed itself "The New York Intellectuals". This group defined itself as socialist and Marxist, but not pro-Soviet. They wrote for *Partisan Review*, *Commentary* and *Dissent*, any of which may be the real life version of Bertram Scudder's *The Future*. Today, one would point to magazines like *Mother Jones* or *The Nation* as candidates.

The names of these intellectuals are a "Who's Who" of that era. Among them were Lionel Trilling, his wife Diana Trilling, Alfred Kazin, Delmore Schwartz, Harold Rosenberg, Dwight Macdonald, Mary McCarthy, Irving Howe, Saul Bellow, Daniel Bell, Hannah Arendt, Susan Sontag, Irving Kristol and Norman Podhoretz. Most of them were Jewish. Irving Kristol and Norman Podhoretz moved right in later years and formed the core of the neo-conservative movement. Sontag spent her last years as a pathetic self-parody, finally skewered by Camille Paglia in a brilliant essay.

Students of the era may enjoy a cruel parlor game looking at the rogues' gallery of intellectuals at Hank Rearden's party and guessing whom they were based on.

- Balph Eubank, author, none of whose books has ever sold more than 3000 copies.

- Claude Slagenhop, president of Friends of Global Progress.

- Bertram Scudder, editor of *The Future*, whose speech contains the definitive manifesto, *"Property rights are a superstition."*

- Mort Liddy, composer, whose film scores are kitsch classical and whose modern symphonies are unlistenable.

- Simon Pritchett, head of the Philosophy Department at Patrick Henry University and apparently the father of the modern philosophical school of Nihilism.

Discussion Topics

- For the past three years, Dr. Simon Pritchett has been the chair of the Philosophy Department of Patrick Henry University. Considering what Rand has said about that school, what does this tell us of the state of American higher education in the novel? In her era? In ours?

- Balph Eubank's comment about Dagny having babies strikes a false note. In the Fifties, such a view would have been considered normal, but not from a New York intellectual – except possibly Norman Mailer. Intellectuals of the Fifties were dismissive of the whole *zeitgeist* of that era when women were expected to cook, sew and have babies. Why has Rand placed this argument in the mouth of this particular character?

- Eubank wants a government subsidy for the arts. Less than a decade after the book was published, Lyndon Johnson signed a law creating the National Endowment for the Arts, National Public Radio and the Public Broadcasting System. What effect has the government involvement had?

- Hugh Akston, former head of the Philosophy Department at Patrick Henry University, retired and disappeared nine years ago. That's contemporaneous with Richard Halley. And Hank's foreman has disappeared. It's time to increment the body count.

- How does one dare oppose the will of the majority? Contrast Dan Conway's use of that question with Francisco's.

Chapter VII: The Exploiters and the Exploited

Synopsis

We meet Mr. Mowen of Amalgamated Switch and Signal of Connecticut, who needs training from Rearden's men before he can handle Rearden Metal, all the while agonizing aloud about whether the metal is real or a fraud.

In Colorado, Dagny is having problems with the Rio Norte Line. Project manager Ben Nealy isn't up to the job, and she and Hank have had to buy up bankrupt companies and shuttered plants to make the necessary equipment. Her chief engineer balks at reinforcing an ancient bridge with Rearden Metal.

Hank Rearden arrives in his new car, a Hammond of Colorado, and his attitude toward Dagny is back to where it was when they were working together at his steel mill. They spar verbally, and Dagny is pleased at her emotions. Hank designs a new bridge of Rearden Metal on the spot with an estimated cost of less than half what her chief engineer has projected. He intends to confront the doubts about the safety of Rearden Metal by building an entire bridge out of it.

Hank is in Colorado looking for a copper mine because he doesn't want to deal with Francisco, whom he considers unreliable after the Mexican debacle. Hank and Dagny enjoy a sense of accomplishment, but when Dagny asks Hank for a lift in his plane to New York, Hank tells her he is flying to Minnesota. When she shows up at the local airport, she discovers that Rearden has taken off for New York after all. He is avoiding her. Why?

Back in New York, Dagny and Jim go to a dinner and conference at the New York Business Council where Dagny has been told she is scheduled to speak about Rearden Metal. The National Council of Metal Industries, headed by Orren Boyle, has condemned it as a threat to public safety. The union is not sure it wants its members to work with it. A convention of grade school teachers in New Mexico has passed a resolution that children should not be permitted to ride the Rio Norte Line because of it. As Jim complains, Dagny notices that every good, reliable piece of equipment on the streets of New York has originated in Colorado.

She is furious to discover that Jim has tried to get Dan Conway to sell his railroad to Taggart Transcontinental; Jim's rationale was to use Phoenix-Durango's steel on the Rio Norte Line to avoid using Rearden Metal altogether. Jim wants to bid for Conway's rail, but his looter friends at the National Alliance of Railroads are attempting to get their own hands on it.

Things grow tense when Dagny discovers that instead of simply speaking, she is there tonight to debate Bertram Scudder on nationwide radio on the topic, *"Is Rearden Metal a lethal product of greed?"* It is a maneuver offensive both for its crudity and its subject; Dagny says the question is not debatable, and she jumps out of the car. She takes refuge in a diner in the shadow of a deserted ruin of an office building and orders coffee. An old bum gives Dagny a sermon on nihilism; in the middle of it the counter boy comments, *"Who is John Galt?"* Another bum tells Dagny yet another legend of Galt, this one about finding a fountain of youth and being unable to bring it back; so he remained where the fountain resided.

Dr. Potter of the State Science Institute sits in Hank Rearden's office and asks him not to upset the economy by introducing Rearden Metal. Hank is not bothered by the disapproval of his metal by the Institute. Potter believes that if the metal is not a physical danger, it's a *social danger* to the country. He offers to buy the rights to the metal from Rearden for a lot of government money to keep it off the market. Rearden refuses, and Potter issues a veiled threat.

Mowen withdraws from the project and refuses to make any more switches of Rearden Metal because too many people don't like it.

Dagny discovers from Eddie Willers that the State Science Institute has warned people against using Rearden Metal but has not really said why. Taggart stock has crashed, Nealy has quit and the union won't let its members work with the metal.

Dagny visits the Institute in New Hampshire to meet with Dr. Robert Stadler, once the head of the Physics Department at Patrick Henry University and one of the nation's leading scientists. Stadler has not even read the Institute's report on Rearden Metal. He knows that there is nothing wrong with it but says that there are

47

other non scientific, i.e. *"social"*, factors. He is concerned that the Institute, with all its government funding, has not been able to come up with anything useful. But Rearden *did*, and that makes the Institute look bad. The survival of the Institute is more important than the survival of Hank Rearden.

Stadler tells Dagny of the three great students he and Hugh Akston shared at Patrick Henry University. One star was Francisco, the other was Ragnar Danneskjøld – and the third was a man who, Stadler complains sadly, is probably a second assistant bookkeeper somewhere.

Dagny finds a drunken Jim hiding at the old Taggart estate on the Hudson. Jim has been using his pull in Washington, first to get the government to seize Dan Conway's railroad, and then to convince the Alliance to let Conway run his line for another year. But Conway has refused. Dagny tells him she is going to start her own company and build the Rio Norte Line for Taggart Transcontinental on a turnkey basis. Eddie Willers will take over Taggart Operations while she is so occupied. Dagny intends to call her company the John Galt Line.

But Francisco will not help fund the line, nor will he tell Dagny why. When Dagny offers to crawl, Francisco comes over to her and tenderly kisses her hand. Realizing he has given away too much, he snaps back into his guarded, caddish persona. He is horrified to discover that Dagny is going to name the line after John Galt, and he tells her that Galt will come to claim it.

Dagny meets with Hank to confirm the orders for the John Galt Line. The financiers are the Colorado industrialists whom the line will serve. Even Ken Danagger of the Pennsylvania coal company is in, and Hank signs on. Wyatt and Danagger have already agreed to purchase Rearden Metal simply because of the State Science Institute's partial condemnation of it. Stockton Foundry of Colorado is going to finish the switches that Mowen wouldn't make. The union won't try to stop the line because there are so few union jobs available.

An Atlantic Southern freight train carrying copper for the Rearden mills slams into a passenger train in New Mexico, and the railroad can't do anything but make excuses. Hank puts together a rescue effort that gets the copper moving again, although Hank decides to move his ore in the future via Taggart Transcontinental.

Hank's mother appears at the mill and asks him to give his brother Philip a job that he doesn't deserve. He throws her out.

Hank now tries to find some steel for the Ward Harvester Company of Minnesota, but he is interrupted by the news that the National Legislature has enacted the Equalization of Opportunity Bill. Wesley Mouch is nowhere to be found.

Hank suddenly comes up with a new design for the rail bridge. He calls Dagny in Colorado and tells her about his new design, which will outperform any bridge ever built and cost no more than a culvert. There is a hint that Dagny has broken into tears.

Dagny's Management Skills

Let's be frank – Dagny's man Ben Nealy is a slug. In the real world a manager that cowardly and ineffective would never have gotten a project of this scope off the ground. Dagny, on the other hand, is a supremely capable woman who seems far happier in her role as a driving project manager than as Taggart Transcontinental's Vice President of Operations, which in real life would call for a considerably different skill set. One wonders if Rand actually knew that. Dagny, as senior management, has no business making decisions over the amount of bark on railroad ties – that's not her job. *Her* job is firing Nealy and she doesn't do it.

What she does is to take up the reins herself, shedding her mantle at Taggart to become the high-powered builder in which role she seems far more comfortable. That she is capable of running Taggart simultaneously through her minion Eddie Willers is probably a bit unrealistic, but it speaks volumes about real managerial ability: his, not hers.

The Trap of the Word "Social"

Dagny rejects the very legitimacy of the "debate" between herself and Bertram Scudder over the merits of Rearden Metal. Everyone may have a right to an opinion, but that does not mean that all opinions have equal merit. To Dagny it is clear that the metal either does what it's supposed to or it does not. That is all that is relevant, not some nebulous concept of *social* impact.

But Scudder's approach isn't to be avoided. It crops up during a conversation in Rearden's office by one Dr. Potter, a representative of the State Science Institute, which has published a statement that Rearden Metal is a menace to the economy. It is not the technical merits of Rearden Metal that are at issue here, but:

"It is the social aspect that I am asking you to consider, Mr. Rearden," the man said softly.

Here one feels compelled to come to the defense of what must be the most abused adjective in the English language, the word "social," used when a charlatan wants the noun to which it is applied to mean the opposite of what it does. "Social welfare," for example, wherein neither the welfare of society nor its constituent individuals actually improves, but that of the administrator does; "social justice," for another, which means simply "theft."

It isn't really so much that Rearden Metal is likely to damage the economy, as Potter suggests, rather the opposite. Its fatal drawback is that it will be outside the control of those who intend to direct that economy and the people within it. It is a matter of political power, not technical merit. That is, after all, what this usage of the word "social" is intended to effect, then and now. It is the bait on the barbed hook of a lie.

Discussion Topics

- Taggart Transcontinental's original Chief Engineer left five years ago. Increment the body count.

- Dagny: *"I've hired you to do a job, not to do your best – whatever that is."* Ben Nealy: *"That's an unpopular attitude, Miss Taggart..."* What has happened to make quality unpopular?

- Dagny: *"The bedbugs will stop crawling from out of unlikely corners, because they won't have the incentive of a big company to bite."* Discuss this statement and the rise of our predatory legal system.

- Mrs. Rearden: *"If you loved your brother, you'd give him a job he didn't deserve, precisely because he didn't deserve it... If a man deserves a job, there's no virtue in giving it to him. Virtue is the giving of the undeserved."* Discuss the merits or lack thereof, of Mrs. Rearden's case.

- When, in the real world, the Union Pacific lost its route through the Oregon Cascades due to a mountain-slide during a blizzard, it had crews on the line as soon as weather permitted, stabilizing the mountain. Then it moved an army of workers and hopper cars into the area until the line was rebuilt, all the while rerouting traffic by sending freight as far away as Salt Lake City. Contrast this with the Atlantic Southern's attitude when a mere 1200 feet of track is torn up in a collision.

Chapter VIII: The John Galt Line

Synopsis

Eddie Willers brings the Anonymous Rail Worker in the corporate cafeteria up to date. Dagny's work on the John Galt Line is going so well the newspapers refuse to report it. The United Locomotive Works has gone bankrupt, and Dwight Sanders of Colorado has bought the plant. Dagny has moved into a little office near the back of Taggart Terminal, and Eddie feels very uncomfortable sitting in Dagny's chair and taking credit for her work.

The office of the John Galt Line is on the ground floor of a half-collapsed building and is strictly a no-frills operation. Dagny rushed to New York upon hearing that Dwight Sanders had retired – and there was no trace of him to be found. In her office, an exhausted Dagny permits herself a small moment of weakness, longing for a man who can share her meaning of the world. Outside she sees the shadow of a man lingering near the door. Someone is watching her. Dagny rushes outside but sees only the rear entrance to Taggart Terminal.

Hank Rearden is forced to sell his ore mines to Paul Larkin to get around the Equalization of Opportunity Bill. Larkin is consumed with guilt, but Hank is not interested in his rationalizations. Hank had earlier sold his coal mines to Ken Danagger, who was willing to sell his coal to Rearden at cost, even though that was illegal. Hank's concern was not cost, but supply.

Wesley Mouch resigns rather belatedly from Rearden's employ to become the Assistant Coordinator of the Bureau of Economic Planning and National Resources. He has made the transition from private industry to government, and his star is rapidly ascending.

Hank and Eddie Willers have breakfast at the Wayne-Falkland. With the railroad in such poor financial shape, Hank wants to give Eddie a moratorium on the first payment for Rearden Metal; from his perspective it's just good business. Eddie takes the offer, feeling badly that this will help Jim Taggart and his friends. Hank says not to worry about them.

The public has been made to be worried about whether the Rearden Metal bridge will stand, and they curse Hank and Dagny for caring about nothing but money. Simon Pritchett, Claude Slagenhop, Orren Boyle and Bertram Scudder are manipulating public opinion while claiming that it arises spontaneously. Balph Eubank and Mort Liddy are the first signers of a petition from the Committee of Disinterested Citizens asking for a government study of the line before it can open.

But Dagny is thrilled to be so close to success. A union boss announces that he is not going to let his men run a train on her tracks, and Dagny throws him out of her office. Every engineer on the system volunteers to run the first train. Pat Logan, engineer of the *Comet* on the Nebraska Division, gets the "demotion" to freight. Dagny intends to ride in the cab.

At a press conference, Dagny gives the details of the opening of the John Galt Line. She and Hank make it clear that their motive is profit, much to the discomfiture of the press. The first train will be a 4-locomotive mixed freight of 80 cars running the entire way at 100 mph. Hank volunteers to ride in the cab with Dagny and the crew.

Everything goes perfectly, exhilaratingly. At 100 mph, the train streaks through the countryside and right through the Denver yards and station. It roars across the Rearden Metal bridge and comes to a halt at Wyatt Junction. Ellis Wyatt is positively giddy; he takes Hank and Dagny off in his convertible to his home. Over dinner, Wyatt tells them he is planning to extract oil from shale only five miles away in a magnitude previously unheard of. Hank, Dagny and Wyatt make great plans.

As they head for separate bedrooms, Hank pulls Dagny into his arms and kisses her brutally. Then he takes her into his bedroom and makes passionate love to her.

The Loci of Corruption

The press has been enlisted as an accomplice in the bureaucratic attempt to stop Rearden Metal. A press so exploited, even willingly, is a press corrupted, both in Rand's world and ours. It is a corruption often dated from the Sixties, but the rot had set in long before. By 1957 Rand was already sketching it with far too much verisimilitude for her to be accused merely of making it up out of whole cloth.

The general policy of the press had been stated by a famous editor five years ago. "There are no objective facts," he had said. "Every report on facts is only somebody's opinion. It is, therefore, useless to write about facts."

Here, once again, we encounter Nietzsche, whose comment read "...it is precisely facts that do not exist, only interpretation." (Notebooks, Summer 1886 – Fall 1887)

That is sadly familiar to the contemporary eye. What matters now is journalism's social effect – that word "social" again – not whether its facts are correct. What matters now is whether the reporter and editor have "made a difference." Journalism no longer intends to reflect, it attempts to shape.

It certainly makes that effort in *Atlas Shrugged*. Journalism is a knowing conduit of the smear campaign directed against the John Galt Line:

"I don't say that the bridge will collapse," said the chief metallurgist of Associated Steel, on a television program, "I'll just say that if I had any children, I wouldn't let them ride on the first train that's going to cross that bridge. But it's only a personal preference, nothing more, just because I'm overly fond of children."

And from social critic Bertram Scudder:

"I don't claim that the Rearden-Taggart contraption will collapse...the important issue is: what protection does society have against the arrogance, selfishness, and greed of two unbridled individualists...? These two, apparently, are willing to stake the lives of their fellow men on their own conceited notions about their powers of judgment, against the overwhelming majority opinion of recognized experts. ...Should society permit it? ...It has always

been the belief of this column that certain kinds of horses should be kept bridled and locked, on general social principles."

That word again, not to mention claims of a phony "scientific" consensus that is sadly reminiscent of present-day ecological controversies. We have, inevitably, a petition from an "expert" committee, and of course the mandatory public opinion poll:

A few businessmen...did not hire metallurgists to examine samples, nor engineers to visit the site of construction. They took a public poll. Ten thousand people, guaranteed to represent every existing kind of brain, were asked the question: "Would you ride on the John Galt Line?" The answer, overwhelmingly, was: "No, sir-ree!"

It is all too familiar: a public relations campaign undertaken by political thugs and abetted by journalist sympathizers who want nothing more than to share the power. The railroad unions do their part by threatening to prohibit their members from running the train. Dagny calls this for what it is:

"You want a stranglehold on your men by means of the jobs which I give them – and on me, by means of your men. You want me to provide the jobs and you want to make it impossible for me to have any jobs to provide."

Politicians, academia, the literati, the media, and now the labor unions. It is 1957 in the real world and yes, the rot has set in. Here in this chapter we have the précis of the novel: that the main impediment to achievement is the political power of those who cannot achieve themselves but intend to control it and everything else, and the only way to break that control is to remove from the system the means of allowing that political power into the hands of the unproductive.

The union backs off – it has little choice. Every single operational individual on the Taggart system volunteers to ride Dagny's chariot of fire. And they provide an armed escort, one per mile of track.   That part isn't ceremonial.   Dagny's opponents would not stick at sabotage and everyone knows it.

The Ethics of Employment

It seems only fair to point out that the Taggart employees, here celebrated for their independence and courage, are the same ones cursed earlier in the novel for enervation, incompetence and ennui. It's a bit of a stretch on Rand's part to attempt to have it both ways. It brings to the fore a question that Rand touched on in the person of Francisco: is the relationship between employer and employee strictly on the basis of largesse – *"jobs which I give to them"* as Dagny put it – or is there an element of reciprocity, a responsibility on the part of the employer toward an effective and ethical employee?   And if there is the latter, at what point is Atlas shrugging an action that is impermissible by the very morals that mandate it?

We have already seen Francisco d'Anconia's view of that issue. It is that he provided the jobs for people who couldn't do that for themselves – point taken – and that he allowed them to be defrauded by the system in which they were participating.   Were there no ethical employees in that arrangement, no one who did what he paid them to do honestly and effectively?   And if there were, did he not betray them, judged by his own standards?   It would appear that he does feel that he betrayed them and that it haunts him, a deplorable but inevitable cost of his own shrugging. We have already seen within Rand's ostensibly atheistic world the artifact of soul, and now we encounter the concept of sin.

Dagny's Ride to Glory

For a dozen pages we read Rand's best effort at descriptive writing nearly uninterrupted by dialogue.   It is the exhilaration of speed, the expression of high achievement in a train doing no less than a hundred miles an hour over untested rail.   It is a metaphor for the sort of life the immovable movers lead, the reward due them for their own personal excellence and that of their followers for their faith.

It's quite a performance, although those who live in the west might look askance at the notion of a freight train hurtling through a small town at a hundred miles an hour, traffic being protected by nothing more than an occasional cross-buck sign. Stop, look and listen – or else.

At last there is a triumphant arrival, a climax to this crypto-sexual Ride of the Valkyries that is consummated later in Dagny and Hank's physical congress in Ellis Wyatt's house. Earlier in the chapter Hank's wife has scoffed at the notion that Dagny is his mistress, and yet here they are in one another's arms. It shouldn't be a surprise. They are two people very much alone, and very much alike. They thirst, they ache for peers. And it is those peers who, one by one, are disappearing from the face of the earth.

The Issue of Rail Speed Limits

At the time of the publication of the book, railroads were entirely responsible for speed limits on their tracks. A 1910 law, most recently upheld in 1996, refused permission for towns to restrict train speeds.

On the John Galt Line, blocks were two miles long. In the real world of railroading, blocks are of variable length. Each block begins with a signal tower that conveys the aspect of the block by a red, yellow or green signal. There is no standardization of block signals in America today; each railroad has its own unique customs. A railroad engineer is issued a booklet with each block on the line listed by milepost and with its designated speed limit. Railroads also use speed limit signs that are often coded separately for freight and passenger trains. The speed limit on a given block is determined by factors such as curvature of the rail and the number of grade crossings. Rail yards have much lower speed limits unless the yard possesses a separate bypass track.

As recently as the Fifties, a dispatcher might radio an engineer and say, "You own the railroad tonight." This was a signal for the engineer to use his own judgment on following the posted speed limits. Today every rail line has track-side sensors, and every train has a FRED Unit ("friendly rear-end device") where the caboose used to be. These tools gather data and use telemetry to pass it to the dispatcher. Thanks to these innovations, engineers with a heavy hand on the throttle are a thing of the past.

The Federal Railroad Administration now sets maximum speed limits on America's railroads. The maximum speed for freight trains is 70 mph, and for passenger trains, 79 mph. Passenger trains on certain types of track with in-cab signals are permitted to go 110 mph, and Amtrak's Northeast Corridor has its own speed limits with sections rated at 120 to 150 mph.

It is obvious that turning the Rio Norte Line into the John Galt Line involved a complete re-engineering. Dagny's train runs around curves and grades, through heavily populated Denver, the Denver station and its yard at 100 mph, which today is simply prohibited.

Discussion Topics

- Contrast Hank's dealing with that old pirate Ken Danagger versus dealing with the sweaty Paul Larkin.

- This time it's Dwight Sanders. Why Sanders? Increment the body count!

- Rather than open the John Galt Line, a "citizen's committee" demands a government impact study first. What is frighteningly familiar about this?

Chapter IX: The Sacred and the Profane

Synopsis

Dagny is awash in the afterglow of a fine night in bed with Hank. Hank, however, is contemptuous of Dagny and of himself for what he has done. Dagny laughs at him, not with anger but with delight. She wants him just as badly, and her proudest attainment is that she has slept with Hank Rearden and, interestingly, has earned the right.

Jim Taggart has sat through a triumphal meeting with his board of directors while Taggart stock has skyrocketed. Yet through the fine speeches, he perceives the board's contempt for him and for themselves. Walking through the rain and realizing he has lost his handkerchief, Jim enters a dying five-and-ten to buy tissues and meets a salesgirl who recognizes him.

Cherryl Brooks is under the impression that it is Jim Taggart's courage, tenacity and hard work that have produced the success in Colorado. Cherryl is the victim of hero worship, views Jim as a Great Man, and is thrilled when he asks her to accompany him to his apartment for a drink. He is attracted to her because she is innocent and genuine, not attempting to play the games that all the other women around him seem to play.

At the apartment over drinks, Jim expresses anger with Hank Rearden for making Rearden Metal a success. Rearden didn't deserve it, says Jim, and did it for his own personal profit. Cherryl has no problem with profit as a motive, and thinks that Jim should glory in his, Rearden's and Dagny's success. She thinks especially highly of Dagny, which Jim finds infuriating. Dagny enjoys her work, therefore to her brother there is nothing to admire. Why serve industrialists in Colorado when there are blighted areas that need transportation? Why should anybody spend ten years to create a new metal? Somebody needs to see beyond his own wallet, says Jim.

But he cheers up when he remembers Orren Boyle's reaction to the success of the John Galt Line: Boyle turned green and holed up in a disreputable hotel with crates of booze and a gaggle of prostitutes. Dr. Floyd Ferris of the State Science Institute was not pleased but turned the issue around by demanding that Rearden give something back to the country. In an unprecedented moment Bertram Scudder refused comment. Simon Pritchett spread a story that Rearden stole the formula for the metal from a penniless inventor whom he then murdered.

Jim gives his opinion of his sister Dagny, who is coming back to New York tomorrow, to Cherryl, who can't believe that Jim could hate Dagny so much. Jim believes that nobody is any good, that man should spend his life on his knees begging to be forgiven for his very existence, and that unhappiness is the true mark of virtue. Cherryl chooses to interpret this as Character and looks up to Jim. He considers a sexual overture, but realizing that he has no desire for her tonight, he takes her home. Cherryl is pleased that he didn't try to seduce her, and Jim is insufferably pleased with his own nobility.

At Dagny's apartment, Hank drops in to compliment her on her work on the John Galt Line. Rearden is inundated with orders for his metal. Dagny's achievement has opened the way for new wealth and a new future. Hank recites Dagny's praises in the press, then takes her brutally. Afterward, Hank asks about her sexual history. She mentions one other partner she had in her teens where the relationship lasted some years. But she won't mention Francisco's name. Hank demands an answer and gets only a smile, which prompts him to take her again. Brutally.

Mr. Mowen of Connecticut watches a worker loading railcars at the Quinn Ball Bearing Plant. He engages the worker – who turns out to be none other than Owen Kellogg, who left Taggart Transcontinental in the first chapter – in conversation about people going to Colorado when other Eastern states are suffering. Quinn is moving to Colorado because of the Equalization of Opportunity Bill, which places severe limits on the freedom of action of industrialists. Mowen condemns Colorado for taking away everyone's business and complains that the state provides very little in the way of government. Mowen also complains that he can't get Rearden Metal because the backlog is too long, and he blames Rearden as well for his inability to procure steel from Orren Boyle. He states that it isn't fair that people can't compete with Ellis Wyatt; there should be a limit placed on his output – and yet New York is running out of oil.

The John Galt Line has been turned over to Taggart Transcontinental as per contract, and Dagny's headquarters building has been demolished. Hank drops in at Dagny's apartment in his tuxedo. He has left a banquet to which Dagny was invited, but chose not to attend so as not to be seen in public with Hank. The theme of the banquet had been that everybody needed Hank, as though they were making a potential claim on him.

Dagny makes great plans for laying track made of Rearden Metal across the entire Taggart system. Hank plans to open mills outside Pennsylvania, believing that the Equalization of Opportunity Bill, which would prohibit such expansion, will collapse of its own weight.

Hank and Dagny decide to take a road trip together as a vacation, but it is a vacation with a purpose. America's decaying network of two-lane highways is described in detail. There are no billboards, few houses, fewer cars, and weeds growing between the cracks in the concrete. What Dagny misses most is the sign of fresh paint.

Ted Nielsen of Colorado intends to build diesel locomotives but can't find the necessary machine tools. Thinking of a closed factory in Wisconsin where Nielsen could scrounge machine parts, Dagny suggests a trip there. Much of the road to Starnesville has actually been torn up and perhaps sold elsewhere. The town itself appears to have been dismantled except for the few inhabited dwellings scattered about at random. Above the town on a hill stands the plant of the Twentieth Century Motor Company, abandoned ten years earlier.

Dagny and Hank ask for directions from a swollen and shapeless woman who lives in a house with a useless gas stove and cooks over a stone fireplace. Her light comes from candles, and her children look like savages. She is not sure where the factory is or how far it is to the next town.

Rearden asks for directions from a man who is drawing water from a squeaky pump at a communal well. Hank offers to pay him ten dollars, but the man refuses the money, stating that the money is worthless. The people of Starnesville use barter among themselves and don't trade with other towns. The man can't give them decent directions, but at last they do find their way to their destination.

The Twentieth Century Motor Company's plant is a ruin. Dagny's exploration turns up the wreck of a motor and a paper description of its purpose. It is like no motor she has ever seen, except in college, where it was said that such a thing was impossible. It is a motor that runs off static electricity. Hank and Dagny realize that no one but the designer could make it work, and Dagny suspects the designer is dead, else why would he abandon it? They decide to send a crew to retrieve the motor and anything else that might be salvaged from the plant.

Cherryl Brooks and the Culture of the Thirties

The documentary film "Forbidden Hollywood" covers movies made in the Thirties before Will Hays and the Production Code censored American films for 34 years. One pre-Code classic was 1933's "Baby Face", with Barbara Stanwyck as Lily Powers. Lily is the daughter of a speakeasy owner in Erie, Pennsylvania, who has paid off local law enforcement by pimping her since she was 14. One night, Daddy's still blows up, killing him, and Lily goes to New York with her black girlfriend – fairly provocative in 1933 – to make her fortune.

She gets a job by bedding the personnel chief at Gotham Trust and sleeps her way to the top. One man she beds and abandons early on is a bank clerk played by the young, unknown John Wayne. At each seduction and abandonment, the camera plays on the bank building, going up floor by floor. The film is done in a breathless "Mothers, don't let your daughters do this!" style. Today's audiences laugh and root for Lily.

Although there was no mandatory code yet for the motion picture industry, the film ran afoul of the New York State Censorship Board which objected to some sexually suggestive scenes – but really bridled at Lily's reading Nietzsche! The producers cut and added footage, and tacked on a moralistic ending to satisfy the board. The uncensored version turned up in a vault in 2004 and has been named one of the best 100 movies of the past 80 years.

In the popular culture of the Thirties, it would have been the perfect comeuppance for Jim Taggart to be taken down by a little guttersnipe from Erie.   But Rand, who worked as a script doctor in Hollywood, avoids the clichés of the era and reaches for deeper meaning.   Cherryl Brooks is not Lily Powers, far from it; in fact, she is the anti-Lily.

Cherryl left her family in Buffalo because they were lazy incompetents who blamed their station in life on bad luck, rather than seeing that they themselves were responsible.   She recognizes that she "comes from dirt," but she doesn't intend to stay in the gutter.   She comes to New York with that great Gershwin spirit, seeing it as the City of Possibilities.   Cherryl does not intend to sleep her way to the top through Jim Taggart – she has a moral code and sticks to it.   It lends a special poignancy to Cherryl's eventual fate.

Hank and Dagny's Relationship

Hank is prey to a fit of post-coital depression and self-loathing, and Dagny rightly laughs at him.   Here Rand presents a question that might have bothered Fifties-era readers more than it does their somewhat jaded successors – should Hank feel badly?   Are the immovable movers exempt from conventional morality due to sheer personal excellence, or only from the corrupt bits of it?   Nietzsche, from whom Rand got the dilemma in the first place, would have answered "all of it."   Rand seems to agree.

But clearly Hank is disgusted at himself for having compromised his wedding vows.   It is the first hint that Hank is slowly, relentlessly, being sucked out of his ethical premises not only on matters of marital propriety but on a far broader front as well.   For now it is Dagny who is helping him.   Who will help her when her turn comes?

At last Dagny dons the bracelet.   This is no longer subtle; the characters know perfectly well what it signifies and say so, Dagny with a somewhat arch aside that she'd have slept with Rearden in order to consummate a necessary business deal if he'd demanded it.

As long as it were he. This isn't prostitution any more than their real intercourse was rape, but it is a prostitution fantasy – just as Rearden's was a rape fantasy – that she finds amusing, yet another insight into her vigorous sexuality. How serious it really is, however, is highly questionable – we remember that she denied both herself and Francisco the re-ignition of their affair under much less trying circumstances. Dagny is no slut and Hank is no rapist, which may be why they can indulge themselves in the fantasies.

The Fifties and Dagny's Sexual History

There is a tendency in popular culture to insist that strict sexual morality was the norm in American society through the Fifties until the Baby Boomers discovered hedonism in the Sixties. It is a silly conceit, actually – the world was, after all, populated somehow before that, and it is entirely possible that sex was involved. A complete study of American sexual mores from the Founding onward is outside the range of current consideration. Let us begin the story *in medias res*, after World War I. The end of the bloodshed and the relief of the survivors prompted a general loosening of sexual morality in Europe and America in the Twenties, and in America the great social error of Prohibition undermined respect for law and morality. American girls bobbed their hair, shortened their skirts, went drinking at "blind pigs", as speakeasies were known, and gleefully discarded their virginity.

There was of course a reaction – in East Texas, for example, the Ku Klux Klan patrolled the parking spots where teenagers were known to congregate. Catching a couple in the act, Klansmen would pull the young offenders out of the car, tie them to a tree and horsewhip them. This was termed "preserving family values" although what it implies about the precise nature of such a family seems questionable to the modern eye.

The pendulum swung the other way with the Depression. People's interests focused more on just staying alive, and extramarital sex became something that criminals, communists and college students did to protest bourgeois morality. With World War II, things loosened up once more, and girls engaged to military men understood that they might not see them alive again once they boarded the troopships. There was some promiscuity among women who worked in the factories and whose husbands were at war, but the role models promulgated by the popular magazines and movies of the period were still, in the words of a contemporary song, "Don't sit under the apple tree with anyone else but me."

Consider this from the perspective of a returning war veteran. He's lived through a tumultuous period of death, depression and social change. Coming home from the war, he wants a job, a house where he and his wife can live away from the parents of either, a car and the classic 2.3 children. He craves stability. That is what the Fifties were about: a breathing space between periods of change, and if those who had survived the bloody chaos of war seemed to overemphasize conventionality in the interest of safety and stability, one can hardly blame them.

It is in that context that we must attempt to understand Hank's reasonable – to him – demand that Dagny reveal the details of her past sexual life. Dagny's laughing refusal is the hint of an approaching age where such details are her business and hers alone. It is often difficult for the inhabitants of a less sexually repressive age to recognize just how radical this was, and just how outrageous this aspect of Rand's novel must have seemed to critics of her time. If she seems to dwell on this overmuch to the modern eye, that may be part of the reason.

Mr. Mowen, Unions and the Third World

"Things aren't right... The Equalization of Opportunity Bill was a sound idea. There's got to be a chance for everybody. It's a rotten shame if people like Quinn take unfair advantage of it. Why didn't he let somebody else start manufacturing ball bearings in Colorado?... I wish the Colorado people would leave us alone. That Stockton Foundry out there had no right going into the switch and signal business. That's been my business for years, I have the right of seniority, it isn't fair, it's dog-eat-dog competition, newcomers shouldn't be allowed to muscle in."

In the Sixties, those words didn't come from business owners like Mr. Mowen. They came from the mouths of union bosses.

To a very great degree organized labor was responsible in the Fifties for creating the American middle class as we know it, and it did so by insisting that unskilled labor be paid the same wages as skilled labor. Following the war, America had the only industrial framework in the world that hadn't been destroyed by bombardment. American unions could demand higher wages, and the rest of the world had no choice but to pay whatever price was demanded for American goods while the devastated countries were rebuilt. That was balanced by the fact that much of the reconstruction was funded out of the pockets of those same American workers. But it was a good time to be one of the latter. An American male could drop out of school, get his union card, sign up at the local plant, marry, have 2.3 children, own a car, house and vacation home, and at age 65 retire with a full pension and go fishing. Good times while they lasted.

In the Sixties, the Third World came on line as a source of cheap labor; in the Seventies, high labor costs caused American goods to be priced out of world markets. The unions had at last lost their pricing power.

In the novel, the divisions expressed by the terms First, Second, and Third Worlds do not exist, because that sort of industrial development pattern had been aborted by an overall acceptance of state socialism. And so, in the novel, it is proceeding in the United States as well, most of it anyway. But there is Colorado, with its minimalist libertarian government, and capitalists move there because it is the last place on the developed planet where there is room enough to breathe. There is room to fail as well, and that frightens our Mr. Mowen. He would be content clinging to what is, but what is, is falling apart.

Starnesville

In AD 476, a Gothic chieftain named Odoacer and the Roman army deposed the last Western emperor. The vast economic structure that was the Roman Empire collapsed. The Roman currency had been clipped and debased to the point where the legions refused the coinage as payment. The Roman bureaucracy soldiered on, pretending that nothing had changed, until at last it gave up the ghost and taxes were no longer collected. On the frontier, Roman legions, now unpaid, deserted, either going home or marrying into the families of the area in which they were stationed.

It was the beginning what is less than accurately referred to as the Dark Ages, a period of time within which the grandeur of Rome retreated, even within the city itself, to those refuges afforded by the surviving manors, the established families, and the grain fields and vineyards that fed them. The heads of these manors were at first scions of the great Roman families, diluted by intermarriage with the newer, more vigorous Gothic and Vandal invaders, who settled down to compose the foundation of modern Europe. There were thanes, barons and dukes, but there would be no kings for nearly four centuries.

It was not exactly an apocalypse, but it forms the basis for an entire genre of post-apocalyptic literature from Procopius to Mad Max. It is typified by despair, vacuum and lack of direction. It is first suggested in *Atlas Shrugged* by Starnesville, Wisconsin.

Starnesville is a vision of hell. The town isn't much more than a ghost town, with no economic base, no school, no gas, no electricity and no running water. Federal Reserve Notes are useless, and people use barter within the town. Nobody trades with other towns, and people aren't even sure how far away the next town is. All we are missing is the local clan chief with his thugs on horseback declaring that Starnesville is his fiefdom. And later in the novel something precisely like that is suggested.

Rand's view of Starnesville after the fall is that of pre-industrial America peopled by citizens with only industrial-age skills. They're starving. And just in case we didn't get the point from *les misérables* with the diapers on the clothesline, Rand ends the chapter with the vision of a post-industrial future:

She looked out at the country. She moaned suddenly...and dropped her head on her arm...

"What's the matter?" he asked.

She did not answer.

He looked out. Far below, in the valley, in the gathering night, there trembled a few pale smears which were the lights of tallow candles.

One understands her horror. It is a hardscrabble existence for its unlucky inhabitants. No power, no food, no hope. But it is, in laudatory lectures from ecological zealots, a "sustainable" lifestyle. So was the Neanderthal's. It didn't help.

What we have here before us in Starnesville happened in the short space of twelve years since the area's economic bubble popped.   Is this believable?   Absolutely, as a visit to contemporary Detroit, or any of the American West's numerous ghost towns will attest. When their economies died, they died, so rapidly in many cases that they seem frozen in time. This is what happens when Atlas shrugs.

Life in the ruins. It has a bittersweet element, a remembrance of things that were, and for most of the inhabitants of Starnesville, a complete misunderstanding of why they are no longer. It is a metaphor, a warning. It is no accident that on the way, Dagny and Hank will have to pass through a place called Rome.

Discussion Topics

- Jim Taggart's soliloquy on virtue is tough on even the strongest stomachs. Compare his – and Simon Pritchett's – philosophy of existence with today's world, particularly with respect to the idea of Deep Ecology.

- Cherryl Brooks' neighbor in Buffalo told her that it was her obligation to take care of her family of layabouts because she was the only one who could hold down a job and because nobody could do anything to change his circumstances in this world. Where does one hear this today?

- Decrement the body count! Owen Kellogg has turned up, and he's working as a common day laborer with a short assignment at Quinn's plant in Connecticut. Why a day laborer, when he could have had an executive position at Taggart Transcontinental? What does it have to do with the disappearance of other executives?

Chapter X: Wyatt's Torch

Synopsis

Dagny and Hank visit the county seat and discover that the Twentieth Century Motor Company is tied up in litigation with two owners vying in court for possession. Mark Yonts of the People's Mortgage Company of Rome, Wisconsin, an institution known for easy credit, had sold the company to a concern in South Dakota and then used it again quite illegally as collateral for a loan from a bank in Illinois. When his company collapsed, Yonts disappeared after stripping the factory of its assets. All records are gone due to a courthouse fire.

They visit Mayor Bascom of Rome, Wisconsin, who had sold the factory to Yonts. The mayor had looted the factory of Jed Starnes' mahogany desk and a manager's luxurious stall shower. He had picked up the factory after the crash of the Community National Bank in Madison. Eugene Lawson, the "*banker with a heart*" who had owned that bank, is now with the Bureau of Economic Planning and National Resources, working with Rearden's ex-employee Wesley Mouch.

Hank and Dagny drive no fewer than 200 miles to find a place where they can make a long distance phone call. Dagny reaches Eddie to ask him to send two engineers to Starnesville to collect the motor. Eddie tells her in a panic that "they," apparently meaning the government, are planning to kill Colorado.

Back in New York, Dagny and Eddie stash the mysterious motor in a vault under the Taggart Terminal.

Hank discovers that Paul Larkin has not kept his word on the shipment of ore to the Rearden mill. He has been shipping it by rail, not lake boat, to support Jim Taggart's failing branch line in Minnesota. And he has shipped it to Orren Boyle. Hank now plumbs the back alleys of the steel business to find the ore he needs.

At home, Lillian enters Hank's bedroom; she wants something. She speaks of the virtue of telling an ugly woman she is attractive and how loving a woman for her virtues is meaningless if she actually possesses them. She notices that Hank has been less

70

tense of late. As she embraces him, he tears himself away from her in revulsion. Hank asks her for her purpose in life. She states that simply *being* is enough for an enlightened person.

Dagny visits Eugene Lawson at his Washington office; he thinks she is there to beg favors of the bureau for her railroad, but Dagny disabuses him of that notion. In fact, she is there to inquire about the Twentieth Century Motor Company. Lawson feels no guilt in the collapse of his bank because he lost everything in the crash; he is proud of his sacrifice. He based his bank's lending policy on *"need, not greed."* Lawson put up the money for the purchase of the Twentieth Century Motor Company because the plant was absolutely essential to the region. While saying that the common worker at the plant was his friend, he can't seem to remember anyone's name. As Lawson sees it, he suffered for an ideal: Love. Dagny asks if he has seen that section of Wisconsin lately, and Lawson becomes defensive, blaming the rich. But Lawson remembers Lee Hunsacker, the man from Amalgamated Services, who bought the plant and is now living in Grangeville, Oregon. As Dagny leaves, Lawson states that he is proud that he has never made a profit. Dagny tells him that is the most despicable statement a man could ever make.

Lee Hunsacker lives in squalor, cadging free space from a working married couple in their home, and he blames the world for never having given him a chance. Jed Starnes, the founder of the Twentieth Century Motor Company, was a backwoods garage mechanic, while Hunsacker came from the New York Four Hundred, the city's richest and most prominent citizens. Hunsacker's mission in life is to complete his all-important autobiography; he has no interest in pulling his weight for the benefit of his hosts. His opportunity at the Twentieth Century Motor Company was his life's dream. The Starnes heirs had run it into the ground, and he went to the bankers to get money to buy the plant, only to discover that the bankers were intent on profit. Midas Mulligan, the Chicago banker, had been particularly rough on him. And Hunsacker says he was the only man who ever beat Mulligan.

Dagny remembers the legend of Michael "Midas" Mulligan, who had bankrolled Rearden Steel in its early days. One never dared mention "need" when one went into his office to ask for a loan. Seven years ago, Mulligan had vanished in the most orderly bank run in American history: everyone who had entrusted Mulligan with his money got it back to the penny before the doors slammed shut.

Mulligan had told Hunsacker that he was unqualified to run a vegetable pushcart. So Hunsacker sued. Judge Narragansett ruled against him, but an appeals court overruled Narragansett and granted him the loan. Rather than comply, Mulligan shut down his bank and disappeared. And very quietly, Narragansett retired and disappeared six months later.

Eugene Lawson granted him the loan, though, but it wasn't enough. The new factory owners went bankrupt when a competitor, Nielsen of Colorado, put out a similar motor at half the price. Hunsacker's top priority was to make the plant's offices prettier for the sake of his mental attitude, which included that luxurious shower in his executive washroom that eventually ended up in Mayor Bascom's possession. He blames the failure on outside conditions beyond his control. But he *does* know the location of the Starnes heirs: Durance, Louisiana.

The Durance police chief tells Dagny that Eric Starnes had killed himself years ago after a life of whining about his sensitive feelings, committing a messy suicide in the house of the 16 year old girl who had spurned him. Gerald Starnes lives in a flophouse married to a whiskey bottle. Ivy Starnes lives in a house by the Mississippi, spending her days inhaling incense while sitting on a pillow on the floor. She is far above the mundane concerns of mere mortals thanks to a trust fund from her father which, curiously, she has managed to retain despite the destitution of her brothers. And she has a story to tell.

Jed Starnes was an evil man, Ivy tells us, because all he thought about was money – hers, as it turns out, although she seems singularly ungrateful, even unaware, of the fact. That he had built a successful business was to Ivy immaterial. Ivy and her brothers felt that they existed on a more enlightened plane, and so the heirs of Jed Starnes implemented "The Plan" for the factory according to a historical precept: From each according to his ability, to each according to his need. Over the space of four years The Plan collapsed into a morass of lawyers, cops and courtrooms. She can only remember the name of William Hastings, the lab chief, who quit as soon as The Plan was introduced and moved to Brandon, Wyoming. He was the second person to quit, and she can't remember the name of the first. Dagny takes her leave of Ivy Starnes, appalled. The woman has learned nothing from the experience, and despite the ruination of everyone involved, herself excepted, she feels the whole thing was a noble effort, pure in intention.

Dagny meets Mrs. Hastings, now a widow. After working for some years in Wyoming, her husband retired. In the last two years of his life he went away for a month every summer and wouldn't tell his wife where he was. Mrs. Hastings remembers the motor, however, and says it was designed by a 26 year old colleague of her husband. Mrs. Hastings had seen the designer as he left on a train along with an older, distinguished looking gentleman. More recently she had seen that same older gentleman working at a diner west of Cheyenne in the mountains.

Traveling to Cheyenne, Dagny finds the older gentleman cooking at the diner, and he cooks the best hamburger she has ever tasted. She offers him the job of head of the Dining Car Department at the railroad, but he refuses. Dagny is upset that she can't find anybody who can do a job properly, and she gets compassion from the cook. She asks him if he knew the engineer at Twentieth Century, and after a pause he says he did – and that she will never find him. The cook is none other than the philosopher Hugh Akston, who last taught at Patrick Henry University. Dagny can't figure out why the leading philosopher of the age is cooking at a diner in the Rockies. She asks about the three students he and Robert Stadler had shared; Akston says that nobody would remember the nameless third man. But he is proud of all three. Akston offers Dagny a cigarette and tells her that the designer of the motor will find her when he chooses. The cigarette is stamped with a gold dollar sign.

At the Cheyenne station, Dagny overhears a conversation about the latest directives issued by the government bureaucracy, apparently authorized by the National Legislature. Alarmed, she grabs a newspaper and discovers that Wesley Mouch has been very busy, issuing a set of directives due to a national emergency:

- Railroads are to slow down and run smaller trains, and to run an equal number of trains in multi-state districts designed by the government for just that purpose.

- Steel mills are to limit production to avoid competition and provide equal shares to all customers.

- Manufacturing companies are forbidden to move out of their home states.

- Railroad bonds are to go into legal default for five years.

- A special tax is to be levied on Colorado to support these measures.

It is the end of Colorado, and Dagny senses that Ellis Wyatt is going to do something rash. She tries to stop him before it is too late, but Wyatt doesn't answer the phone. As her train comes to an emergency stop, in utter horror Dagny witnesses Wyatt's oil fields going up in flames. His last message before his disappearance is, *"I am leaving it as I found it. Take over. It's yours."*

Socialism and the Crooked World of Finance

Dagny and Hank stop in the decaying community of Rome, Wisconsin – the Rome of AD 476, perhaps, that has not yet truly fallen but is in the hands of barbarians – wherein one Mayor Bascom presents an argument that is critical to the understanding of the economic and philosophical underpinnings of socialism. Within a long and frightening list of characters is Rand's own Bernie Madoff, a fraudulent financier named Mark Yonts:

"He wasn't the kind who ever operates anything. He didn't want to make money, only to get it."

That didn't, of course, prevent the Mayor from helping Yonts' plunder:

"There's plenty of laws that's sort of made of rubber, and a mayor's in a position to stretch them a bit for a friend. Well, what the hell? That's the only way anybody ever gets rich in this world" – he glanced at the luxurious black car – *"as you ought to know."*

And there it is, the foundational moral premise of socialism. "Property is theft," said Pierre-Joseph Proudhon, the proto-anarchist, in *Confessions of a Revolutionary*. Interesting fellow, Proudhon. Before his breakup with Marx he was quite the thing in post-revolutionary France, at one point attempting to institute a curious scheme for the redistribution of wealth, a bank that obtained its money from the evil capitalists through an income tax and lending it to the workers at what amounted to sub-prime rates of interest. It failed, of course. Surely nobody would be stupid enough to try that in the United States? Surely they were.

This fundamental article of faith, of received truth underlying socialism, is that wealth is theft, that any movement from the "natural", even distribution of wealth is illegitimate, that the wealthy are *ipso facto* criminal, and that as such it is not a criminal act, but one of "social justice," to steal it back on behalf of the people – and take a prime cut off the top for being clever enough to figure the whole thing out. Is there a thief yet who didn't consider himself cleverer than his victims? Not Mayor Bascom, certainly – he feels he has the whole thing figured out, and Hank has to restrain his hands from the mayor's throat.

A crooked financier, and next a failed bank. The reader is to be forgiven for suspecting that Rand owned a crystal ball.

"Some say it was this motor factory that broke the bank, but others say it was only the last drop in a leaking bucket, because the Community National had bum investments all over three or four states. Eugene Lawson was the head of it. The banker with a heart, they called him."

75

The *"banker with a heart,"* meaning he made loans on a basis of something other than the likelihood of repayment. Banks that do that tend to fail, as we are learning so bitterly of late, having compounded one banker's foolishness to all the banks by governmental mandate. This is something more than prescience on Rand's part; it borders on the eerie.

Marxism and "The Plan"

The Starnes siblings destroyed the Twentieth Century Motor Company by following a set of Marxist precepts that would make an observer of modern history shudder with recognition. The factory was run by workers' councils – the Russians called them *soviets* – that adjudicated compensation on the basis of the employees' abilities to state their need. Naturally where need was rewarded and achievement punished, the achievers departed rapidly, and the needy remained to divide the pie, dwindling because those capable of replenishing it were gone.

Lenin actually tried something like this between 1918 and 1921. His industries went broke nearly as quickly as Rand's fictional one, and the upshot was a new, "realistic" approach named the New Economic Policy. But along with this was a subtle difference that Trotsky pointed out in *The Revolution Betrayed*: "to each according to his need" was shown not to be a feasible principle during this "stage" of historical progress toward communism. It became "to each according to his work," and naturally that work included a premium on the activities of the ruling class, to their enrichment. Stalin followed this with full collectivization and central direction, after which the workers' soviets went the way of the workers' councils at the Twentieth Century Motor Company. Some of their principal members were stood against a wall and shot, blinking, never understanding why their socialist fantasy land had such a grim ending.

The Plot to Kill Colorado

A distraught Eddie Willers, who has been holding Taggart Transcontinental together with his bare hands, describes what to him is simply unbelievable:

"Dagny, you're going to think I'm insane, but I think they're planning to kill Colorado."

He is correct. Eddie understands what the looters do not, that wealth is the product of achievement, not theft, and that when the achievement ceases or is deliberately prevented, wealth is no longer created. Eventually the theft ceases as well, because as we have seen at the Starnes' company, there is nothing left to steal.

But to the looters – we may openly call them socialists now – wealth is a pile of material goods that someone has amassed immorally, to be confiscated and divided by those who have established political control over it. They are killing Colorado because they cannot control it and because it represents a threat to the piles of material goods they do control. On a deeper level, they are killing Colorado so that the achievers – who appear to them only as particularly skilled thieves, although not so skilled as themselves – will have nowhere else to go.

That is, parenthetically, the reason that communism – its own proponents state this – can only succeed if it is established on a worldwide basis. There must be no escape. That is a particularly revealing admission. If communism is, as Marx insists, the acme of human actualization, then why would anyone wish to escape from it? And yet every communist state ever established became a prison camp in pursuit of some mythical, never realized benefit to the prisoners. To the communist the inhabitants wish to escape because they are not yet perfect enough for the system. In no sense must the system be perfect enough for them. It is the collective, after all, that is supreme, not the individuals who compose it. But in fact this is the death of the human spirit, not its transcendence, and that is the point Rand is attempting to convey in *Atlas Shrugged.*

The Bureau of Economic Planning and National Resources makes its move against Colorado, and if this sounds disturbingly familiar, it ought to:

"The laws shouldn't be passed that way, so quickly."

"They're not laws, they're directives...there's no time to palaver when it's a national emergency."

In reply, Ellis Wyatt makes his own move, leaving behind a single derrick that burns with a perpetual flame, his legacy, Wyatt's Torch.   Rand strips us of the romantic hope that persons of achievement must always prevail over the obstacles presented to them by lesser men.   It isn't so.   And a society corrupted to the point where it isn't so, is committing suicide.

Beatniks, Hippies and Existentialists

Following the end of World War II, the bebop movement in jazz gave birth to the beatniks, who became one of the two rebel classes of the Fifties; the other was the greasers.   Rand witnessed the rise of the beatniks, but gave them no space in the book.   What she managed to anticipate, however, is a surprise: Ivy Starnes, prototypical hippie.

Ivy lives in a house by the Mississippi River inhaling the vapors of incense – and probably other things – as she sits on a pillow on the floor contemplating her navel.   She is a practicing communist and will keep practicing until she gets it right.   She attempted to bring Marxism to Wisconsin and destroyed a company and a town in the process, concluding, as communists are wont to do, that it was because the people on whom she inflicted her theories weren't worthy of them.

Rand's other surprise is Lillian Rearden.   When hippies of the Sixties were asked about their purpose in life, they would often reply that it was not necessary to *achieve*, but merely to *be*.   Ivy Starnes would have understood this sentiment.   Lillian says much the same thing to Hank when she is asked this question, and she is as far from a hippie as one could imagine.

That attitude, though, had already been anticipated in the grosser excesses of the philosophical movement named Existentialism, with which Rand was thoroughly familiar. We hear its echoes in the words of Dr. Pritchett, for whom the purpose of life is suffering and futility. A human being need aspire to no purpose higher than being – that is his, or her, penultimate moment.

It is properly a transcendental moment as well, a theme Albert Camus played into a seminal Existentialist essay *The Myth of Sisyphus*, wherein a very Randian Sisyphus is condemned to rolling a rock to the top of a hill forever for the crimes of trickery and thwarting the god of death. It is eternal, fruitless labor, intended to torture through frustration, and if we see a hint of Hank Rearden in all this, it was probably not accidental.

But Camus isn't Rand. Concludes Camus:

"The struggle itself...is enough to fill a man's heart. One must imagine Sisyphus happy."

One must imagine Rand outraged. She will leave absolutely no doubt in the reader's mind as to why.

Lee Hunsacker, Coleman Young and the CRA

Lee Hunsacker attempted to raise the capital necessary to buy the old Twentieth Century factory, but a hard-nosed and highly successful banker, Midas Mulligan, turned him down flat. So what did Hunsacker do? He sued, of course:

"...the state of Illinois had a very humane, very progressive law under which I could sue him... I had a very smart, liberal lawyer who saw a way for us to do it. It was an economic emergency law which said that people were forbidden to discriminate for any reason whatever against any person...[Judge Narragansett threw it out]...but we appealed to a higher court – and the higher court reversed the verdict and ordered Mulligan to give us the loan on our terms."

That is precisely what Congress mandated in 1995 in reformulating the Community Reinvestment Act (CRA). Contrary to Marx, the first and fictional occurrence of this history was the farce; the second – the real one – was the tragedy. The government forced banks to lend money at unacceptable risk for criteria other than ability to repay, and default occurred when the borrower proved incapable of generating wealth sufficient to meet his obligations. It took decades for this to grow from a fictional tadpole to a real-world Leviathan, but grow it did. This was not prophecy; it was a necessary consequence of the sort of corruption Rand was positing and that the United States came later to embrace.

In many respects, the fictional Lee Hunsacker was similar to long-time Detroit mayor Coleman Young. In the Seventies Young noticed that different sections of Detroit had differing degrees of investment, a phenomenon known as "redlining". Bankers would invest in one area but not another, which meant that unelected bankers, not elected officials, were deciding which neighborhoods of Detroit would prosper and which would decline. What the mayor chose to ignore was that banks are businesses that live or die by return of investment. Young's success came from framing the argument in terms of racism and civil rights, which is simply another form of an argument from need.

In 1977 Congress passed the CRA. Banks were not being forced to make risky loans – that was strictly forbidden – but bank lending practices were now placed under government supervision. In 1995 the other shoe dropped, but with the government guaranteeing the loans via Fannie Mae and Freddie Mac, the banks didn't protest.

Coleman Young didn't go to court to beat his own Midas Mulligan, he went to Congress. And Congress did what the appellate court did in *Atlas Shrugged* – recast the basis of business from profit to need. The result was the crisis of the early 21st Century, with sub-prime mortgages and the derivatives intended to protect them.

Discussion Topics

- It would appear that the Federal Deposit Insurance Corporation, created by the government during the Depression, somehow managed to fall by the wayside. When Eugene Lawson, the *"banker with a heart"*, had his bank in Madison fail, the depositors were wiped out just as they would have been before FDR's reforms. But Lawson wasn't the only banker who was free and easy with credit in the name of compassion. Mark Yonts ran an S&L in Rome with easy credit, writing mortgages for people who never should have owned homes in the first place. In this early era, Yonts didn't have the ability to sell those loans upstream by packaging them with derivatives as insurance. Define the pattern of financial corruption in the real world and relate it to Rand's world.

- Martin Armstrong points out that if an economy is balanced, then everyone will be poor because there will be no economic activity. Feudalism was a system with a balanced economy. It is the "unbalances" that create economic activity, prosperity, and wealth. Why would government have an interest in turning free men into serfs?

- Increment the body count by three and decrement by one. Michael "Midas" Mulligan and Judge Narragansett disappeared some years ago. Ellis Wyatt has disappeared after torching his own oil fields. And the celebrated Hugh Akston, once head of the Philosophy Department at Patrick Henry University, turns up running a diner near Cheyenne, Wyoming. It is a waste...or is it? Check your premises!

Part II: Either-Or

Chapter I: The Man Who Belonged on Earth

Synopsis

The title of Part II, "Either-Or," is a reference to Aristotle's *Metaphysics* and to the dilemma Rand is beginning to flesh out: Can a society both possess its achievers and exploit them to death simultaneously? And if it turns out to be one or the other, who will decide?

Dr. Robert Stadler's path to his meeting with Dagny is painful, for he is becoming aware of just how corrupt his assistant Dr. Floyd Ferris is, and how far he has bent the State Science Institute to the will of its political backers. Stadler has finally sensed the nature of his fall, and he's finding it difficult to deal with. He deals with Ferris' book, however:

He picked up the book and let it drop into the wastebasket... A face came to his mind...a young face he had not permitted himself to recall for years. He thought: No, he has not read this book, he won't see it, he's dead, he must have died long ago... The sharp pain was the shock of discovering simultaneously that this was the man he longed to see more than any other being in the world – and that he had to hope that this man was dead.

Ambivalence doesn't come any better than that. There is still no name for this man, this ex-student, this hypotenuse of the d'Anconia-Danneskjöld triangle. But he appears to embody something Stadler finds that he has lost and misses bitterly. So, apparently, does Dagny, for Stadler makes his way to her New York office in search of nothing less than his soul.

[Stadler speaking] *"He [the missing engineer] arrived at some new concept of energy. He discarded all our standard assumptions, according to which his motor would have been impossible. He formulated a new premise of his own and he*

82

solved the secret... Do you realize what a feat of pure, abstract science he had to perform...?"

Intentionally or not, Rand is describing what she herself is attempting to accomplish with respect to philosophy: a new paradigm, a structure built on first principles that leads in a direction entirely different from that of conventional philosophy. Whether she actually achieved that will be the topic of future controversies, but it is quite clear that she is aware that it is what she is attempting.

"I knew a John Galt once. Only he died long ago... He had such a mind that, had he lived, the whole world would have been talking of him by now."

"But the whole world is talking of him."

He stopped still. "Yes..." he said slowly, staring at a thought that had never struck him before. "Yes...why?" The word was heavy with the sound of terror.

Who is John Galt? Ayn Rand is John Galt. Hank Rearden is the man who belonged on earth. The precise sense of how this is true will become clearer in future chapters.

It is in this chapter that we are introduced to the mysterious Project X. Ferris explains that "X" stands for "xylophone", and that it would be most inadvisable for Stadler to mention this top secret project.

Dagny's path to her meeting with Stadler is no less painful. She scratches a Colorado freight train off the roster as she has struck so many others. Lawrence Hammond has retired and disappeared, and Hammondsville will no doubt dry up and blow away as have the towns of Wyatt Junction and Stockton. With Wyatt's fire, new operators had claimed the oil business until prices rose to the point where large customers turned to coal, and the government rationed oil and then levied a special tax to subsidize out-of-work oil hands. Then the government subsidized the oil operators but only those with connections. Coal briefly became king until Andrew Stockton retired, closed his foundry and disappeared. The only thing that Dagny can discover is that somebody spent most of the night talking to Stockton before he vanished.

With the oil shortage, Dagny is reduced to running coal burning steam locomotives and depending on Ken Danagger for fuel. Jim is getting a government subsidy for every train running, and those subsidies produce more revenue than Dagny's hard-fought operations. Jim brags that he is responsible for the best six months in the railroad's history.

Wesley Mouch has unfrozen the nation's railroad bonds but only to certain people. A whole new profession of *"defreezing"* has been created by young wonders just out of college who know how to fill out the government paperwork – and who have connections.

Dagny's engineers, who searched the abandoned plant of the Twentieth Century Motor Company for clues surrounding the miracle motor she and Hank uncovered in the rubble, found nothing; they interviewed people who worked there and learned nothing. The Patent Office was a dead end. Dagny's friend at the Taggart Terminal cigarette stand can't even locate the brand of Hugh Akston's golden dollar sign cigarette.

Dagny attempts to find an engineer to reconstruct the motor and encounters people who don't think it will work, don't care if it will work, want too much money to make it work, or believe that if the motor works, it should be suppressed because of the harm it would do to the egos of lesser scientists. So despite the results of her earlier meeting with Dr. Stadler, she decides to see him again. Despite what he has become morally, his is still a brilliant mind.

Shown the incomplete specifications of the motor, Stadler quickly becomes the consummate professional and is beside himself with excitement as he perceives what the designer has wrought. But Stadler can't imagine who could have designed the motor, why he would have designed it at a factory in rural Wisconsin, and he is even more shocked that the designer didn't seek him out. His statement that even a greedy industrialist with no brains would have taken the motor to make a fortune prompts a bitter smile from Dagny. She asks him to recommend someone who could work on the motor, but Stadler tells her he can't even find the kind of simple talent possessed by a decent garage mechanic. He asks to see the motor.

Dagny takes him to the underground vault. Upon seeing the motor, Stadler states with the innocent arrogance of genius that he is thrilled to see a great new idea that isn't his. He condemns the mediocrities who fear anyone with an idea better than their own and who envy achievement. He and Dagny briefly experience a meeting of the minds. Stadler recommends a young engineer named Quentin Daniels who works at the Utah Institute of Technology; he has no desire to work for the government but only for his own wealth, which indicates he just might be one of the good guys. Utah Tech has gone under, but Daniels is still there. It's a lead that Dagny will follow up.

Hank Rearden refuses an order from the State Science Institute for ten thousand tons of Rearden Metal for Project X. The Fair Share Law has dictated an arbitrary government figure for what he can produce *per annum*, and he now has a backlog of orders for the next fifty years. The rights to Rearden Metal – the modern term is "derivatives" – are being bought and sold on a gray market by speculators with everybody making a profit but Hank. Those speculators who get the rights are those with connections in Washington. Hank Rearden watches as the bounty given to the world in the form of his metal has been expropriated, throttled and redistributed in accordance with current political doctrine. It is not how fortunes are made, but it *is* how they are stolen:

He turned away without a word when anybody mentioned to him what everybody knew: the quick fortunes that were being made on Rearden Metal. "Well, no," people said in drawing rooms, "you mustn't call it a black market, because it isn't, really. Nobody is selling the Metal illegally. They're just selling their right to it. Not selling, really, just pooling their shares."

The modern reader may find this an uncomfortable reminder of the remarkable artifice known as carbon credits. Rand was being exaggeratedly cynical with respect to metal. How incredulous would she be to learn that someone was seriously treating the very

85

air we breathe as a commodity the rights to which may be bartered by those whose only power over them is granted by arbitrary statute? Had Rand placed that scam into *Atlas Shrugged*, people would have laughed at its outlandishness.

We meet briefly a young man known derisively as the Wet Nurse, a government representative empowered to see that Rearden Metal is distributed to the approved recipients. Earnest but deluded, a fully fledged product of the corrupt educational institutions of the day, he retains an innocence that Rearden finds amusing.

"You know, Mr. Rearden, there are no absolute standards. We can't go by rigid principles...we've got to...act on the expediency of the moment."

"Run along, punk. Go and try to pour a ton of steel without rigid principles, on the expediency of the moment."

It is an engineer's answer to some of the sillier excesses of postmodern philosophy – one may happily entertain the argument that there is no truth, that everything is contextual, a matter of interpretive relationship between reader and text, and yet those of us whose lives depend on it would rather not drive over a bridge built on the assumption that the difference in tensile strength between steel and cardboard is merely a matter of opinion.

Hank is visited by a paramilitary representative inquiring about his reasons for refusing the order. Hank won't provide that answer and refuses to sell anything to the Institute for any purpose. The officer explains that Hank must obey the law; Hank tells him to arrest him and steal whatever he wants from the railcars sitting in the steel mill's yard. The individual is horrified, not at the immorality of theft, but at how the public would react, and tells Hank that he will regret his decision.

From this point, Rand digresses into yet another disquisition on human sexuality that is by now becoming a bit tedious. We see Dagny naked before a mirror with a blood-red ruby between her breasts – an image that appears, better done, in one of the most touching of Robert Heinlein's Lazarus Long stories – Dagny half-naked and smothered in a blue fox cape, Dagny as a toy, as a kept woman, pretending to be all of those things she patently isn't, and the two of them turning philosophical somersaults to claim sensuality as the legitimate birthright of the virtuous. It is Rand's approach to sexual liberation, but the reader tires of the rhetoric, and the bed is getting cold.

But there is, placed oddly in the midst of all of this pre-coital pontificating, a statement of one of Rand's central theses regarding the maintenance of the corruption of society – that it requires the sanction of the exploited:

He [Rearden] leaned forward. "What he wanted from you was a recognition that he was still the Dr. Robert Stadler he should have been, but wasn't and knew he wasn't. He wanted you to grant him your respect in spite of and in contradiction to his actions. He wanted you to juggle reality for him...and you're the only one who could do it."

"Why I?"

"Because you're the victim."

It is a sanction that can be withheld, the result being that the looter no longer feels good about himself. For someone for whom self-esteem is deified, that is a deadly blow.

Rand and Religious Morality

Despite Rand's notorious atheism, not all of her characters appear to be of that theological bent. Hank Rearden expresses his approval of Ellis Wyatt:

...the words which he had not pronounced, but felt, were: God bless you, Ellis, whatever you're doing!

This isn't a slip-up on Rand's part, nor is the balance of *Atlas Shrugged* relentlessly anti-God. Far from it, many of her ethical dilemmas are foundational issues in all the great religions, discussed at length by their intellectual giants. Christianity, Judaism, Islam, Buddhism, Zoroastrianism – all of these and more have to deal with the existence of evil and the true source of human ethics. These are fundamental issues that Rand will not be able to escape by avoiding theology, because it is through theology that Western philosophy gave them their most thorough development. As a student of philosophy, Rand recognized this.

There was a character written into the original draft of *Atlas Shrugged* but out of the final copy, a Catholic priest named Father Amadeus who was to be James Taggart's confessor (Leonard Peikoff, introduction to the 35th anniversary edition, quoting Rand's journals). One might expect him to represent the evils of modern religion to an unrepentant atheist such as Rand, and one would be mistaken; he was, by all reports, a sympathetic character whose dialectical function would have been debate with John Galt himself. Rand explained that his presence would have made the narrative unnecessarily complicated, which it undoubtedly would. Perhaps as well, she did not care to balance her interpretation of Christian doctrine against the real thing. That may be intellectual cowardice, it may be scrupulous honesty, it is certainly prudence, and it surely spared the reader another five hundred pages.

Discussion Topics

- Increment the body count by two. Andrew Stockton and Lawrence Hammond have both disappeared. We now know that a mystery man sat down with Stockton for most of the night before he vanished.

- Rand terms it *"defreezing"*, and young college graduates are going to work as consultants selling their services to investors to fill out the necessary bureaucratic paperwork to get reimbursed for the frozen railroad bonds. An individual defreezer's success is directly proportional to his connections in Washington. How accurately does this reflect the activities in the well-established lobbyist row on K Street in Washington?

Reading the Root of Money Speech

The next chapter contains Francisco's Root of Money Speech, one of the large set pieces of the book. It is a critical insight into Rand's philosophy of Objectivism and a good primer on capitalism. There are three ways one can handle the speech.

- Read it linearly as part of reading the chapter.

- Skim it and read it thoroughly on a second pass.

- Skip it entirely and then read it thoroughly on a second pass.

This is one of the two critical declamations in *Atlas Shrugged*, and the time taken to grasp its principles will reward the reader greatly when it comes time to consider the larger one later.

Chapter II: The Aristocracy of Pull
Synopsis

This chapter introduces the Aristocracy of Pull as a concept, but its membership and operations are only hinted at. Rand has chosen her terms carefully – it is in fact an aristocracy, an insular ruling class with its own hierarchy and internal means of exchange. The chapter also introduces something the reader is not entirely sure that Rand possesses up to now: a sense of humor, and how it echoes through the personalities of the chapter's principal characters.

The men of Colorado disappear one by one until only Ted Nielsen is left; he promises Dagny he is not going anywhere. Dagny considers she is encountering a Destroyer who is performing the reverse of the mystery motor on people, turning driving, kinetic energy back into the potential of the untapped static.

Quentin Daniels, Dagny's hope for somebody capable of revealing the mystery of the motor, is earning his daily bread working as a night watchman. Earlier an engineer sneeringly demanded that Dagny support him at the rate of $25,000 a year, quite a generous salary in 1957, to investigate the thing, hinting openly that it was likely to be a long-lived and fruitless effort – except for the health of his bank account. Daniels, on the other hand, is a risk taker who only expects to get paid for results and paid well if he manages to produce them. That is Rand's idea of a moral business arrangement.

The cigarette stand proprietor catches Dagny as she is leaving the building and tells her that Hugh Akston's cigarette had attributes he had never seen before and was not made anywhere on this earth. It is a playful phrase on Rand's part – in a sense, he is correct, as we shall learn.

Ken Danagger and Hank meet discreetly in Hank's hotel room at the Wayne-Falkland to conclude a deal, now illegal, giving Danagger Coal the Rearden Metal it needs for its mines. Danagger has expanded his operation by acquiring a bankrupt coal company despite the conflicting complaints of bureaucrats that he is a monopolist but yet he needs to expand further.

After Danagger leaves, Lillian Rearden surprisingly arrives; she is in town for Jim Taggart's wedding to Cherry Brooks, which she sees as perfectly ridiculous. She wants to be the center of her husband's life, and although Hank would prefer not to go, he does so to please her.

The courtship of Jim and Cherryl did not include sex, for which Cherryl is grateful. But she is hurt by those who see Jim's involvement with her as being "generous", as if she were an object of pity. She is especially hurt by the reception she gets from Jim's friends, particularly Betty Pope, whose cryptic comments she finds disturbing. When she hears comments about Jim's connections in Washington, she thinks the men hate Jim out of envy, not something the reader finds more likely, such as disgust. Now Cherryl Taggart, she is the beneficiary of the sort of leech-like arrangement in love that Jim appears to have with business. She is the innocent that Lillian thinks Dagny might be, and is cautioned by a nameless newspaper columnist who has befriended her:

"Listen, kid," the sob sister said to her, when she stood in her room for the last time, the lace of the wedding veil streaming like crystal foam from her hair to the blotched planks of the floor. [A lovely word image, actually. Rand should do more of it.] *"You think that if one gets hurt in life, it's through one's own sins – and that's true, in the long run. But there are people who'll try to hurt you through the good they see in you – knowing that it's the good, needing it and punishing you for it. Don't let it break you when you discover that."*

It's good advice that flies far over the head of the naïf. She gets a welcome to the big leagues from none other than Dagny herself:

[Cherryl] "I'm not going to put on the sweet relative act... I'm going to protect him [Jim] against you... I'm Mrs. Taggart. I'm the woman in the family now."

"That's quite all right," said Dagny. "I'm the man."

Touche. That line is unlikely to appear in a contemporary novel due to the tender feelings of feminist gatekeepers whose intellectual attainment appears principally to consist of tender feelings. But we know exactly what she means. She is quite as direct with Lillian. Concerning her continuing to wear the Rearden Metal bracelet:

"I'm sure, Miss Taggart, that you realize how enormously improper this is...don't you think that this is a case where one cannot afford to indulge in abstract theory but must consider practical reality?"

Dagny would not smile. "I have never understood what is meant by a statement of that kind."

Oh, but she does. The sort of abstract theory with which Lillian is most familiar is the sort that issues from the impure mouths of Pritchett the philosopher, Ferris the false scientist, and Scudder the polemicist. It isn't really the sort of stuff in which Dagny tends to indulge. She will have her own confrontation with abstract theory, not that kind, but the real thing, and the time is not yet.

So why does Dagny continue to wear the bracelet in public? It is an acknowledgment of Rearden's achievement, and hence Rearden himself in a non-sexual sense, and it is as well a covenant, a private sign of possession strictly between the two of them. But although she knows that it is also a public statement that she is sleeping with Rearden, she appears not to care. Does she find the inability of those around them to believe that they might be having an affair to be amusing? Perhaps – *"she would not smile"* – but if so, it isn't obvious, and it doesn't strike one as the sort of sense of humor that fits Dagny's straightforward personality. But Rand finds it highly amusing, and so does the reader.

Even Lillian has a sense of humor, dark though it is. She approaches Jim and asks if he likes her wedding gift, which is Hank. It creates the public impression that even the great Hank

92

Rearden has to toe the line with Jim Taggart and serves as a warning to all in the room. Lillian wants Jim to understand that she has the power to deliver Hank.

There is one character among the opposition who does possess a wicked sense of humor – it is the brutal and marvelously cynical Orren Boyle. He is a wolf among sheep and knows it, and enjoys letting the sheep know it as well. He gives us a glimpse of what passes for a medium of exchange in his political circles:

"The ones you buy aren't really worth a damn because somebody can always offer them more...but if you get the goods on a man, then you've got him, and there's no higher bidder and you can count on his friendship...what the hell! – one's got to trade something. If we don't trade money – and the age of money is past – then we trade men."

It isn't only Boyle's opinion:

"We are at the dawn of a new age," said James Taggart from above the rim of his champagne glass. "We are breaking up the vicious tyranny of economic power. We will set men free from the rule of the dollar... We will build a society dedicated to higher ideals, and we will replace the aristocracy of money by – "

" – the aristocracy of pull," said a voice beyond the group.

They whirled around. The man who stood facing them was Francisco d'Anconia.

It is Francisco the playboy, the wastrel, the clown. He has been Loki in Rand's tripartite pantheon, but no one seems to be laughing.

"Senor d'Anconia, what do you think is going to happen to the world?"

"Just exactly what it deserves."

"Oh, how cruel!"

*"Don't you believe in the operation of the moral law, madame?"
Francisco asked gravely. "I do."*

Moral law? That's pretty rich coming from a playboy, and
everybody knows that Francisco is a playboy, don't they? And
now Francisco gets to deliver the opening salvo in the battle that is
being joined. He steps out of the party for a moment and in front
of the proscenium where he makes his Root of Money Speech.
This small part seems hauntingly pertinent:

*"Do you wish to know whether that day [of reckoning] is
coming? Watch money. Money is the barometer of a society's
virtue. When you see that trading is done, not by consent, but by
compulsion – when you see that in order to produce you need to
obtain permission from men who produce nothing – when you see
that men get richer by graft and by pull than by work, and your
laws don't protect you against them, but protect them against you –
when you see corruption being rewarded and honesty becoming a
self-sacrifice – you may know that your society is doomed."*

Are we doomed, then? It is no idle question. In order to run
a commercial enterprise in the United States one may soon need to
purchase a remarkable contrivance known as carbon credits from –
and obtain the kind permission of – men who produce nothing.
Consider that from Rand's point of view – we have here a group of
political operators who have created a web-work of real law
around a scientific fiction and are drawing from it the power to
dictate every aspect, not only of commercial enterprise, but of the
lives of human beings unfortunate enough to come under their
sway. Rand has not yet expounded on morality – she will – but
she has described obscenity with sufficient accuracy for us to
recognize it when it appears before our astounded eyes.

The Root of Money Speech is the first indication that Rearden
gets of Francisco's true nature and game. But he already knows
that Francisco is far more than he appears.

"What are you doing at this party?"

"Just looking for conquests."

"Found any?"

His face suddenly earnest, Francisco answered..."Yes – what I think is going to be my best and greatest."

He means Rearden himself, of course, but Hank doesn't make the connection.

Rearden's anger was involuntary, the cry, not of reproach, but of despair: "How can you waste yourself that way?"

The faint suggestion of a smile...came into Francisco's eyes as he asked, "Do you care to admit that you care about it?"

And Hank does care, because he senses a kindred spirit under the tuxedo and suntan.

"I wish I could permit myself to like you as much as I do."

"When you'll learn the full reason, you'll know whether there's ever been anything – or anyone – that meant a damn to me...and how much he did mean."

He, who? We suspect, of course, but Rearden does not – yet. We also know where the looters have been keeping their ill-gotten gains, safely invested – or so they think – in d'Anconia Copper stock, a company that has never failed. That is why Francisco is systematically ruining it.

No one listening seems to take this disquisition very seriously, although it is not entirely the sort of talk one might expect to hear at a wedding party. Francisco is putting on a show, but it is a show for a very select audience. He is a select audience as well, being the only one at the party who knows both Dagny and Hank well enough to realize that they are lovers. That knowledge in the face of the stubborn denial of lesser souls would be the sort of thing that would appeal to his own mordant sense of humor. That it is the woman he loves might appeal to his sense of irony. Loki, indeed.

He returns to that character so quickly that no one other than Hank and Dagny seems to notice, starting a run on his own stock with the mere suggestion that it is about to fail, the guests scattering from the exclusive wedding party like cockroaches exposed to the light. It is sordid – and very funny. Certain of Rand's characters may lack a sense of humor, but their author definitely does not. Hers just happens to be a very dark one.

Discussion Topics – Francisco's Root of Money Speech

This speech is an audition for Hank Rearden, and it has the desired effect. There are lines that bubble up from memory long after one has put the book back on the shelf.

- *"An honest man is one who knows that he can't consume more than he has produced."* Considering that this describes American behavior since 1933, why should this make the modern reader squirm?

- *"The verdict you pronounce upon the source of your livelihood is the verdict you pronounce upon your life."* What happens when an honest self-examination produces a verdict of "moocher" or "looter"?

- *"The lovers of money are willing to work for it. They know they are able to deserve it."* "Able" to deserve it implies that others are unable to. Who is, and who isn't, and how can we know?

- *"Destroyers seize gold and leave to its owners a counterfeit pile of paper... Paper is a mortgage on wealth that does not exist, backed by a gun aimed at those who are expected to produce it. Paper is a check drawn by legal looters upon an account which is not theirs: upon the virtue of the*

96

victims. Watch for the day when it bounces, marked: 'Account overdrawn.'" The "gun" is the term "legal tender", which has lost its original meaning of "forced tender". What forced tender means is, "See this piece of paper? It doesn't look or feel like money because it isn't made of gold or silver. But I say it is money, and it *is* money because I have the guns and the military forces to back that statement up." The modern term for this is "fiat currency." This critical bit of our founding history is little-explored today. What happens *"the day the check bounces,"* when the central bank monetizes vast amounts of debt because foreigners won't buy it anymore?

- *"You stand in the midst of the greatest achievements of the greatest productive civilization and you wonder why it's crumbling around you, while you're damning its life-blood – money."* Why is this thesis right or wrong?

Further Discussion

- The body count is getting out of control. Add an undisclosed number of Colorado men now that Wyatt's Torch has taken the place of Wyatt Oil. Ted Nielsen promises to stay, yet in the next sentence Dagny fantasizes a Destroyer come to collect them all. Why would Nielsen be next? What would The Destroyer gain by recruiting Nielsen? What chain of events would that set off?

- After the Root of Money Speech, a lady tells Francisco that she feels he is wrong, not over facts but feelings, which to her are more important. Where are there instances of this philosophical approach in today's popular culture?

Chapter III: White Blackmail

Synopsis

Lillian condemns Francisco for what he has done and for shooting off his mouth at the wedding, with its messy complications. She takes the train home while Hank heads for Dagny's apartment.

Hank is sorrowful that Dagny had to see him with his wife, but Dagny is more sorrowful that she had to witness Hank's agony in the presence of that woman. Dagny views her relationship with Hank as a fair trade with each drawing joy from the other. Hank wants to know the identity of Dagny's mysterious first lover, but Dagny intends to keep that private.

Dagny thinks that Francisco has intentionally engineered the disaster that is going to break tomorrow, but she can't figure out why. She ought to feel that Francisco is depraved, but for some reason she can't, and neither can Hank, who is starting to like Francisco despite himself.

Hank returns to the hotel to find Lillian awaiting him. Caught! Well, Hank is, anyway. Too obtuse to recognize in Dagny a successful rival for her husband, Lillian makes fun of Henry the Monk who has not touched her for the past year and asks if his mistress is a manicurist or a chorus girl. Hank is ready to give Lillian anything she wants except for one thing: he won't give up his paramour. She refuses divorce in favor of what is clearly important to her: *"...my home, my name, my social position...",* but considers that their relationship is altered. He knows better, and so does the reader, who knows Lillian. In another sort of novel her body would have washed ashore somewhere by now and the reader would be rooting against the detective.

One cadence Rand picks up with frightening fluency is that of evil. Dr. Floyd Ferris is clearly a major power broker now and is chosen by the powers that be to present their case to Rearden, and he does so with a bluntness that is, after so much dissimulation, positively refreshing.

"Now, would you care to be a martyr for an issue of principle, only in circumstances where nobody will know that that's what you are – nobody but you and me – where you won't be a hero, but a common criminal...either you let us have the Metal or you go to jail for ten years and take your friend Danagger along, too."

Rearden said calmly, "In my youth this was called blackmail."

Dr. Ferris grinned. "That's what it is, Mr. Rearden. We've entered a much more realistic age."

It is an echo of what Orren Boyle has revealed to us in the preceding chapter:

" ...but if you get the goods on a man, then you've got him, and there's no higher bidder and you can count on his friendship...what the hell! – one's got to trade something. If we don't trade money – and the age of money is past – then we trade men."

Ferris clearly is in the business of trading men, and has become a man of considerable influence himself in view of what he now offers Rearden:

"Don't bother with Jim Taggart, he's nothing...want us to step on Orren Boyle for you? ...to keep Ken Danagger in line? Just let him understand that if he doesn't toe the line he'll go to jail but you won't because you've got friends he hasn't got...now that's the modern way of doing business."

"But after all, I did break one of your laws."

"What do you think they're for?"

What Ferris says next is Rand's central thesis about the relation of law and power in an age of decadence.

"We want them broken. We're after power and we mean it. There's no way to rule innocent men. The only power any

99

government has is the power to crack down on criminals. Well, when there aren't enough criminals, one makes them. One declares so many things to be a crime that it becomes impossible for men to live without breaking laws...now, that's the system, Mr. Rearden, that's the game..."

That and selective enforcement compose an exercise of power that is the basis for every police state ever devised. It is the ability of those in power arbitrarily to designate a non-cooperative citizen a criminal, to silence, to imprison. It is raw, sanctioned coercion.

Here there are no rights, only privileges, and government attains its aims and maintains itself by granting or denying those privileges. For example, a citizen of California might consider the Second Amendment in the Bill of Rights to mean that he is entitled as much as his fellow citizens to bear a concealed firearm. In that citizen's state, however, that is regarded as a privilege to be conferred by the local police, to be withheld by default, to be granted for fame or favor or cold hard cash. As a right it is the basis of society; as a privilege it is the basis of corruption.

The French economist and political philosopher Bertrand de Jouvenel described this very thing in *On Power*:

"...the mounting flood of modern laws does not create Law. What do they mirror, these laws, but the pressure of interests, the fancifulness of opinions, the violence of passions? When they are the work of Power which has become, with its every growth, more enervated by the strife of factions, their confusion makes them ludicrous. When they issue from a Power which is in the grip of one brutal hand, their planned iniquity makes them hateful. The only respect which they either get or deserve is that which force procures them. Being founded on a conception of society which is both false and deadly, they are anti-social." [*On Power*, Ch. 16, pt 4]

That is law in these days of decay. And so Rearden has his loyal secretary, Gwen Ives, show Dr. Ferris the door. Something has changed for him. Between what Francisco said and what Ferris said he is beginning to find his way.

Eddie Willers appears entirely aware of what is going on and refers the matter to his confidante in the Taggart cafeteria, the Anonymous Rail Worker to whom Eddie has come to pour out his heart.

"I feel that someone is screaming in the middle of the streets but people are passing by and no sound can reach them – and it's not Hank Rearden or Ken Danagger or I who's screaming, and yet it seems as if it's all three of us...Rearden and Danagger were indicted this morning. They'll go on trial next month. No...no, I'm not shaking, I'm all right, I'll be all right in a moment... That's why I haven't said a word to her, I was afraid I'd explode and I didn't want to make it harder for her...it's not Hank Rearden that she's afraid for, it's Ken Danagger...she feels certain that Ken Danagger will be the next one to go...he's a marked man...she says there's a destroyer, that she won't let him get Ken Danagger..."

Those might be imprudent words in the wrong ears, perhaps, but then the fellow is only a rail worker after all, isn't he?

Dagny cools her heels in Danagger's anteroom, and when she is finally allowed admittance to his office, he's gone. The strongest pillar supporting her collapsing world. He's sitting in front of her, but he's gone. The Destroyer has come and gone, taking Danagger with him. And all he has left behind is a gold-stamped cigarette butt.

"I won't say goodbye," he [Danagger] said, "because I'll be seeing you again in the not too distant future."

"Oh," she said eagerly, holding his hand clasped across the desk, "are you going to return?"

"No. You're going to join me."

Never! But the pillars of her world are now one fewer.

An author is always entreated "write what you know," and one must question gently Rand's ability to convey in authentic terms the relationship of man to man. In the previous chapter we learn that Francisco has changed his life on the basis of how much one man – we don't know who he is, but we can guess – meant to him. In this chapter we hear Danagger stating that he loves Rearden and that Rearden loves Francisco. This is not, as certain modern critics might insist, a case of unrequited homosexual desire, it's simply a woman placing a man's sentiment into a man's mouth with a woman's vocabulary. It's evocative enough, but it doesn't quite ring true to the modern ear, at least to the modern male ear.

As he prepares to leave the steel mill, Hank finds Francisco waiting for him in the reception area. Now begins a parallel conversation that would have made Dagny, still waiting anxiously in Danagger's reception area, frantic had she known of it. It is a Destroyer speaking to receptive ears. Are there then two of them?

Francisco knows how lonely Hank is this evening with the loss of the one man who counted so much both to his business and to his morale. Hank says he will have to work that much harder now that Danagger has gone, and Francisco asks just how much he can take, telling Hank he is the last moral man left in the world. He has placed moral action into material form at the steel mill, but he has not held to the purpose of his life as clearly as he has held to the purpose of his mills. Hank developed Rearden Metal to make money but has not. The fruits of his labors were taken from him, and he was punished for his success. He had wanted his rail to be used by those who were his equals in action like Ellis Wyatt, those who were his moral equals like Eddie Willers, but not by the looters and failures of the world who proclaim that Hank is their slave because of his genius. The people reaping the fruits of Hank's labors are those who proclaim a right to another man's effort, who require that Hank live for their benefit. Francisco explains that Hank is putting his virtue into the service of evil. He has left the deadliest weapon in the hands of his enemies: their moral code. He has made the mistake of accepting undeserved guilt. He has accepted the need of the looters as a reason for his own destruction.

"Mr. Rearden," said Francisco, his voice solemnly calm, "if you saw Atlas, the giant who holds the world on his shoulders, if you saw that he stood, blood running down his chest, his knees

102

buckling, his arms trembling but still trying to hold the world aloft with the last of his strength, and the greater his effort the heavier the world bore down upon his shoulders – what would you tell him to do?"

"I...don't know. What would you tell him?"

"To shrug."

And there it is, the source and meaning of the novel's title. This is barely a taste, a three-page taste to be sure, but by Rand's standards it's only a hint of what The Destroyer must say to his victims. Francisco d'Anconia's recruitment of Hank Rearden is almost consummated when an alarm goes off, signaling an industrial accident: the side of a blast furnace has been breached, and the white-hot metal is flowing out to consume everything in its path. And Francisco shows himself to have held at least one more honest job in his life: he knows how to stem the flood with fire clay, an art form Hank thought had died out years ago. Hank joins him and watches Francisco grinning widely; he realizes he has met the real Francisco d'Anconia at last. But Francisco misjudges a throw, loses his balance, and Hank saves him from incineration.

But oddly, Francisco has failed, because Hank believes that with the kind of joint effort he and Francisco have just shown, they can beat the looters. Hank offers Francisco a job as a furnace foreman and says that will get him to appreciate his copper company properly. Francisco declines politely, thwarted for the moment. He can't finish what he had to say to Hank because Hank isn't ready to hear it.

But Rearden now knows what we have known all along. Francisco is no playboy, but a player in a game as big as the world on Atlas' shoulders.

Rand and Godhead

There is a special image in this dramatic sequence that has implications as large as the novel itself. The topic is morality, the voice Francisco's, speaking to Rearden:

Francisco pointed to the mill... "If you want to see an abstract principle, such as moral action, in material form – there it is. Look at it, Mr. Rearden. Every girder of it, every pipe..."

A girder as a moral statement? Yes. What Francisco means by it is that the girder is a product designed in accordance with the laws of the universe – the laws of gravity, of material science, of tensile strength and chemical formulation, of the mathematics of the distribution of forces, and it is the recognition of those laws by men that make the girder possible. They are not opinions; they are not negotiable. They simply are, and to Rand and Aristotle, to acknowledge that is the first act of philosophical clarity; to deny it, intellectual death. A Dr. Pritchett, for whom no knowledge is possible, could not have made the girder.

It is objective reality: the grudging acknowledgment that the world is not simply an artifact of human perception, that on the contrary there is something there to be perceived independent of human existence. That is the basis of Aristotle's philosophy and Rand's view of morality. The girder's very existence is an acknowledgment of law.

Whose law? Human law? No, for then it would be subject to the approval of such creatures as Dr. Pritchett. The law of the universe? Yes, that describes it, but then who put it there? Are we to believe that it simply *is*, and that although we may discover it we may not inquire as to its origin? Those laws are the structure of the universe and they do not depend on human approval. Why are they, then?

Whose law? Rand simply cannot bring herself to say "God's" but Aristotle did. That is the reason for his "unmoved mover." For Aristotle, God is simply the unavoidable and logical consequence of his system of understanding the world.

Recall that Rand, along the lines of Nietzsche, attempted to relocate godhead into the person of man. Her industrialists are her immovable movers. There is no God. But she hasn't avoided the problem of the origin of the laws of the universe in doing so, and those laws, she states, are the very basis of her own system of

104

moral judgment. It seems a rather glaring deficiency in logic. What are we to make of this?

Aristotle's is not, actually, the proof of the existence of God; if it were, God's existence would be contingent on a system of reason. Aristotle's Western interpreters, the Medieval Schoolmen, concluded that it is the other way around: reason is the gift of God; God is not the gift of reason. But in order to dispense with God as Rand desires, one has to dispense with the logical system under which His existence is a necessary consequence. It can be done, of course. There are a number of non-Aristotlean logic systems from which to choose. But one can't embrace Aristotle's without acknowledging its implications, and that's what Rand is trying to do. One can't have it both ways. "Either-Or."

This is a rather fundamental philosophical problem, and throughout the rest of the novel we will see how Rand deals with it and must decide whether we're satisfied with her solution.

Divorce in the Fifties

Before the era of no-fault divorce, different states had widely different standards for ending a marriage. Some, like New York, had only grounds of adultery. To simplify this, a wife would pay detectives to barge into a cheating husband's love nest to take pictures of the adulterous couple in action. Sometimes, cheating husbands would pay detectives to do the same thing to expedite the process.

In other states, a divorce was impossible unless both partners to the marriage agreed to it. Lillian's decision not to grant Hank a divorce gives her power over him. It is power that she prefers to a significant divorce settlement. That turns out to be a mistake.

"A Speedy Trial"

The Sixth Amendment to the Constitution affirms the accused the right to a speedy trial. Today, trials come years after the arrest. Back in the Fifties, this was not the case. For Hank and Ken Danagger to come to trial a month after their indictments was not unusual in that era. But the trial, when we see it, will look very strange to people who expect such things to follow the Constitution.

Discussion Topic

- Francisco has torn a gaping hole in the universe from which Hank can perceive the heart of darkness. This is the key topic of this chapter and one of the most important themes in the entire book. Francisco's attempted recruitment of Hank gives a clue to what The Destroyer said to Ken Danagger – and Midas Mulligan – to make them both joyful at the prospect of disappearing and leaving their enterprises behind. What exactly did Francisco say to Hank that might have this effect? Explore this in detail.

Chapter IV: The Sanction of the Victim

Synopsis

At Thanksgiving dinner, Hank dines in the bosom of his family of moochers and vipers. Hank's mother's prayer describes a country where the people lack food and housing. The Reardens have been fortunate, and Mrs. Rearden thinks Hank should toast the American people who have given him so much. Brother Philip chirps the customary progressive drivel about the evils of business:

"Businessmen are taking advantage of the national emergency in order to make money. They break the regulations which protect the common welfare of all...grow rich by defrauding the poor of their rightful share...they pursue a ruthless, grasping, grabbing anti-social policy... I think it's contemptible."

It is, to say the least, indiscreet to refer to one's host in such a manner, especially when he is about to be put on trial for precisely those things. Hank calls him on it, and Philip discovers very quickly that there are now, where there weren't before, some distinct lines drawn with respect to Hank's toleration. Hank is changing, hardening before their eyes, becoming less malleable, less susceptible to the crude manipulation they have been practicing on him. Along the way Hank throws off this rather interesting statement:

"You concluded that I was the safest person in the world for you to spit on, precisely because I held you by the throat."

It is a behavior common to those who are manipulating other people through a scheme of contrived obligation and guilt. This behavior requires the sanction of the victim. Without that sanction it has no power, and Hank is slowly coming to the realization that it is a crime, a betrayal and an act of immorality for the victim to grant that sanction.

Lillian's great concern is that Hank might make a stand at his trial tomorrow. He says he intends to, which prompts a remonstrance from his mother that is rich in irony: why can't he play by the rules, like Orren Boyle? Lillian thinks that concepts like right and wrong are irrelevant, and Hank is conceited for trying to take a stand on principle. The men whom Hank will face at the trial are weak, and their only way of getting rich is to grab the fruits of Hank's labors. To Lillian that is the human condition. She advises Hank to abandon the illusion of his perfection and accept the system for what it is, complaining that Hank has no thought about going to jail or what it will do to his family.

Lillian attempts to play on the guilt she believes Hank feels for having an extramarital affair. It is one more case of lead-like density from a woman who has little else going for her but her ability to pull the strings on a puppet that seems busily occupied in cutting them. Lillian's stock in trade is her ability to "deliver" her own husband to other people. But Hank simply does not feel the guilt for his affair that she is counting on. The reason for this will become clearer later when Rand spins her theory of the nature of human sexuality.

It is an uncomfortable scene, broken when Hank decides he'd be better off spending the balance of the last day before his trial in New York in a more congenial environment.

Hank recalls that the Wet Nurse had failed to turn him in for the Danagger sale and couldn't explain why. That fellow is in the midst of his own existential crisis, and we learn two things: first, he is a metallurgist by training, not an administrator and certainly not a spy; second, he has a conscience, a real one.

At the office Dagny and Eddie Willers are working through Thanksgiving as Hank shows up. Hank tells Dagny that she is going to get Rearden Metal, not steel, for the money she has spent and more of it than she paid for. He intends to give Dagny plausible deniability by tangling up the bookkeeping to the point where no auditor could hope to figure it out, except possibly to blame it on Hank. The two raid the illicit bar of the traffic manager and down a pair of brandies to drink to the real

Thanksgiving, the holiday established by productive people to celebrate the success of their work.

The trial of Hank Rearden is another set-piece, a departure from reality necessary in order to support Rearden's expression of his current philosophical state, of which Rand, as a witness to the great Soviet show trials of the Thirties, was certainly aware. For one thing, a refusal to enter a plea would most likely have resulted in a plea of "not guilty" being entered for him – in an American court, anyway – and for another, no judge charged with the mission this sort of trial entails would allow the victim to make a defiant, three page declamation. It is not a real courtroom, of course, it is a stage, and it is not a real trial, it is a dialectic, and the reader will be more comfortable simply accepting that. The trial is not conducted under Constitutional law. It's an administrative panel presided over by three judges from the Bureau of Economic Planning and National Resources with no jury; however, this tribunal, empowered by the directives of Wesley Mouch issued under a state of emergency, has the power to send people to prison. One judge acts as prosecutor.

Hank refuses to recognize the right of this so-called court to try him, nor does he recognize his actions as criminal – he is, after all, complying with the law to the letter; his property may be disposed of without his consent. He does not wish to be a party to this farce. Told that he must defend himself, Hank tells the court that a defense is only possible if there are objective principles that bind him and the judges to the law; in the absence of such principles the court may do as it wishes.

The judge condemns Hank for opposing the public good. Hank tells him that "good" was once a concept determined by moral values, and no one had the right to violate the rights of another. If men may sacrifice Rearden and steal his property because they need it, how does this make them any different from a burglar? At least a burglar doesn't ask for sanction. The judge asks if Hank holds his interests above those of society. Hank replies that such a question can only arise in a society of cannibals. If people wish to decrease his profits, they should refuse to buy his metal; anything else is the method of the looter. If the judges wish to impose punishment, then impose it. The judge says Hank's only alternative is to throw himself on the mercy of the court. Hank refuses; he will not do anything to validate this farce.

A judge demands that Hank try not to make it look as if he is being railroaded. Realizing his mistake, the judge stops cold, but someone in the audience whistles: the cat is out of the bag. Rearden explains that they are choosing to deal with men by means of compulsion. This court is only possible when the victim permits it to be possible. If the judges wish to levy punishment and seize his property, then let them do so publicly at the point of a gun. Hank makes it clear he is working for his own property and profit; he does not seek the sanction of others for his right to exist, nor does he recognize the good of others as a justification for the seizure of his property.

"If it is now the belief of my fellow men, who call themselves the public, that their good requires victims, then I say: The public be damned. I will have no part of it!"

The crowd bursts into applause.

A judge now tells Hank that the court wishes to approach him in the spirit of amity, but Hank declines. The judge tries to place the blame on the missing Danagger, but Hank isn't having any of that either. The judge tries to get him to say he was working for the good of the people, but Hank refuses that escape too. Realizing that the government has badly misplayed its hand, the judges fine Hank five thousand dollars – but suspend the sentence. The crowd applauds Rearden and jeers the judges. The curtain comes down on the farce.

Dagny misses the point entirely.

"Hank, I'll never think that it's hopeless... I'll never be tempted to quit. You've proved that the right always works and always wins..."

Does it? Rand has already shown us that there are motivations for quitting other than hopelessness. It will take both Dagny and Hank a long time to realize that, but realize it they will.

The Wet Nurse is undergoing a push toward clarity all his own.

110

"Mr. Rearden, what's a moral premise?" "What you're going to have a lot of trouble with." The boy frowned, then shrugged and said, laughing, "God, that was a wonderful show! What a beating you gave them, Mr. Rearden!..." "How do you know it was a beating?" "Well, it was, wasn't it?" "Are you sure of it?" "Sure, I'm sure." "The thing that makes you sure is a moral premise."

A very minor note for writers of dialogue: this is a reproduction of the form of the dialogue in the paragraph above, a rapid-fire exchange that eschews the normal paragraph-break-per-quote form found in the rest of the novel. It is a curious departure, and it's not clear what to make of it. Perhaps at that point even Rand had had her fill of dialectic.

But this is another of Rand's moral premises: in an objective reality, what counts is a conviction that to do one thing is right and another in its place, wrong, and that the principle does not change as a function of who is doing it. Special rules for special people need not apply. That may seem strange for one whose imagery is so heavily Nietzschean, and it is one reason that Rand is not really Nietzschean after all. This moral premise applies to everyone, stock boy to stockbroker, policeman to politician. Were it otherwise, the looters would always be in the right. That is all that stands in the way of a consensual victimhood, in the way of an outright use of force: a moral premise. The reason that Atlas must shrug is that the moral premise now is held in contempt and will not serve to protect the victim.

Hank seeks out Francisco. They're pals now, and Rand uses this particular sounding board both to suggest very broadly what Francisco's real game is and to present in his mouth her theory of human sexuality.

A triumphant Rearden determines to defy all the looters and is sorely tempted to kick the moochers out of his house. He'll make as much metal as he likes and sell it to whomever he pleases and keep the country running despite the worst efforts of those who are trying to tear it down. Well, he intends to. His pal's copper, on which he had based these hubristic plans, resides at the bottom of the Atlantic courtesy of Ragnar Danneskjøld and quite obviously with Francisco's collusion. Hank is furious, of course, but the reader is unmoved. He was warned, after all.

Hank Rearden's Show Trial

Here is Rand's case: that the ethical system under which looting is permissible requires the victim's sanction to masquerade as anything but naked coercion. In a cultural sense this is very powerful – to refuse to grant the moral standing of those who feel that "social justice" entitles them to expropriate your property is to expose them for the bullies and thieves that they are should they do so. In Rand's world they hesitated; in ours they will do so enthusiastically, self-righteously and in the spirit of class vengeance. Rearden is let off with a minor fine, suspended, which he suspected he would be from the very beginning. His counterparts in the great Moscow show trials were shot, as they knew they would be from the very beginning.

That is the nature of a show trial, after all, not a masquerade for power but an open expression of it. A real show trial is a public display that one side is triumphant and the other both disgraced and helpless. Justice has absolutely nothing to do with it and political theater, everything.

And the truth is that, pacè Rand, the state and the people behind it will not be in the least reluctant to resort to naked coercion; they revel in it, in fact, that's the point of the exercise in the first place. Coercion is the nature of the state. Rand, a Russian expatriate, knew it better than most people of her time. Rearden's triumph here – he walks, of course – will not and cannot be a final victory. He has refused to grant the sanction of the victim, and it leaves the state only with the resort to naked force. Is he naive enough to think that the state will not use it? Perhaps he is, but Rand knows better.

Francisco's Sex Speech

Rand's Theory of Sexuality isn't anything the reader hasn't figured out by now, but it was perhaps because it was so unconventional for her time that she felt it necessary to present in such theoretical detail. Briefly it consists of the idea that sexual attraction is perfectly normal and is one manifestation of intellectual admiration; that to the virtuous the ultimate aphrodisiac is virtue. Francisco informs us at length in one unbroken stream of pop psychology running to 618 words – he never pauses for breath – that the reason for imperfect coupling is an imperfect view of self, low self-esteem and a lack of personal actualization. As those improve, so apparently does one's focus on the ideal mate. It's a beautiful idea, one supposes, but not one held in much favor by anyone who has actually observed the maddening, contradictory, baffling complexities of human sexuality in action in the real world.

If the frequent visitation of this particular issue seems a bit too insistent to the modern reader, we must remember that the Fifties, although not quite as sexually repressed as certain contemporary commentators like to think, still were quite repressed in terms of public expression of matters sexual. "Pregnant," for example, was not a word uttered on the public airwaves. At the time of writing, Rand's philosophy of sexual liberation was just as radical as her philosophy of economic liberation, and presumably the same philosophical considerations that free people from guilt over making money, free them from guilt over making love. Not, presumably, from the responsibility of making babies – reliable chemical birth control was still in the future as of the writing of the novel as the FDA did not approve the first hormonal contraceptive until 1960 – and one notices that the complication of pregnancy never arises within its sexually liberated main characters.

Francisco is still carrying a torch for Dagny based on that premise of attraction, and so is Hank, her current partner in the making of the two-backed beast, and so, one suspects, is that mystery admirer who has haunted Dagny's surroundings from time to time. Three – at least – worthy admirers, and only one will be chosen. One sees Rand projecting herself into Dagny here after the manner of a medieval romance: the woman is the transcendent, the desired, the unattainable. It isn't one of her more admirable moments. "Love pure and chaste from afar" is a nice turn of phrase but a fellow can get awfully lonely occupying a permanent and hopeless second place on Superwoman's list of finalists.   And he can, in this system, desire no other.   It's simply not how people really behave.

Discussion Topics

- Lillian and Philip Rearden lecture Hank on the folly of making a stand at his trial.   How are their arguments applicable to trials in the real world, and do the mechanics and rules of evidence in a modern trial prevent or facilitate their arguments?

- The trial of Hank Rearden is written in the literary form of dialectic.   Compare it to Francisco's monologue on the Root of Money.   Which of the two forms makes for the better communication of ideas, and why?

Chapter V: Account Overdrawn

Synopsis

It is a particularly cruel winter, five months after Francisco threw down the gauntlet at James Taggart's wedding with his Root of Money Speech. It has not been a time of success for the central planners of the Aristocracy of Pull. Danagger's replacement cannot deliver coal, Taggart cannot run trains without it, and Rearden cannot produce metal without it either. Danagger's withdrawal is proving to be a crucial, strategic blow to the production of the surplus that keeps the looters in business. Honest production – that is, the sort that is not covered by centralized planning – now being illegal, Rearden finds himself purchasing coal on the black market, produced by men desperate to feed their families. The machine is running down.

- Blizzards descend without snow removal in a world of unheated houses and stranded trains in which people freeze to death.

- The Danagger coal bound for Taggart Transcontinental goes to the People's State of England whose problems are even worse. That means trains with California produce are stuck on sidings, and the wilted produce ends up, not at the Hunts Point Produce Terminal in Brooklyn, but in the East River. The growers go out of business, and nobody cares because they are private concerns. The Danagger coal meant for England never arrives; it ends up in the holds of Ragnar Danneskjøld's ships. Then Danagger's mines shut down for lack of lubricant.

- Mr. Quinn of the Quinn Ball Bearing Company, formerly of Connecticut and now of Colorado, shuts down his plant and disappears. The Quinn shutdown contributes to business collapses in Michigan, Oregon, Iowa and Illinois.

115

- Blizzards in the Rockies shut down the Taggart line through Colorado when the snow plows break down. The reader will recall that Ellis Wyatt himself warned of this probability. The new plows have not been delivered because the manufacturer couldn't get the steel from Orren Boyle. Three Taggart passenger trains are stuck in the snow for six days in Colorado, and rescue trucks break down on the way.

- Wesley Mouch rations coal to permit heating houses for only three hours per day and closes all sources of entertainment. Professors burn their books and growers burn their trees while Bertram Scudder extols the privations and sacrifices that make a people strong. Francisco's critical comments about Scudder are not printed by the press.

- Dr. Simon Pritchett witnesses a woman holding a son who has starved to death, and attempts to console a volunteer worker by telling her, *"Reality is only an illusion. How does that woman know that her son is dead? How does she know that he ever existed?"*

- Evangelists undergo a sudden surge in popularity.

- Orren Boyle sells steel intended for the Atlantic Southern to the People's State of Germany. The steel is seized by Danneskjøld, but the media never report it.

- The Atlantic Southern's bridge across the Mississippi collapses into the river. The chief engineer had warned that the bridge was unsafe, and the only parts that held were those sections reinforced with Rearden Metal. Two other bridges across the Mississippi are condemned and closed. One railroad goes out of business, but the other and the Atlantic Southern lay track to get to the Taggart Bridge at Bedford, Illinois.

- Due to the copper shortage, Wesley Mouch forbids the occupation of any building above the 25th floor. The tops of American cities go dark.

We learn something curious about the Aristocracy of Pull: it is an international ruling class, presiding over the *immiseration* of entire countries. That is a term popularized by Marx to describe his prediction of the steadily declining fortunes of the workers under capitalism; in fact, under capitalism those fortunes steadily grew, and it is, on the contrary, socialism that has produced that process in the real world and is producing it now within Rand's. That is, apparently, what one abandons when one abandons the Aristocracy of Money for the Aristocracy of Pull: one abandons nothing less than civilization itself.

There is a new man at the Taggart Transcontinental board meeting, one Clem Weatherby, who is from the government, and that is all anyone knows. Whether he is a guest, adviser, or the government's rail czar, no one dares ask.

Jim wants to raise freight rates, but Weatherby cuts him off and explains that Wesley Mouch wants to discuss the unions' demand for a pay raise and the shippers' demand for a freight rate cut. While Mouch likes Jim, he feels it might be necessary to sacrifice his personal feelings and friendships for the welfare of the public. The unions can call on five million votes, and with the current inflation the members need something to offset the cost of living. But the shippers can't survive with the current freight rates either.

Jim is aghast because the National Alliance of Railroads has taken a stance against the unions, and all signatories are required to stay on board. Weatherby wants Jim to drive a wedge into the Alliance for Mouch's sake. Jim fears what a court would do, but Weatherby explains that Mouch controls the courts. But the railroad can't afford it, Jim moans. Weatherby asks Jim if he wants the government to run his railroad. Everyone now understands that it would be best to tear up the John Galt Line and use the Rearden Metal rail to maintain the rest of the network. Weatherby stops them by saying they need government approval to close a branch line, but if Jim gives Mouch something in return, like the raise for the unions... Jim still can't break with the Alliance, so Weatherby explains that the government could easily call the Taggart bonds. Jim protests, of course – his meal ticket is in jeopardy – but Weatherby holds the whip hand. Jim is caught very neatly here – his free money has a cost after all – so he accedes to the salary raises that will kill his company in return for permission to pull up rail sufficient for that death to be delayed as long as possible. That rail exists only in one place, the Rio Norte Line, its first use and now its last reservoir. The John Galt Line, to name it truly, must die, and they want Dagny to give it the death sentence. She declines to make the decision for them.

The sanction of the victim has been withdrawn. Dagny has learned the hard way, but she has learned. After considerable dithering they summon the courage necessary for the death sentence and then hand Dagny the responsibility for the execution, at least in part because she's the only one present who could accomplish it. She is predictably devastated at the loss, the death of her achievement, and not only hers, but Rearden's as well.

Upon leaving the board meeting, Dagny runs into Francisco, who has been waiting for her. He asks her to go out with him for a drink, and slowly and carefully begins her recruitment. His share of blame is not mentioned, nor is it necessary. But blame does come up, and it lands in a surprising quarter:

"Dagny, the men of your Board of Directors are no match for Nat Taggart, are they? ...Then why is it that throughout men's history the Nat Taggarts, who make the world, have always won – and always lost it to the men of the Board?"

"I...don't know."

"Dagny, he fought with every weapon he possessed, except the most important one. They could not have won, if we – he and the rest of us – had not given the world away to them."

She misinterprets.

"Yes. You gave it away to them. Ellis Wyatt did. Ken Danagger did. I won't."

He smiled. "Who built the John Galt Line for them?"

Dagny is a fighter, it isn't in her to give up, and she is so very stubborn. One comes to admire and deplore it in her. That is why she makes herself a willing victim for the leeches, food for the vultures. It's all futile anyway. *"Who is John Galt?"* she asks Francisco, and to her surprise he answers.

"I can tell you who is John Galt. John Galt is Prometheus who changed his mind. After centuries of being torn by vultures in payment for having brought to men the fire of the gods, he broke his chains and he withdrew his fire – until the day when men withdraw their vultures."

It is imperfect mythology, but the point is made. There, in three sentences, is the précis of *Atlas Shrugged*. The rest is, as a certain infuriating old professor of mathematics used to smirk, "merely procedure."

Dagny and Hank tour Colorado looking to pick up whatever machinery can be found in the state's closed factories. Colorado's machine has run down.

- Ted Nielsen, as we suspected, has disappeared and abandoned his plant.

- Roger Marsh's appliance factory has shut down, and Marshville is becoming a ghost town.

- The Wyatt reclamation project has been abandoned.

A crowd lines up at the station for the last passenger train on the John Galt Line before its removal. Dagny runs into people who scream that the rich should be destroyed, and Hank saves her by leading her to her private car.

Lillian Rearden has lunch with Jim Taggart in New York. Jim tells Lillian that Hank needs to have his attitude adjusted, or really bad things will happen to him – and to her. The men in Washington think that Jim has some pull with Hank, and they are leaning on him to bring Hank into line. Jim is furious at Hank's performance at his trial, and Lillian replies that she didn't double-cross him but tried to deliver Hank and failed. The only thing that Lillian wants out of the meeting is the knowledge that she had the pull to get Jim Taggart to meet with her.

Lillian goes to Hank's suite at the Wayne-Falkland and calls the mill, asking Hank's whereabouts. He is on the *Comet*, she is informed, so Lillian asks for flowers to be delivered to his compartment at the stop in Chicago. But the flowers go undelivered, and Lillian deduces that Hank is on the train with his mistress. Lillian meets the *Comet* at the Taggart Terminal and sees Hank walking alone. Then she spots Dagny exiting her private car, and it all comes together for her.

At the hotel Lillian confronts Hank, and he admits that Dagny is his paramour. Lillian now understands Hank's performance at the trial. She demands that Hank give her up, and he refuses. Hank quietly tells Lillian he will keep Dagny even if it means Lillian's life; he wants a divorce. Lillian is furious, accusing Dagny of bedding every man on the railroad; Hank informs her coldly that he has reached his limit of toleration and that she risks physical assault. Lillian won't grant him a divorce. She leaves, and Hank feels a sense of deliverance.

Rand's Political and Sexual Theories

We are made aware of the linkage between Rand's theories of matters political and personal: in neither arena may one human being properly demand that another live for him or for her. Lillian finds this out when she demands that Hank and Dagny end their relationship:

"But I have the right to demand it! I own your life! It's my property. My property – by your own oath... I hold first claim! I'm presenting it for collection! You're the account I own!"

120

It is a rather stark and unattractive description of what remains in marriage when the love has drained away, and it is the emotional leverage she must employ in order to "deliver" her husband in exactly the same way as Orren Boyle or Wesley Mouch delivers another man. She too is a dealer, and Hank is her stock in trade. Up to now.

"Whatever claim you may have on me," he said, "no human being can hold on another a claim demanding that he wipe himself out of existence."

We will hear those words later from another mouth and in another context, but Hank has arrived. When he comes to believe that about his whole life, and not just about the confines of his married life, he will have taken the last moral step.

Discussion Topics

- Increment the body count. Quinn, Nielsen and Marsh have deserted their posts and disappeared. The Destroyer is a busy fellow. Who will be next?

- Buzzy Watts, Chick Morrison, Tinky Holloway and Kip Chalmers. There is a sense that Rand is playing with the reader, but in fact she is making a point. Such nicknames were common at the Ivy League schools of her day and elsewhere in a rich, idle stratus of American youth, and remain so. How is this stratus similarly influential in contemporary politics?

Chapter VI: Miracle Metal

Synopsis

At last the Aristocracy of Pull makes its move. And what a move it is!

"But can we get away with it?" asked Wesley Mouch.

No one answers him right away, and at last the only one with the courage to do so is one Mr. Thompson, in whom Rand personifies the legitimate government, for whatever that term is worth at this point. Thompson is the *"Head of State"*. Rand does not use the term "President," largely after the pattern of the European countries that are all now *"People's States."* It's all the structure needed for the moment for it is apparent that the true power lies elsewhere. In fact, most of it is in the room: Wesley Mouch, Eugene Lawson, Jim Taggart, Dr. Floyd Ferris, Orren Boyle, Clem Weatherby, and Fred Kinnan, who is head of Amalgamated Labor of America. It is their moment.

Why the trepidation? They have the official if tacit support of the sitting government, the media, the academics, and in another bit of Randian prescience, the popular entertainers. What could they have to worry about?

Responsibility. There is a truism of military command that one can delegate authority, but never responsibility. That stays with the delegator, but not in the Aristocracy of Pull, whose residents are adept at precisely the opposite: maintaining authority while passing responsibility. It is the ladder to the top of a very unstable structure.

They're going to take over the economy and hence the country itself, and they're going to establish a centrally-planned and centrally-directed economy by simple fiat. This is Directive 10-289:

1. *All workers are bound to their jobs and can neither leave nor be fired under penalty of one year in prison. The Unification Board, reporting to the Bureau of Economic*

Planning and National Resources, possesses judicial authority. All citizens upon turning 21 must register with the Unification Board which will assign them jobs in the best interests of the nation.

2. *All businesses must remain in operation and cannot close under penalty of nationalization and confiscation of property.*

3. *All patents and copyrights are to be turned over to the government by the use of "voluntary" Gift Certificates. The Unification Board will license those processes to all applicants to eliminate monopolies. All brand names and private trademarks are abolished.*

4. *No new inventions shall be produced or invented. The Patent Office is suspended.*

5. *All business establishments will produce the same amount every year as they did in the baseline known as the Yardstick Year, to be enforced by the Unification Board.*

6. *All citizens must purchase the same amount of goods every year as they did in the Yardstick Year, to be enforced by the Unification Board.*

7. *All wages and prices are frozen.*

8. *All cases arising from this directive are to be decided by the Unification Board.*

It is an economy built on the classical Fascist model – the means of production remain nominally in private hands, but their control and their product are strictly in the hands of the State. It is a frantic attempt to freeze a collapsing economy in a state of pre-collapse. It is also an outright *coup d'etat* on behalf of this Unification Board, whose membership will wield an arbitrary, dictatorial control over the country from which there is no appeal.

Membership on this board is the acme of power, and the bureaucrats consider that to be reserved for themselves.

Fred Kinnan brings them all down to earth: the Unification Board is to be staffed with his men exclusively. Orren Boyle objects that this will give Kinnan a stranglehold on every business in the country, and as an industrialist he insists on his property rights. Kinnan smiles and agrees about the stranglehold; he tells Boyle that if he wants Point Three, there should be no further talk about property rights. Kinnan is forcing the gang of self-deluders to face what they really are doing. He certainly knows what he is doing.

"Only I'm not going to say that I'm working for the welfare of my public, because I know I'm not. I know that I'm delivering the poor bastards into slavery...and they know it, too. But they know that I'll have to throw them a crumb once in a while if I want to keep my racket, while with the rest of you they wouldn't have a chance in hell... I'm a racketeer – but I know it and my boys know it, and they know that I'll pay off. Not out of the kindness of my heart, either, and not a cent more than I can get away with, but at least they can count on that much. Sure, it makes me sick sometimes, but it's not me who's built this kind of world – YOU did – so I'm playing the game as you've set it up and I'm going to play it for as long as it lasts – which isn't going to be long for any of us!"

It seems a bit ironic to observe that this arrangement is essentially indistinguishable from that between employer and employee in Rand's ethical world, although the latter is expressed in somewhat more idealistic terms. These are the terms under which Rearden is purchasing black market coal. Kinnan is a brute observing an ineluctable law of the universe; Rearden and d'Anconia are refined intellects observing that law as well, and the law remains the same. Kinnan knows he must keep his word, or else. And because of that, Rand may have considered Kinnan a more moral individual than the bureaucrats who were trying to disguise the fact that they were jobbing the system for their own good on behalf of the People. They're playing under two sets of rules. For Kinnan, words have meaning, and for the others, they don't. But the latter is only an intellectual fantasy, and it comes at a price. Where words have no meaning, evil becomes very difficult to recognize as it sits down to dine.

Dr. Ferris suggests off-handedly that the death penalty be applied to industrialists who vanish after the practice meted out to military deserters, but Kinnan stops him. They weren't quite that reluctant in Soviet Russia, which is where Rand learned most of this process. And once it started they weren't reluctant in the least. For those for whom words have no meaning, "death" is one of those words – as long as it happens to somebody else. For the elite, death is simply another of those abstractions that may be played with like counters on a board, an unfortunate necessity – no, not always that, but a necessity – for the building of an imagined world whose inhabitants are as abstract as the words that denote them: *bourgeoisie,* capitalist, counter-revolutionary, wrecker, spy. Kulak. Jew. Not real people, merely abstractions. This is a culture of death, and Rand calls it by name. "The death of one man is a tragedy," famously observed Stalin, "the death of millions, a statistic."

The copyright issue will cause problems with intellectuals, Lawson points out. Kinnan says that intellectuals are cowards; they were the first to sell out European nations to committees of goons like those in this room. A longshoreman may someday remember he is a man and take action. But intellectuals? Ferris agrees, and recommends putting a few intellectuals on the government payroll to buy them off.

But Ferris is worried about the whole issue of Gift Certificates; they have to look voluntary. They worry that Hank Rearden could blow their whole plan apart. Jim drops a bombshell when he says he can deliver Rearden. This heartens Mouch enough to give him his rate increase, much to Boyle's discomfort.

All leave the room with a window view of the Washington Monument.

Dagny unintentionally sleeps over at her office. She wakes and starts working, all the while wondering why her staff has not approached her this morning. She reads a report from her chief engineer: repairs to Colorado track have been shelved in favor of repairs to the Miami line due to a three hour delay created by a derailment that caused government bureaucrat Tinky Holloway to be late. Although the rail on the Miami line is in better shape than Colorado, there is a social need for the Miami line repairs to have a higher priority. Dagny slashes pungent remarks on the margins.

Francisco calls and tells Dagny to check the newspaper. Eddie Willers brings her the paper and tells Dagny that no one wanted to be the first to break the news. Upon reading Directive 10-289, Dagny's reaction is more than shock; it is a surreal out-of-body experience. Only her anger grounds her. Dagny walks into Jim's office and resigns; she returns to her office and breaks the news to her staff. She is going to her cabin in the Berkshire Mountains. She tells Eddie not to communicate any information about the railroad and to tell only Hank where she is. She calls Hank and delivers the news; when she ready to return, Hank will come for her. Dagny leaves the building with a sense of finality.

Hank Rearden's rolling mill foreman quits. The sides are lining up now, and Rearden's minder, the Wet Nurse, has made up his mind which one he's on.

"Mr. Rearden," he said, "I wanted to tell you that if you want to pour ten times the quota of Rearden Metal or steel or pig iron or anything, and bootleg it all over the place to anybody at any price – I'll fix it up. I'll juggle the books, I'll fake the reports, I'll get phony witnesses, I'll forge affidavits..."

"Now why would you want to do that?" asked Rearden, smiling, but his smile vanished when he heard the boy answer earnestly:

"Because I want, for once, to do something moral."

"That's not the way to be moral – " Rearden started, and stopped abruptly, realizing that it was the way, the only way left, realizing through how many twists of intellectual corruption this boy had to struggle toward his momentous discovery.

The Wet Nurse begs Rearden not to sign over his ownership of Rearden Metal to the government. He knows it isn't right. He thinks there is no right or wrong, and yet he knows it isn't right. That is a contradiction. The young man is in the process of checking his premises.

More and more of Hank's men disappear, but the personnel office isn't notified. Instead, new men using the names of the former employees take their places at the mill. Unnumbered industrialists vanish, but the press won't report it.

Dr. Floyd Ferris arrives to obtain Hank's signature on the Gift Certificate in time for the nightly news. Hank looks ironically at the Gift Certificate with the Statue of Liberty on it and the name "Rearden Metal" replaced by "Miracle Metal". Ferris' lever is the evidence of Hank's adultery with Dagny Taggart; he points out to Hank that with experts in the art of smearing like Bertram Scudder called to the task, Dagny's reputation will be ruined. It is the Orren Boyle School of Management – they have the goods on him, courtesy of James Taggart, who got those goods from Lillian Rearden. She has closed her transaction with the Aristocracy of Pull and has delivered her husband to them.

Hank hasn't the least concern that a scandal will damage him, but he knows full well it will hurt Dagny. It is a vulnerability he has handed them. And so Rearden has to decide which he cares for more: his life's work, or the woman who represents the ideals under which it was achieved. He thinks back to their first encounter. Even then she was brave, free and admirable; now she is his lotus floating spotless in a pool of filth. The decision is not a difficult one. His reverie is broken by a peremptory demand.

"Well, Mr. Rearden? Are you going to sign?" asked Dr. Ferris.

"Oh, that?" said Rearden.

He picked up a pen and with no second glance, he signed his name at the foot of the Statue of Liberty and pushed the Gift Certificate across the desk.

And so Rearden Metal becomes Miracle Metal with the stroke of a pen. No more trademarks. It is Point Three of Directive 10-289, and now it's the law.

The Never Ending State of Emergency

In 1933, as one of his first acts as president, Franklin Roosevelt placed the country under a state of emergency via executive order and navigated his way around the Constitution. Successive presidents signed one executive order after another, declaring overlapping states of emergency.

Following the Watergate scandal in 1974, Congress decided to examine presidential misuse of states of emergency and executive orders, repealing many of them, but not all. Congress understood that if it removed all states of emergency, it would lose much of its own power and reduce the overall power of the federal government. The result would be Congress meeting for three months every year and then going home; this was considered unacceptable. And so both state of emergency and presidential directive remain as weapons in the arsenal of the State.

Wage and Price Controls

Upon entering World War II in 1942, Franklin Roosevelt imposed wage and price controls upon the country. This was only a small part of the conversion of America from a depression economy to a wartime economy. Full socialist industrial planning turned consumer product factories into war materiel factories.

Among so many other things, war is an exercise in credit. To keep money flowing into war bonds a comprehensive advertising campaign was utilized. ("It's bonds or bondage!") Rationing was established to prioritize certain resources for the military, and war bonds represented the logical and patriotic destination for savings. One good thing that developed from this was that war bond money moved into the economy in a controlled pace for 25 years after the war as those bonds matured, the foundation for a slow but continuing prosperity. It was not until 1970 that the country finally had to face the travails of an entirely postwar economy.

Truman removed wage and price controls in 1946.

In 1971 Nixon re-imposed controls to address runaway inflation and closed the gold window to foreign payments. Unlike World War II, there was no rationing, and that led to shortages. The controls interfered with the seasonal refinery switches from gasoline to heating oil and back, hence the summer of 1972 saw occasional gasoline shortages.

The "floating" of the dollar caused a massive devaluation that in turn caused Middle Eastern oil suppliers to increase their prices. Although the government shied away from the politically unpopular position of directly rationing fuel, there were other forms of rationing such as purchase limits at the pump and customers limited by license plate numbers to purchase on specific days of the week. Upon the removal of controls in 1974, a wave of labor unrest swept the country as wages, which were adjusted less frequently than prices, failed to keep pace with double-digit inflation.

In Rand's world, the government is about to repeat the mistakes of the Seventies, with catastrophic consequences.

Discussion Topics

- Head of State Thompson expanded the powers of his office because it was expected of him by those who had pushed him into office. Why is this a classic pattern in politics?

- Labor racketeer Fred Kinnan is the only honest man in the room; he is almost likeable. He knows he is a crook, but that's what his membership wants. All he needs to do is produce for his people as Jimmy Hoffa did in the old days in the real world. Has this changed today, and if so, why?

- Serfs were bound to the land; now under Directive 10-289 people are to be bound to their jobs, and the Unification Board will draft Americans to do jobs based on national need, particularly young Americans just about to enter the job force.   What happened to freedom?

- The media in *Atlas Shrugged* are useless and biased.   Rand had no patience with journalists; the only honest one in the book is fired for it.   Has this changed since the 1950's, and if so, how?

Chapter VII: The Moratorium on Brains

Synopsis

Eddie Willers sits down with the Anonymous Rail Worker in the Taggart corporate cafeteria and updates him with respect to the following:

- People are deserting their jobs and getting arrested, but the police can't find the resources to feed them.

- On the railroad, the best men have left and are being replaced by scum. And Dagny, the only one who could hold the railroad together, is gone. Jim is keeping it secret lest his friends in Washington condemn him for having a deserter in the family. Clifton Locey, a friend of Jim, is sitting in Dagny's office doing his best not to get caught working. Locey has already framed two employees for his mistakes and let the Unification Board do the rest. Locey leans on Eddie for help but treats him like dirt.

- Chick Morrison, the government's Morale Coordinator, got a special train, and the Unification Board let him ignore the government's speed limits. For his train, Morrison even got the reserve diesel locomotive which is stored for emergencies at the mouth of the Taggart Tunnel at Winston, Colorado.

- Orren Boyle refitted his furnaces at a plant in Maine to produce Rearden Metal, but Ragnar Danneskjøld shelled the plant from out at sea using long range naval guns. The press has maintained total silence, and the government is denouncing the report as a scurrilous rumor.

- Dagny is at a secret location in the Berkshires.

The Anonymous Rail Worker says he'll be gone for a month; he has taken a month off every summer for the past twelve years. Eddie is envious and remarks that it is quite a vacation for a track worker.

Hank Rearden takes a walk after dark in the countryside with a revolver in his pocket. It isn't the act of a prudent individual, but by now Hank really doesn't care. He is waylaid by a blond highwayman who instead of robbing him, presses a gold bar into Hank's hands representing a down payment on all the money that was stolen from him by the looters – in this case, through income taxation. It is one of Rand's better dramatic moments when we learn his name. He is none other than the notorious pirate Ragnar Danneskjøld.

It is an interesting conversation, another outreach by a Destroyer, and yes, there do appear to be three of them, which should surprise no one at this point. It is amusing to learn that Danneskjøld wishes to slay Robin Hood – not the real character, but his false contemporary image promoting the virtue of stealing from the rich and giving to the poor. In fact, Danneskjøld is not stealing from the poor and giving to the rich but stealing from the looters and returning the loot to its rightful owners. Hence the gold. The rest of Hank's gold, the pirate tells him, is deposited in the Mulligan Bank, which is not in Chicago; Ragnar suggests that Hank will soon know its true location. The gold is intended to start the rebuilding of the world out of the ruins after the final collapse. Danneskjøld goes just a bit farther in preventing Orren Boyle from profiting from the theft of Rearden Metal by shelling the factories Boyle had readied, knowing that the theft was imminent.

Danneskjøld is uncharacteristically far inland, standing in for an unnamed friend who would otherwise have been at Rearden's side. Suicidally so, in fact, for the police are hot on his trail, and Hank, although he expresses open contempt for criminal activity – this is a fellow who would not steal a piece of fruit when, at age 14, he was starving – finds himself covering for Danneskjøld by claiming him to be a new bodyguard. It is, in at least a sense, not altogether a lie. There is one jarring moment:

[Policeman] "Did you happen to see a man anywhere around these parts, a stranger moving along in a hurry?"

"Where?"

"He'd be either on foot or in a battered wreck of a car that's got a million-dollar motor."

This won't do. The clear implication is that Danneskjøld is running his jalopy on the mystery motor whose wreckage was discovered in the Twentieth Century rubble, whose tragedy was that nobody recognized it for what it was. It isn't impossible that its inventor made another one for Danneskjøld, in fact, as we shall learn later, it might even be likely, but it is quite impossible for a policeman to know of it. That editor that Rand did not use might have spotted this anomaly. It's a tiny point, really – curable by the excision of a single phrase – but a telling one in the overall consideration of whether *Atlas Shrugged* could have used a sympathetic editor with an unsympathetic ax. The novel would have been the better for it, or at least shorter, which is frequently the same thing.

Kip Chalmers is on a tight schedule – he has been granted a private car attached to the *Comet* for his trip to California where he hopes to solidify his position in the Aristocracy of Pull by being formally elected a legislator, although it is a little vague what that title might entail. Chalmers' place in the bureaucracy depends on it, he has dawdled to attend a cocktail party and now finds himself on the wrong side of the Rocky Mountains with the campaign rally looming. It shouldn't be a problem, really, at least until a rail splits and the engine pulling the *Comet* ends up on its side.

At the Winston station, the agent, who had been a drifter only a few days before, gets word of the problem and passes the buck to the night supervisor at Silver Springs, who passes the buck to his boss. Division manager Dave Mitchum is the brother-in-law of Claude Slagenhop and owes his job to a bit of blackmail between Jim Taggart and Wesley Mouch involving Mouch's sister. Mitchum is an old railroad hand who blames a conspiracy of the

Big Boys for his many career failures, and characteristically he is at a loss as to what actions to take in this emergency.

Bill Brent, the dispatcher, says they aren't going to send a coal burning steam locomotive into a tunnel built for diesels. They don't dare delay the Army munitions train to use its diesel to haul the *Comet*. Nobody wants to take responsibility and make a decision with Locey and the Unification Board watching. Brent says they need to take the diesel from an eastbound freight, which is on its way, after it exits the tunnel, and use that diesel to move the *Comet* through the tunnel. Then they can use a coal burner to get the *Comet* to the West Coast; it will be eighteen hours late. Everyone knows that blame is going to be delegated from New York and does not desire to become the point at which it comes to rest.

When the *Comet* reaches Winston, hauled by a switching engine, and Chalmers gets the bad news, he is outraged. His electoral success depends on an arrival on time, and he knows which levers to pull to ensure that he does not miss it. The orders drift back down from New York to Mitchum, and every employee down the line who executes them knows that the orders are wrong, but if the Unification Board rules against them, they and their families will starve to death.

Mitchum tells Brent he is taking a track motor up the line to Fairmount, where he thinks there may be a diesel engine available. In fact, it is obvious that he is merely excusing himself from the scene. Mitchum tells Brent to wait thirty minutes and then send the *Comet* through the tunnel with a coal burning steam locomotive. Brent refuses, demanding a written train order, which Mitchum won't provide, screaming that he will bring the law down on him. Brent demands that Mitchum repeat his train order in front of witnesses, and Mitchum assaults him. Brent leaves, and Mitchum gives his orders to the call boy, who executes them after major misgivings.

At Winston, the engineer of the coal burner refuses to drive the train and vanishes into the night. The station agent hands the job to an alcoholic employee who is a friend of Fred Kinnan and who has already survived a bout with the Unification Board. As the train departs with Chalmers' car in tow, the conductor slips off the train and disappears.

Some chapters ago the question was broached: Are there no innocent victims? By amazing coincidence, the passengers in the first class section of the *Comet* include a professor of sociology who teaches collectivism, a journalist supporting the use of compulsion because his feelings justify it, a schoolteacher who has corrupted the minds of innocents, a newspaper publisher who believes in fascism, and a businessman who received his big break from the Equalization of Opportunity Bill. There are more, many more, on this Train of Fools. As it enters the tunnel, the last living vision of its passengers is of Wyatt's Torch.

An eerie and symbolic image, and into the darkness they go, never to return. We are left unsatisfied by Rand's description of grim recompense. There were at the very least two children aboard whose only crime was to be those of a bureaucrat, and Rand's nascent theology rejects the idea of Original Sin. Or does it? We face the question of whether there are, in the act of Atlas shrugging, no innocent victims. Rand here implies that there are not, at least insofar as this particular tragedy is concerned, yet her narrative clearly describes them. For the rest it is a form of cosmic justice; for the children it is a tragedy. There will be more, far more, as the country collapses. The true cost of the culture of looting is measured in the blood of the innocent, and the redemption, if any, had better be worth it.

It is a grim and disturbing chapter, and it was meant to be.

The Two Economic Models

It is more than the titular *"moratorium on brains"*; it is, in effect, a moratorium on new economic activity and a contradictory and impossible insistence that the old economic activity proceed as it did before. The reason for this is that there are two different conceptions of economics both in *Atlas Shrugged* and in the real world: first, the dynamic model wherein wealth is created, risk and reward are balanced, and inequities in distribution of wealth cause the flow that is economic activity; second, the notion that wealth is static, that it is a pie to be sliced up in even portions, and that if the portions are uneven, it is up to the State to rectify the matter. That the pie itself might shrink or expand is irrelevant to the "social justice" involved, and hence it is resolutely ignored until at last there is no pie at all and the last recourse is to find a scapegoat.

Nations move back and forth between those models depending on which of their adherents is in power. Those that thrive on the first model build up enough capital for the disastrous consequences of transitioning to the second model to be masked for a time. The Soviet Union lasted seven decades under those conditions; Zimbabwe, seven years.

It is the latter conception that resulted in Directive 10-289. Both production and consumption are commanded to proceed unchanged while the underpinnings of the economy are expropriated by the Aristocracy of Pull, quite as nonsensically as if a waterwheel were ordered to continue turning while the river is stopped because there would be social consequences if it didn't.

Railroad Technology

Taggart Transcontinental's tunnel is based on the real life Moffat Tunnel, opened in 1926, and built by the Denver & Rio Grande. Thanks to multiple mergers, it is owned today by the Union Pacific.

A track motor is a powered handcar, now replaced by the ubiquitous high-railer, which is a truck or SUV fitted with railroad wheels. Today, even large trucks, such as vacuum trucks that clean rights-of-way and culverts, carry high-rail technology, and railroads designate them as trains on their dispatching systems.

Telegraphers, local dispatchers and call boys disappeared with the addition of radio to the railroads' arsenal in the Fifties. Today, advances such as data telemetry and the Internet permit railroads to have up-to-the-minute information, which is why railroads utilize single location dispatching.

Discussion Topics

- Ragnar Danneskjøld: *"Gold is the objective value, the means of preserving one's wealth and one's future."* In

1957 it was illegal for Americans to possess gold but not Europeans. But in the book, the people of the European people's states are not permitted to possess gold either. How does gold define the difference between a free man and a serf, a citizen and a subject?

- Ragnar's gold is intended to restart the world after the final collapse. If a recession descends into a depression and then morphs further into disintegration, how would a nation's economy – or the world economy – restart? Are precious metals, or some form of hard currency, the only solution? Diecuss whether yet another fiat currency could fill the void, or whether hard money is the only answer.

- In Stephen King's epic novel *The Stand*, there is a long passage enumerating the less significant people who died of the Captain Trips virus, and each is kissed off with the sentiment that his death was no great loss. Rand does the same thing but with a tone of malevolence. These people had it coming, and they got it; it was their long delayed comeuppance. Discuss whether she is justified in this conclusion.

Chapter VIII: By Our Love

Synopsis

In this short chapter Rand isolates one issue and addresses it with one crisis of conscience. She has certainly made her point concerning the abuse of the producers by the looters, of the achievers by the leeches, so much so that the reader is probably wondering why the whole system hasn't already collapsed. Why do the victims persist? Why can't they let go? Why hasn't everyone slipped into seclusion and let the whole rotten edifice fall down? They are held in harness by love, by a form of white blackmail.

Dagny has finally had enough. Directive 10-289, the *"moratorium on brains,"* has sent her flying in disgust and revulsion to an old cabin in the wilderness where she can think it all out, an ancient plot device wherein the author can speak to us directly through her protagonist's internal dialogue. It isn't any surprise that Dagny finds it impossible to turn her previous life off like a light switch. She is in the frame of mind reported by many retirees, feeling like a roaring engine whose load has suddenly been removed. Both engines and people can fly apart under those conditions.

She's game about the whole attempt, though, building paths to assuage her relentless drive to build something, fighting the ennui of a shopkeeper by making the simple suggestion that she move her produce out of the sun. The latter is so worn down by it all that she answers bovinely, *"It's always been there."* It is what much of the world is becoming, and Dagny doesn't fit into that world at all, so she retreats to the cabin where her old friend and lover Francisco arrives to comfort her; Dagny could swear he's whistling the theme from Halley's Fifth Concerto. He knows the price of giving up what one loves – and will relearn it through the rest of the novel. Dagny is only now getting her first taste.

She wonders how he found her and asks if Eddie, the only person in whom she has confided her location, has told him. He hasn't seen Eddie for more than a year, but Rand gives us a clue that something or someone is a go-between, for the chatterbox

Eddie was in fact the only one who did know where she was until he blabbed it – to someone.

Francisco takes Dagny in his arms and kisses her, but Dagny pulls away. Francisco tells her that he can now explain everything. He should have intercepted her when she quit and spared her the past month in seclusion. Dagny wishes that The Destroyer had come for her, and she was surprised when he didn't. Francisco reminds her of that night, twelve years ago, when he warned her in agony about what was going to happen that he couldn't talk about.

"I am destroying d'Anconia Copper, consciously, deliberately, by plan and by my own hand."

And he is doing it to prevent his company from sustaining the cosmic fraud that is the looters' creed. Like Ellis Wyatt he intends to *"leave it as I found it,"* not as he personally found it but as his ancestor did. Dagny is astonished to realize that the knowing destruction of what he most loves has become his life's work. To Dagny that is inconceivable in the exact sense of the word. Builder that she is, it strikes her as profoundly immoral, a rejection of everything that man is.

It is at this moment that a radio broadcast of a symphony is interrupted by a news bulletin about a train wreck in the tunnel in Colorado.

As we left the *Comet* in the last chapter, it had entered the tunnel pulled by a coal burning steam locomotive. Three miles into the eight mile bore, the crew felt the effect of the fumes, and the engineer threw the throttle wide open to gain enough speed to surmount the heavy grade. As the passengers felt the effect of the fumes, one panicked and pulled the emergency stop cord, breaking the locomotive's air hose and stopping the train midway through the tunnel. The fireman fled through the tube, reaching the western portal when he was flattened by the blast of an explosion behind him. Apparently, the Army munitions train had been cleared to proceed because the tunnel's signaling system was defective, and it plowed into the *Comet*, setting off an explosion that demolished the tunnel and most of the mountain with it.

Dagny screams at this horrendous revelation and flees, and Francisco begs her not to go back, but to no avail.

Jim Taggart stares at the letter of resignation he hopes to avoid signing. Most company officers are avoiding the office. Jim decides to hide in his, and even Wesley Mouch knows better than to call him. But finally galvanized into action, Jim accosts Eddie Willers and demands to know where Dagny is; Eddie won't answer. Jim tries to intimidate Eddie, accusing him of treason, but Eddie won't budge.

Then Dagny walks in. And she is back, their savior, as if there were anything left worth saving. This is not an act of sacrifice on Dagny's part; it is an irresistible, existential moment. The situation is a challenge, a drug to an addict, the sound of guns to a warhorse not yet ready to be put out to pasture. To give it up would be to give up not just Taggart Transcontinental, but herself. No wonder she can't do it.

Jim screams that the disaster is all her fault, but Dagny pointedly ignores him and gives orders to Eddie. She quickly discovers that key personnel on the railroad have quit and disappeared. While Jim slinks off to shred his letter of resignation, Dagny asks what has been done since the disaster. Nothing, says Eddie, because the first person to act would have set himself up for the Unification Board. The entire Taggart system is in chaos.

Dagny opens up a rail map and tells Eddie to route trains over the tracks of other railroads, even to buy abandoned railroads and put them back into service. To fill gaps in the map, she tells Eddie to hire local crews to build new rail lines; bribe the Unification Board goons if necessary. Then she tells him to get the pre-tunnel system map out of the archives to see how they can reclaim the old route through the Rockies.

Eddie updates Dagny: Hank has signed the Gift Certificate, Quentin Daniels hasn't been heard from, and trains have been abandoned on the system with the crews disappearing into the night.

Wesley Mouch calls Dagny, making the official excuse that her health was the reason for her absence. She sloughs Mouch off and demands to talk to Clem Weatherby. She tells the rail czar that Mouch is never to call her again; she will deal exclusively with *him*.

Weatherby balks until he realizes that Dagny is handing him *preferment*, the right to use her as an item of pull. She is going to start breaking laws immediately, and Weatherby tells her the laws are certainly flexible in such a situation. Finishing the call, she looks at Clifton Locey's collection of progressive magazines and sweeps them off the coffee table in one stroke.

After giving the orders that will put the railroad back in working order, Dagny calls Hank.

"Hank, I don't think they care whether there's a train or a blast furnace left on earth. We do. They're holding us by our love of it, and we'll go on paying so long as there's still one chance left to keep one single wheel alive..."

"By our love." Rand has answered the question suggested by the chapter title. She should have stopped there.

"...when the flood swallows it we'll go down with the last wheel and the last syllogism..."

The thud of that clunker hurts the ears, and unfortunately the chapter ends two sentences later, so that it reverberates like a lead weight falling down the basement stairs. The last *what?* If there's one thing a high-tension railroad executive isn't going to be invoking with her world in flaming wreckage around her, it's a syllogism. If the word even occurred to Dagny at that moment one would have to reach for the straitjacket.

But it would occur to Rand the philosopher. Here the author has so closely identified with her protagonist that there is no longer a filter of fiction between thought and utterance. This is odd, because Rand was a perfectly competent Hollywood scriptwriter, and dialogue was second nature to her – but this one rings horribly false. It is Rand speaking, not Dagny, and when Dagny has lost her own voice, we lose Dagny. And we don't want to do that at this point, because we like her and she's placed herself right back in the fray. Something she loves too much to give up is a chain that she's put on herself, stronger than the one of Rearden Metal that she wears on her wrist, and her enemies hold the other end.

Aristotle and the Straight Line

But the work of building a path was a living sum, so that no day was left to die behind her, but each day contained all those that preceded it, each day acquired its immortality on every succeeding tomorrow. A circle, she thought, is the movement proper to physical nature...but the straight line is the badge of man, the straight line of a geometrical abstraction that makes roads, rails, and bridges, the straight line that cuts the curving aimlessness of nature by a purposeful motion from a start to an end.

There are Earth-worshipers would shrink in horror from such blasphemy. And yet the straight line is not really an artifact of man, but his imitation of the horizon. The horizon isn't perfectly straight, of course, either in terms of curvature or of granularity, but then neither are the lines made by men. In this, man is one with his world whether he likes it or not.

Consider that standard of straightness, a plumb bob. Under examination the string is revealed, even without a lens, to be coarse, its boundaries pocked and porous, its internal fibers twisted and lumpy. Nothing about it is really straight. It is only straight when one backs up enough to consider it as a one-dimensional object, which it is only in the mind: this is pure Plato, Aristotle's teacher, and now this piece of Rand's new philosophy is revealed as a strange admixture of Plato and Nietzsche. Straightness, as Rand stated, is an abstraction, an *a priori* concept that is one of the laws of the universe that form the foundation of her epistemology. It is real, but we can only imitate it in such worshipful constructions as a railroad track reaching toward the horizon. To Dagny that makes that track's destruction, either deliberate or merely by allowing it to happen, an act of apostasy.

Philosophically this is like dipping one's toes in a mile-deep ocean, and it is crucial to an appreciation of Objectivism as a philosophy. This idea of straightness, defined as a one-dimensional line describing the shortest distance between two points, themselves abstractions – is it an invention of man, or was it always there and man merely its discoverer? *A posteriori* or *a priori*? Inventor or discoverer? It makes a fundamental difference in one's view of the universe. And Rand, like Aristotle, like Plato, like Kant – whose main theses she angrily rejected – must come down on the side of *a priori*.

And yet, as we have seen, Rand parts company with Aristotle on the topic of teleology. For her the laws of the universe simply are, and for him they are caused. Her place between Nietszche and Aristotle is in whose mind such abstractions as straightness, such laws of the universe, really reside: Man's or God's. It is a philosopher's question, not an engineer's.

That she considers the destruction of that track an act of apostasy is why Dagny is not yet ready despite Francisco's hopeful overtures. One feels for the fellow – he has not only become such an apostate himself, but has given up the woman he loves in doing so. Does he hope to win her back now that the charade is known? For she is close, so very close to the realization that abnegation of all of this is the price that they must pay for the sin of selling it too cheaply.

Discussion Topic

- The buck passing in the previous chapter now moves to Taggart headquarters in New York. No one wants to answer the phone because of the possibility of having no one to pass the buck to. Eddie says the buck stops with him, and only Dagny's arrival saves Eddie Willers from the Unification Board. The one man glad to accept the buck is Clem Weatherby because it now guarantees him extra pull; he has exclusive access to Dagny and the railroad. Where does this currency of access have a counterpart in today's politics?

Chapter IX: The Face Without Pain or Fear or Guilt

Synopsis

Dagny is back in the fight after a month of self-exile. It is the railroad that has drawn her out of her refuge, but she finds herself caught between the poles of two men: one, her old lover Francisco d'Anconia, who wishes to pull her out of it all; the other, her current flame Hank Rearden, who quite inadvertently is pulling her back in. The railroad is the trump card in this, and she's shackled to her desk because she has locked the thing in place with her own two hands.

It is Francisco who comes to her first. Here there is the wistful action of a man who has lost his love but hopes in the end to win her back. There is also the sympathy and loyalty of an old friend who knows she's in need of one at the moment, and it isn't the first time. One must admire that loyalty whether directed at a dog, who merits it, or Dagny, whom one might be tempted to wonder about. Both she and Francisco share the same values, beliefs, and yet they are pursuing them in opposite directions. Why?

"Dagny," he [Francisco] said slowly, "I know why one loves one's work...what is it you see when you think of a moving train?"

She glanced at the city. "The life of a man of ability who might have perished in that catastrophe, but will escape the next one, which I'll prevent...the kind of man who is what we were when we started, you and I. You gave him up. I can't."

Clearly Dagny does realize that her passengers are her trust and that there were innocents aboard the doomed *Comet*. It is a rather grudging moral epiphany, but it's something. And yet Rand will have none of it. Is Dagny serving that hypothetical *übermensch* by saving his life if it means perpetuating the system that enslaves him?

"All right, Dagny. I won't try to stop you. You will stop on the day when you'll discover that your work has been placed in the service, not of that man's life, but of his destruction."

"Francisco!" It was a cry of astonishment and despair. "You do understand it, you know what I mean by that kind of man, you see him too!"

"Oh, yes," he said simply..."Why should you be astonished? You said that we were of his kind once, you and I. We still are. But one of us has betrayed him."

Our question as to whether there are innocent victims is answered in stark terms: yes, there are, and it doesn't matter. To Rand the system is a moral abomination, and its cessation is worth the price paid in blood no matter who pays it; to maintain it does not avoid paying that same price and worse. We will encounter this moral absolutism frequently. Atlas may fight this conviction, but when finally he comes to accept it, he shrugs. There is a charm, even nobility, in Dagny's stubborn insistence on keeping a dying machine running. But for The Destroyer's program of renascence to take shape, the societal machine must halt. And she is keeping it running.

"Until then, Dagny, remember that we're enemies. I didn't want to tell you this, but you're the first person who almost stepped into heaven and came back to earth... It's you that I'm fighting, not your brother James or Wesley Mouch."

"Francisco!" she cried, in desperate defense of him against herself. "How can you do what you're doing?"

"By the grace of my love" – for you, said his eyes – "for the man," said his voice, "who did not perish in your catastrophe and who will never perish."

An odd usage, that. Coupled with a phrase dropped earlier in this same conversation concerning *"that man"* permitting no tribute to Caesar, permitting no Caesar, we realize that Francisco is not speaking of an individual here but an archetype, which is well, because very few individual human beings are likely to survive an ammunition train explosion and a mountain being dropped on them. Once again we see that Rand has pressed godhead onto her idealized perfect human being, her *übermensch*.

"I wish I could spare you what you're going to go through," he said, the gentleness of his voice saying: It's not me that you should pity. "But I can't. Every one of us has to travel that road by his own steps. But it's the same road."

"Where does it lead?"

He smiled, as if softly closing a door on the questions that he would not answer. "To Atlantis," he said.

So does he still love her? Of course he does.

"I'll always wait for you, no matter what we do, either one of us."

It is the loyalty of a gentle soul, warding off the bleak image of a lonely future with a scrap of hope.

The present, however, bursts through the door in the person of Hank Rearden, who imagines – despite his previous insight into Francisco – that the latter is there to make Dagny one of his petty conquests. It is a brutal scene, one of accusations that cannot be answered, of false assumptions that may not be challenged. Perhaps it is Dagny's presence that works to madden Rearden, but it is not at all a flattering moment. And at its end comes an admission out of context that causes Rearden to put Francisco to his greatest trial.

...he asked, pointing at Dagny, his voice low and strangely unlike his own voice, as if it neither came from nor were addressed to a living person, "Is this the woman you love?"

146

Francisco answered, looking at her, "Yes."

Rearden's hand rose, swept down, and slapped Francisco's face.

Francisco forces himself to take the blow unanswered.

He was looking at Rearden, but it was not Rearden that he was seeing. He looked as if he were facing another presence in the room and as if his glance were saying: If this is what you demand of me, then even this is yours, yours to accept and mine to endure, there is no more than this in me to offer you... She knew that what she was witnessing Francisco d'Anconia's greatest achievement.

It is a disturbing image. Francisco is a complete believer, a dedicated revolutionary striving for utopia. But in this paragraph his dedication is not directed at an ideology, and apparently, no longer at an archetype. It is unmistakably directed at a specific *man*. What man? We don't know yet, but we certainly aren't short of clues. This is the devotion of a religious follower worshiping that godhead that is embodied in the person of a man of achievement, the man Dagny is running her trains to save, the man Francisco is destroying his mines to free. But this case, this particular man, is real. He is godhead taken unto flesh. For an atheist, Rand certainly doesn't skimp on the Christian imagery. But this is no Christ. And Francisco's religious fervor is more than a little disturbing.

Nevertheless, Hank has delivered the blow, and realizes too late that he would give anything to retract it. Dagny chooses to reveal that Francisco was no threat to her, that in fact he was her first lover. Francisco has departed with what dignity is possible in such a shattering situation, his mouth bleeding. In the next few moments, Dagny fears that Hank will beat her to death and seems to accept the idea with a most uncharacteristic submission, but instead they couple violently.

The building superintendent arrives to deliver a letter that he has been holding in Dagny's absence. It's from Quentin Daniels, and it prompts her to grab the phone and call Utah in a panic.

Daniels has come to his own independent conclusions concerning the propriety of giving the miracle motor to an unappreciative and exploitative society. He too has traveled the road that Francisco predicted for Dagny, and at its end is the abnegation of the flesh for the good of the soul. One more Atlas has shrugged, and lest we miss the significance of this moral epiphany, Rand drives it home with another curious image. Daniels isn't actually going anywhere, he's continuing as a janitor, but he's just giving up working on the motor.

The contrast between the two cases of the sober Daniels and the Francisco-Hank-Dagny triangle of whatever it is – the term "love" seems inadequate – could not be any clearer. Rand has at last returned to her very formidable case, and it has taken the monk-like asceticism of Quentin Daniels to bring her there. The reader might be forgiven for suspecting that to be a revelatory moment lost on its own author, especially in the light of what follows.

There is a railroad to be rebuilt, the full weight of which has fallen on the shoulders of poor Eddie. She is off to chase Daniels to attempt to convince him to re-enter her tumultuous and failing world, and all Eddie has to do in the meantime is handle the entire reconstruction of a transcontinental railroad. It is no real surprise that under such pressure Eddie seeks out his own safety valve, his Anonymous Rail Worker confidante in the company cafeteria. And the Worker has, as a plateful of cigarette butts attests, been waiting for him. He is still voiceless but now we are made aware of his appearance.

"Do you know what's strange about your face? You look as if you've never known pain or fear or guilt."

At last Rand validates what we have suspected all along – this Worker is something more than he appears. This time he shows a reaction – the fellow is, after all, due to commence his month-long vacation, so perhaps that's it. Or perhaps it's the knowledge that Quentin Daniels has made landfall on Atlantis on his very own, perhaps the notion of Dagny launching herself out on a hazardous mission to Utah. Or perhaps it's Eddie's sudden and embarrassing admission that the woman that Eddie, too, has discovered that he loves, is sleeping with Hank Rearden. Eddie is undoubtedly a magnificent manager of projects, but he possesses all the private discretion of a giggling schoolgirl on Valentine's Day. And he is clearly in the grip of his own existential crisis.

"Why is there nothing but misery left for anyone? What are we doing? What have we lost? A year ago I wouldn't have damned her for finding something she wanted. But I know that they're doomed, both of them, and so am I, and so is everybody, and she was all I had left...the world is perishing and we cannot stop it. Why are we destroying ourselves? Who will save us? Oh, who is John Galt?!"

One suspects that it might be from the distraught Eddie's uncomfortable and contrived monologue that the Track Worker flees suddenly. One would certainly forgive him.

Infidelity and Rand's Understanding of Male Psychology

The slap was a momentary failure on the part of Hank, instantly regretted, and received with an inhuman restraint by a Francisco in the grip of all the fervor of martyrdom. Rand feels his departure dignified; most male readers will consider it ignominious. Hank seems to understand the enormity of the insult, and so he and Dagny dash through the streets of New York in pursuit of Francisco to tender an abject apology for an unforgivable act... Well, no, they don't. What they do instead is to copulate like a pair of spring rabbits. But it's all right with Dagny, because...

...she felt Francisco's presence through Rearden's mind, she felt as if she were surrendering to both men, to that which she had worshiped in both of them...which had made of her love for each an act of loyalty to both.

An act of *what?* Perhaps in Dagny's endorphin-soaked brain this is some sort of cosmic double play, but in plain point of fact one fellow is bedding her with the enthusiasm of a sailor fresh off a six-month cruise, and the other fellow is walking through the streets with a bloody mouth. Those are the facts; the rest of it is sophistry that even Dr. Pritchett would be embarrassed to bleat.

It is here that Rand's sexual theories reach the far shore of adolescent fantasy. Dagny is not being disloyal for the simple reason that she is not having sex with another human being, but with an idea, and as long as she remains true to the idea, the human being in whom it is embodied at the moment is essentially irrelevant. It is a credo that is consistent in its internal logic, personally convenient, and perfectly monstrous. It is a portable morality with a padded, ergonomic handle. It is simply another manifestation of that preference for the exigencies of the moment that Rand professes to find distasteful when it is applied by her villains anywhere else.

Again we face an apparent deficiency in Rand's knowledge of men's relationships with other men. Francisco is, by Rand's specific description, a scion of old world honor, and here he has been offered a physical blow by the successful rival to the love of his life in her very presence. Rand regards this as the provocation that it is, but one doesn't get the impression she fully appreciates just how outrageous. It is insufferable, unforgivable, a mortal insult in the precise sense of the term. Men in Francisco's culture died for it and still do.

Yet Francisco withdraws from the confrontation like a whipped pup, not in fact an alpha dog suddenly turned beta, but one who has been a beta dog for quite some time. Should Dagny's idealistic bed-hopping land her in another hutch – it's almost inevitable by now – Rand apparently feels the two men will be able to shake hands and be pals again, secure in the happy status of eternal beta-dom. It is a resolution as unlikely in real life as a gargoyle suddenly sprouting wings and littering the landscape with rose petals.

Discussion Topics

- This chapter occurs in Dagny's apartment with the presence of a former lover and a current lover. What do we learn about Rand's philosophy from these interactions?

150

- How does Rand really feel about the death of the children aboard the *Comet*? Are they innocent victims or do they share their parents' guilt? What if Galt had been aboard the train?

Chapter X: The Sign of the Dollar

Synopsis

The *Comet* rolls across Nebraska with Dagny's private car. The train traverses a Middle America as imagined by Hieronymus Bosch, islands of normality punctuated by signs of decay.

...she saw the ghosts between, the remnants of towns, the skeletons of factories with crumbling smokestacks, the corpses of shops with broken panes, the slanting poles with shreds of wire...she saw an ice-cream cone made of radiant tubing, hanging above the corner of a street, and a battered car being parked below, with a young boy at the wheel and a girl stepping out, her white dress blowing in the summer wind – she shuddered for the two of them, thinking: I can't look at you, I who know what it has taken to give you your youth, to give you this evening, this car, and the ice-cream cone you're going to buy for a quarter...

It is a bittersweet image, a sense of ingratitude for a plenty taken for granted, and of how fragile that plenty can be in the face of that ingratitude. It is a sentiment common to many post-war novels.

Dagny hears the shout of the conductor throwing a hobo off the vestibule of her car, but she rescues him and asks him to be her dinner guest. A hobo is not a bum, nor is he a "tramp" as Rand incorrectly terms him; he is a traveling man who supports himself with odd jobs, and Rand has already placed words of import into the mouths of vagrants. This one has a mouthful himself, twelve pages fleshing out a single story that we already know. One might think that would qualify it for the cutting-room floor. Hardly; it may be the twelve most important pages in the book.

Dagny gives him a ride, buys him his dinner, and in reward he tells her a story, the story of the six thousand workers at the Twentieth Century Motor Company and how they degraded and wasted their patrimony. He is on the road – there is no work for him in the East anymore; everyone is watched, no one is allowed to succeed unless it is through connections with the Unification

Board. And everywhere he does manage to find a few weeks' work, closes. And the odd catchphrase of despair and futility, *"Who is John Galt?"* that has danced through the novel?

"That's it, ma'am. That's what I'm afraid of. It might have been me who started it."

There are enough versions of this fable around already: a woman's at a cocktail party, Francisco's (at least two of them, Prometheus and Atlantis), Hugh Akston's, and now this, in the mouth of a vagrant, hardly a place to inspire confidence, and yet it's the one true story. It is the story of a great enterprise's slide into pride, sin and failure. In twelve pages we have a precise description of a Randian fall from grace. No external entity may be blamed, no force of tyranny imposed from afar. The workers voted for fairness, and what they got was slavery.

It was a simple plan, forwarded by the Starnes children, the new owners of the company. Each worked to his ability, each was compensated on the basis of his need. Twice a year, the Twentieth Century workers voted on whose need was foremost – after all, weren't they all one big family? But need is misery, and soon everyone became a beggar jealous of his needs, valuing his miseries above his fellow workers'. And need was not the only variable in the equation – ability was, as well. As production fell, the workers voted on who were the best and set their work quotas even higher.

As a consequence people watched each other like hawks, hiding their abilities, accentuating their needs. They had been told that the world of capitalism was vicious, but it was nothing like this, where people competed to do the worst job possible. People turned to drink, had children only to increase their allowance; the sick that drew too heavily on the resources of the collective disappeared, evicted or perhaps even murdered. The Plan had been put in place in the name of love and brotherhood, and now people hated one another.

The best men left, the company fell apart, and after four years the experiment ended as the company collapsed. The employees went to their fate gleefully, defiantly, and it is not accidental that the hobo casts it in quasi-religious terms.

"You know, ma'am, we are marked men, in a way, those of us who lived through the four years of that plan... What is that hell is supposed to be? Evil – plain, naked, smirking evil, isn't it? Well, that's what we saw and helped to make – and I think we're damned, every one of us, and maybe we'll never be forgiven."

"They let us vote on it, too, and everybody – almost everybody – voted for it. We didn't know. We thought it was good. No, that's not true, either. We thought that we were supposed to think it was good."

A nice turn of phrase, that. A tragic number of American citizens dispose of their vote based on that feckless premise.

"We had just voted for the new plan and we were in an edgy sort of mood, making too much noise, cheering the people's victory, threatening some kind of unknown enemies and spoiling for a fight, like bullies with an uneasy conscience... Gerald Starnes yelled through the noise. 'Remember that none of us may now leave this place, for each of us belongs to all the others by the moral law which we all accept!'

'I don't,' said one man and stood up.... 'I will put an end to this once and for all,' he said. 'I will stop the motor of the world.' Then he walked out..."

"When I hear them repeating that question, I feel afraid. I think of the man who said that he would stop the motor of the world. You see, his name was John Galt."

Twelve years. It is a length of time that has been noted frequently throughout the novel with respect to a number of seemingly unconnected events.

Dagny gives her berth to the hobo and sits alone, knowing that what she has just heard is the truth. She drifts off to sleep, and then awakens to silence. The train is *"frozen"* somewhere on the tracks of the Kansas Western, meaning it has been abandoned by its working crew in the middle of nowhere with a full complement of passengers onboard. It is all done by the book: the fires of the steam locomotive banked, the brakes set, and a warning lantern placed at the rear of the train to guard against the approach of the next one. That might, in these times of decadence, be days. In the logbook of the locomotive Dagny finds a familiar name: Pat Logan, her engineer when she risked her life at breakneck speed to prove the worth of Rearden Metal, logging out of his last Taggart ride. She'll walk for help, then – she has to get to Utah.

I'll get there in time, she thought. I'll get there first. I'll save the motor. There's one motor he's not going to stop, she thought...

Dagny has all the information the reader has, but she hasn't made the connection yet. It is not her motor after all. It is literally John Galt's.

But there are outlaws, raiders – *"deserters"* in these days when the only legitimate employment is for the looters – and the road is no longer safe. Who should turn up but her old employee, the mystery man Owen Kellogg, a fellow who does seem to turn up at the oddest moments? But this one is legitimate and Kellogg a perfectly legitimate passenger. He's off for a month's vacation at an undisclosed location, and it's the most important thing in his world.

He's the only one willing to accompany Dagny – except for one other. It's the hobo, whose name is Jeff Allen. She hires him on the spot to take charge of the abandoned train and its passengers until help arrives. Good help has, as the saying goes, become so very hard to find.

Kellogg is maddeningly evasive about what he has been doing since he left the railroad. He isn't talking, but Dagny is thinking. She wants him back desperately, but Kellogg's brain is not on the market.

She stood looking at him, her face growing harder. "You're one of them, aren't you?" she said at last.

155

Yes, he is. And he's laughing at her. Infuriating male! They walk, finally locate a working phone box, and she summons help for the gaggle of fools left on the abandoned train after a frustrating argument with the night dispatcher of the Kansas Western, a man afraid to do anything until Dagny takes responsibility for his actions. She has laid her charge to rest. Next is her mission. But along the way Kellogg absentmindedly offers her a cigarette, and it's stamped with a gold dollar sign. Dagny wants to know the source, but Kellogg won't tell her. What does the dollar sign stand for?

"For a great deal. It stands on the vest of every fat, piglike figure in every cartoon, for the purpose of denoting a crook, a grafter, a scoundrel – as the one sure-fire brand of evil. It stands – as the money of a free country – for achievement, for success, for ability, for man's creative power – and precisely for these reasons, it is used as a brand of infamy... Incidentally, do you know where that sign comes from? It stands for the initials of the United States."

Yes, actually, it does. Those who take that sort of thing for granted and place their beliefs in something their political enthusiasms tell them is a "higher truth" do so at the risk of the sort of ingratitude that will bring the entire system crashing to the ground. That is Rand's warning. That is the point of *Atlas Shrugged.*

"Do you know that the United States is the only country in history that has ever used its monogram as a symbol of depravity? Ask yourself why. Ask yourself how long a country that did that could hope to exist, and whose moral standards have destroyed it."

Well, the country didn't. Certain of its self-appointed intellectual leaders have, just as they have in the novel, under the fatuous assumption that it is the currency that is being venerated and not the ability to earn it. It is, properly, a measure of merit,

156

not merit itself. A lot of people possessing large quantities of it tend to forget that fact just as easily as an editorial cartoonist.

A short distance from the tracks, in the middle of nowhere, is a bright beacon that marks an airstrip on which sits a Dwight Sanders plane, unaccountably abandoned. The airport attendant is no smarter than the night dispatcher of the Kansas Western, so Dagny writes him a check for fifteen thousand dollars and darkly hints at a secret mission from important men in Washington. Kellogg has remained, cheerfully taking responsibility for putting proper closure to the train full of demanding customers. Dagny continues her mission, taking off in the darkness. Here Rand's descriptions are obviously by an individual who has sampled the exquisite moments of general aviation, but not as a pilot. They are evocative nevertheless. Dagny finds herself using as a checkpoint the brave flickering of Wyatt's Torch.

She arrives at Afton, Utah, minutes too late. A fellow gestures to a departing airplane, now carrying Quentin Daniels, who went with a man who had flown in for him three hours earlier. It's impossible. It's The Destroyer! They know! How? No one outside her select circle knew about Daniels, and absolutely no one knew about his letter – except for Eddie Willers. And a certain Anonymous Rail Worker.

She gives chase, of course, through the mountains, and mountains can be very dangerous flying country. Off course, low on fuel, this is the stuff of disaster. Downdrafts can easily exceed the climb capabilities of a light aircraft, and when that happens, the aircraft descends, and where the ground is as much vertical as horizontal, that can mark a very unhappy ending. Even her Sanders plane is struggling to keep up.

Just when she thinks the plane with Daniels should climb, it banks and prepares to land, but where? The landscape appears to be jagged peaks. Then the plane disappears entirely. Dagny drops and circles, trying to find the plane, but discovers that the view of the valley floor hasn't changed at all, and the light doesn't seem right. It's an image – a reflection of a nearby peak. And below her is a secret valley, a Shangri-La in the Colorado high country. Dagny is about to land there because a sudden flash of light has disabled her engine, and one thing a pilot really doesn't want to see is the propeller that's supposed to be pulling her along, suddenly stationary over the cowling.

Dagny goes in for a dead stick landing, fighting it to the ground, because that's what you do if you're a pilot *in extremis*. You trade airspeed for altitude, altitude for distance, and along the way you're hoping for that nice, green, smooth spot that in the end, Dagny espies. Before she strikes, she knows she's got it, and the last thing to go through her head is a derisive, "*Oh, hell! Who is John Galt?*"

There is a truism that one shouldn't ask questions whose answers one isn't ready to hear.

Discussion Topics

- Hobos? Raiders? There hasn't been anything like this since the Great Depression. What can one expect to witness as an economy collapses?

- How does life at the Twentieth Century Motor Company under The Plan resemble life at a modern, unionized automobile factory? How does it differ?

- The motto of the New Socialist Man in the Soviet Union was, "As long as they pretend to pay us, we will pretend to work." Connect that to the Twentieth Century Motor Company and to certain occupations today.

- Today the standard is not one of *need*, but of *victimhood*. But there are legitimate victims, and there are pretenders. Gresham's Law may apply to victims as well as to money: illegitimate victims may drive legitimate victims out of the market. Explore the ramifications of this, both in the marketplace of money and the marketplace of ideas.

Part III: A is A

Chapter I: Atlantis

Synopsis

Dagny awakens to the face of John Galt! He is surprised that Dagny braved his protective device to reach the valley. It is too painful for her to walk, so Galt picks her up and carries her. She hears the strains of Halley's Fifth Concerto, played by the composer himself, coming from his house.

On a granite column is a three-foot Sign of the Dollar made of solid gold, Francisco's gently mocking tribute. It is the logo on the cigarettes and their package, the totem of a world that is formed around moral propositions that are the opposite of those of the looters. In 1982 in the real world, there was another huge dollar sign, a floral arrangement twice that size that was laid on the grave of Ayn Rand. In what is likely an accidental irony, she and her beloved Frank O'Connor are buried in Valhalla, New York.

A car arrives, driven by Midas Mulligan, with Hugh Akston as his passenger. Akston is stunned by her arrival, having previously told her that she would never find the designer of the motor, and now finding her in his arms. Mulligan gives her a rich, profane tongue lashing for having endangered her life by crashing into the valley rather than entering by the front door. John Galt takes responsibility for Dagny; she is there, she is welcome, but because she has not reached it by virtue of intellectual and moral conviction, she is profoundly an outsider, a "scab" in terminology deliberately derived from trade union cant.

Parallels to the versions of Paradise described by various religions are quite deliberate, and were Rand not quite so deadly serious about the thing, one might almost say satirical. Dagny has a near-death experience and wakes up in a perfect world, in the arms of a perfect man, in the company only of good people, the bad ones being banished. Heaven, of course. Or Valhalla.

As they drive along, Dagny finds that Mulligan owns the valley, Galt works there, and Akston is one of Galt's two "fathers". The final piece slips into place for her. It is this John Galt who was the mysterious third student of Akston and Stadler, the second assistant bookkeeper, the designer of the motor – and The Destroyer.

At Galt's house, the famous Dr. Hendricks, who had disappeared six years before, tends to Dagny's injuries. As John cooks and serves breakfast, Dagny finds that each of the Gulch's luminaries has a second occupation in this new world: Lawrence Hammond runs a grocery store, Dwight Sanders a pig farm, and Judge Narragansett a dairy farm. John Galt is merely the handyman. Dagny realizes that Galt's motor is the power source for the valley and desires to see it in action. She is astonished that Mulligan is charging John 25 cents to rent his car; she quickly learns that the word "give" is banned in the valley.

Quentin Daniels delivers the car. He apologizes to Dagny for skipping out without notice and tells her how Galt had come to his lab, erased his work and written down one simple equation. After that, he would have happily followed John Galt to the ends of the earth. With pride, he tells her that he is now a janitor and hopes to rise to the position of electrician!

The first stop on John Galt's grand tour of the valley is Dwight Sanders, who agrees to fix her plane for a mere $200 – in gold. But she can't buy the gold, and all her cash and stock is worthless in the valley.

The second stop is Dick McNamara, the former rail contractor, who is in charge of the valley's utilities.

As they drove on along the edge of the lake, she asked, "You've mapped this route deliberately, haven't you? You're showing me all the men whom – " she stopped, feeling inexplicably reluctant to say it, and said, instead – "whom I have lost?"

"I'm showing all the men whom I have taken away from you," he answered firmly.

At the third stop, we meet for a moment a nameless, beautiful young woman who is fishing for a living. She is, tellingly, a novelist.

Dagny jerked her head to look back and saw the glance with which the young woman stood looking after Galt. And even though hopelessness, serenely accepted, was part of the worship in the glance, she experienced a feeling she had never known before: a stab of jealousy.

Jealousy in Dagny is a side of her we haven't seen before. For Lillian Rearden she felt only contempt, but then she had already taken Lillian's husband for her own at that point. Galt is not hers, at least not yet, but here we have the first indication that she'd like him to be.

The fourth stop is Ellis Wyatt's shale oil facility. One of Wyatt's two employees is the young brakeman caught by Dagny whistling the theme from Halley's Fifth Concerto; he is now Halley's best student. Wyatt is producing two hundred barrels of oil a day from shale.

Wyatt tosses off a sentence that has since become an Objectivist aphorism: *"...there's no such thing as a lousy job – only lousy men who don't care to do it."* Like many of Rand's asseverations it's true to a point, but not always. One of this book's authors knew a distinguished Japanese gentleman in the business of high-tolerance machining who had spent World War II in an old torpedo factory, and his job had been to smack test fuses with a hammer to ensure they didn't go off prematurely. That was a lousy job.

Along the way she discovers that Ted Nielsen runs the lumber yard and Roger Marsh grows vegetables. The fifth stop is at Andrew Stockton's foundry; he had to ruin a competitor, who is now his employee, to run it. Stockton says he would be happy to be ruined by Hank Rearden, who would revolutionize life in the valley. Ken Danagger turns out to be his foreman.

The sixth stop is the valley's Main Street, home to Hammond Grocery, Mulligan General Store, Nielsen Lumber, and Mulligan & Akston Tobacco. Actress Kay Ludlow, who had disappeared five years earlier, now runs a cafeteria. Down the street are Mulligan Bank and Mulligan Mint, which produces coins of gold and silver like those from America's past.

The seventh stop is the house of Francisco d'Anconia. Dagny now understands that John Galt was the man to whom Francisco had pledged his life twelve years ago.

The eighth stop is the powerhouse. On the building is the inscription, *"I swear by my life and my love of it that I will never live for the sake of another man, nor ask another man to live for mine."* As Galt pronounces the oath, the door to the powerhouse swings open, but he closes it quickly. When Dagny is ready to say those words and accept the consequences, he will show her the motor.

Mulligan invites all of Dagny's old friends to dinner at his place to honor her arrival, and he introduces her in the traditional Navy manner by the name of her command, "Taggart Transcontinental".

She laughed suddenly... "This looks like...you know, I had never hoped to see any of you again, I wondered at times how much I'd give for just one more glimpse or one more word...now this is like that dream you imagine in childhood, when you think that someday, in heaven, you will see those great departed...from all the past centuries, the great men you would like to meet..."

"And that's one clue to the nature of our secret," said Akston. "Ask yourself whether the dream of heaven and greatness should be left waiting for us in our graves – or whether it should be ours here and now on this earth."

It is a highly significant statement, the reason that Rand may rightfully claim her philosophy to be life-affirming. There are difficulties, of course. It would be wonderful to spend an afternoon drinking with the likes of Franklin, Washington, Montaigne, Alcibiades, Edmund Burke and Oda Nobunaga. That would be quite outside the confines of the here and now – that is the point of Paradise, after all, to transcend the here and now. But it is heaven on this earth that is Rand's aim, a heaven she clearly feels is within the capacities of men, a heaven denied by the profound moral error that is the credo of the parasites, the looters, the moochers, that has so twisted and warped its host society that no remedy less than the latter's dissolution will suffice. Atlas shrugging is that dissolution.

"Given up?" said Hugh Akston. "Check your premises, Miss Taggart. None of us has given up. It is the world that has... All work is an act of philosophy. And when men will learn to consider productive work – and that which is its source – as the standard of their moral values, they will reach that state of perfection which is the birthright they lost."

Each gives a brief disquisition on the reasons for his going on strike, including a longer speech from John Galt.

"My refusal to be born with any original sin... That night, at the Twentieth Century meeting, when I heard an unspeakable evil being spoken in a tone of moral righteousness, I saw the root of the world's tragedy, the key to it, and the solution. I saw what had to be done. I went out to do it."

"I went out to become a flame-spotter. I made it my job to watch out for those bright flares in the growing night of savagery, which were the men of ability, the men of the mind – to watch their course...and to pull them out, when I knew that they had seen enough."

"Our sole relief were the rare occasions when we could see one another. We found that we liked to meet – in order to be reminded that human beings still existed. So we came to set aside one month a year to spend in this valley – to rest, to live in a rational world, to bring our real work out of hiding, to trade our achievements... Each of us built his own house here, at his own expense – for one month of life out of twelve. It made the other eleven easier to bear."

It explains the persistent references to one month's vacation at a mystery location. That's all it was in the beginning, when the valley was a resort in the precise meaning of the word. It is now a self-sufficient community courtesy of the industrialists who made their last stand in Colorado and now need somewhere to hide, literally, for they face imprisonment for the crime of striking – *"deserting,"* as Dr. Ferris put it, who wishes to have them shot for it.

"We started with no time limit in view," said Galt. "We did not know whether we'd live to see the liberation of the world or whether we'd have to leave our battle and our secret to the next generations... But now we think that we will see, and soon, the day of our victory and our return."

"...when men see that neither their hearts nor their muscles can save them, but the mind they damned is not there to answer their screams for help...when they have no pretense of authority left, no remnant of law, no trace of morality, no hope, no food, and no way to obtain it – when they collapse and the road is clear – then we'll come back to rebuild the world."

That's the plan, anyway. Like most utopian schemes it is far more specific on how the present is to be broken down than it is on how the future is to be built. The former is by far the easier of the two, as many a socialist revolutionary has found to his eventual dismay. But at least here we have the possibility inasmuch as these men and women already have built something in their lives. Che Guevara never did anything but destroy.

The dinner ends, and Dagny is escorted back to her host's house for the evening. The guest room is a curious one – it is the purgatory where each of the strikers spent his first night after severing ties with the outside world. It is a place of sleepless pain, of renunciation, with graffiti on the walls to prove it.

And here she is, with her perfect man, and she can't have him.

Hank who? Francisco who? Here, in the person of the nameless fisherwoman, we see their fate and the upshot of Rand's flawed conception of human sexuality: it is *"hopelessness, serenely accepted."* In no other aspect of human life would Rand permit this sort of inert fatalism.

Thus the two of them do *not* wind up in Galt's bed after all, although she contemplates his door as he contemplates her body. Sexual self-denial, in Rand? Yes, of course. Sex is the consummation of intellectual convergence, and Dagny is still not ready. It isn't a case of a monastic renunciation of the world and the flesh, it turns out to be a choice between the one or the other. St. Augustine would have laughed to tears: Dagny's desire is for the very opposite of chastity, but like St. Augustine's, her qualification is, "but not yet."

Rand's Schoolgirl Crush on John Galt

John Galt turns out to have some remarkably Christ-like characteristics, being after all the man *"without pain or fear or guilt,"* stepping completely formed from the unknown as Akston – Galt's "father", who did not conceive him – describes it later. It is as near as Rand could get to virgin birth without being named in a plagiarism lawsuit by St. Matthew.

Nor are we spared a description of his physical perfection that might have been culled from a Danielle Steele novel:

The light cloth of his shirt seemed to stress, rather than hide, the structure of his figure, his skin was suntanned, his body had the hardness, the gaunt, tensile strength, the clean precision of a foundry casting, he looked as if he were poured out of metal, but some dimmed, soft-lustered metal, like an aluminum-copper alloy, the color of his skin blending with the chestnut-brown of his hair, the loose strands of the hair shading from brown to gold in the sun, and his eyes completing the colors, as the one part of the casting left undimmed and harshly lustrous; his eyes were the deep, dark green of light glinting on metal.

That is a single sentence. When finally we get to dialogue, it's actually quite good, every sentence holding a double meaning, an allusion to what came before. Through the chapter, we discover that as long as we can keep from drowning in Rand's schoolgirl gushing over him, Galt is rather a likable fellow after all. That turns out to be a bit of a challenge.

Aware with abnormal intensity of the pressure of his hands against her body, of the gold and copper threads of his hair, the shadows of his lashes on the skin of his face a few inches away from hers...

We're not quite two pages into the chapter. Hank has become a distant memory. One touch of Randian weirdness:

...but she had always known that an emotion was a sum totaled by an adding machine of the mind...

No, it isn't, although that grotesque metaphor does explain a good deal about Dagny's love life. Of the hundreds of metaphors for emotion resident in human literature this, it is safe to state, is the very first likening it to an adding machine. It may be unique. It ought to be.

The sole suggestion of luxury was the color of his hair – the strands stirring in the wind like liquid gold and copper...

We get the point. John Galt must be an angel – or an android.

Rand and Science Fiction Technology

The valley itself is protected by the illusion of a nearby mountaintop projected overhead that was, as Galt puts it:

"...calculated against everything – except a courage such as yours... you hit the ray screen. Some of the rays are the kind that kill magnetic motors..."

It is, incidentally, one of the few dated moments in this 50 year old novel, this "ray screen" that kills "magnetic motors." There are components of certain modern aircraft engines that are magnetic in nature – "magnetos" – that produce the necessary current to induce fuel ignition. The precise nature of a "ray" that might affect this process is best left to fiction.

Later there will be similarly dated allusions to technologies that a contemporary perspective may make us a little too ready to mock, as well as to ones we cannot mock because they have become reality. For example, the idea of extracting oil from shale was barely a glimmer in an oil man's eye in the Fifties; not until the Seventies did the price of oil rise to the point where recovery from oil shale might be profitable. By the turn of the next century it was common practice. Here Rand was ahead of her time.

America's Mixed Relationship with Gold

The medium of exchange in Galt's Gulch was gold, a pure metallic element shaped into coins in the Mulligan Mint. At the time of the writing of *Atlas Shrugged* the employment of a gold coinage was not the distant memory it seems to contemporary readers. It has, in fact, a long and fascinating history.

After of the Treaty of Paris in 1783, tensions with Britain eased, and the country got around to governing itself under the Articles of Confederation. But the war debt caused major problems, not the least of which was a deflationary depression. A few states took their debts seriously, but others engaged in partial or total repudiation. At the same time, the Continental Dollar, supposedly backed by one Spanish Milled Dollar each, was collapsing in value because there was no real backing except for a nebulous promise to pay. Enlisted men in the Continental Army had been paid in paper dollars, and they expected those dollars to be honored at full value.

There were only three banks in the entire country. These banks didn't care about the farmer, the shopkeeper, or the wage slave, but only the owner of the textile mill in Lawrence, Massachusetts, the import-export business in Manhattan, or the iron foundry in Batsto, New Jersey. It was for these that the banks operated, while ordinary Americans held their wealth in their mattresses and under their floorboards. Without a genuine coin of the realm, people relied on coins of gold and silver minted in Spain, England and France, along with base metal coins minted by the states. Coins of precious metal were often "clipped", so merchants weighed them to see just how much gold and silver were really present.

While farmers and shopkeepers could survive without a coin of the realm, the owners of the banks and large businesses could not. How could a capitalist perform the Italian art of constructing a balance sheet or an income and expense statement if there is no standard by which to measure value?

The states that wanted to treat their war debts honorably had a problem. The basic unit of governance in America was the county. The county collected the property tax, and a voter had to show his tax receipt at election time to the county clerk in order to vote. It was the county that built the roads and maintained the poorhouse for indigents. States collected taxes for their own purposes, but repaying war debts would require a major hike in taxes, the very thing over which a war had just been fought.

There is an old saying in the world of taxation: "Don't tax him, don't tax me, tax the guy behind the tree." The states that wanted to retire their war debts found a way of taxing the guy behind the tree – they taxed the residents of other states. After all, residents of other states could not vote in state elections, so the states charged tariffs on goods crossing state lines. The Connecticut farmer who loaded his wagon and took his produce to New York to sell now found himself confronted at the state line by a New York customs agent who slapped taxes on his produce. Quickly other states took up the idea, and a full scale trade war erupted.

The issue of the legality of the Continental Dollar came to a head when Massachusetts refused to accept it in payment of taxes in spite of the words "legal tender". And that led to Shays' Rebellion, which led to the Constitutional Convention.

In 1790, Alexander Hamilton, now Secretary of the Treasury under Washington, pushed for *assumption*, the act of taking the debts of the states and nationalizing them. What Hamilton wanted was financial ballast. A ship without ballast is unstable and tends to capsize in rough waters. Hamilton believed that a properly managed national debt would act as ballast and be a blessing. In this, Hamilton copied Sir Robert Walpole who established the Bank of England's fiat currency in 1694. The key was "properly managed". Hamilton saw a national debt as a way of encouraging a basic conservatism in American finance. By rolling the state debts into a national debt, Hamilton effectively monetized all that Continental paper. On a weekly basis, Hamilton's clerk at Treasury went down to the New York Stock Exchange and either bought or sold Treasury bills, thus managing the money supply in a manner similar to the Federal Reserve today. Was the new American financial paper backed by gold or silver? Not at first: America's initial bonds and banknotes started out as a fiat currency.

This was a point made by Ragnar Danneskjøld in his evening conversation with Hank Rearden on a back road outside Philadelphia. It was also a significant point made by Francisco d'Anconia in his Root of Money Speech. Rand knew her American financial history.

It was Hamilton's intent for the US Mint in Philadelphia to fix the gold and silver problem. Congress established gold and silver coins of different denominations, and people who owned foreign coins or bars of gold and silver could take them to the Mint, which would smelt them to the correct purity and mint coins of the realm, which would in turn be handed back to the owner to be placed in circulation.

Hamilton's consolidated war debt was paid off by James Monroe's first term, and the new debt accrued during the War of 1812 came close to being paid off by the end of Andrew Jackson's first term. That led to a problem. Under Nicholas Biddle, the Bank of the United States had put aside its function of neutral arbiter of capital allocation and had played favorites. Biddle saw this as a prudent form of industrial planning.

When Jackson ran for reelection in 1832, his campaign slogan was "Jackson and No Bank". Jackson referred to the Bank as "The Monster" and made its abolition the cornerstone of his second term. Biddle inadvertently helped Jackson when he fought the president in Congress by allocating capital to congressmen who were the Bank's friends and punishing its enemies via foreclosure. It was a fatal mistake. With the end of the Bank, the national debt was gone – and so was the financial ballast. And the sharp practitioners of Wall Street were ready for a world under a gold exchange standard.

169

In the world of finance, there is Smart Money, Stupid Money, and Widows' and Orphans' Money.

- Smart Money can read a balance sheet and income and expense statement and park its money in an asset class as it first begins to appreciate. Smart Money's participation defines Phase 1 of a bull market, known as the "stealth" phase. Smart Money comes early to the party and knows enough to leave early, rarely getting caught when the inevitable bubble bursts.

- Stupid Money follows the Smart Money but always late, thus defining Phase 2 of a bull market, known as the "mainstream" phase. Stupid Money is late to the party and late leaving which is why it gets lost.

- Widows' and Orphans' Money is more interested in capital preservation than income, so it functions best when invested in good, safe government bonds, America's financial ballast. When the Widows and Orphans abandon their safe investments and jump in, establishing Phase 3 of a bull market, the "mania" phase, the price of the asset goes parabolic, and no asset can survive that. Then comes the crash, and the Widows and Orphans take the worst losses of all.

With the end of good, safe government bonds, an asset bubble formed on Wall Street in stocks. The Smart Money had already staked a claim, and the Stupid Money followed; next came the Widows and Orphans. It should be noted that the primary business of Wall Street is to fleece investors by inflating and bursting bubbles, known as "pump and dump" in the trade.

The bubble in stocks created the illusion of prosperity, and Jackson never understood what he had wrought. With the luck of the Scots-Irish, Jackson left the presidency to Martin van Buren before the Panic of 1837 erupted. People lost their savings, their homes, their farms, and froze to death in the cities. The road back was slow, arduous, and interrupted by other financial calamities, such as the Panic of 1857, when a ship full of gold coins minted in San Francisco was lost at sea in a hurricane off the coast of South Carolina. That hole in the money supply launched a panic from which the Cotton South recovered more rapidly than the industrialized North. In 1860, that led to a fatal miscalculation by the southern states.

To avoid usurious interest rates from the House of Morgan, Abraham Lincoln issued a paper fiat currency known as the *greenback*, which was to finance the Civil War and then get mopped up via federal tax collections afterward. Upon being withdrawn from circulation, the disappearing fiat money triggered deflation and the Panic of 1873, which set off a long depression.

In 1913, America established the Federal Reserve, which was not exactly a national bank because it was owned by a cartel of private banks. But the country was still on the gold standard. The calamity of October 1929 and the events that followed inadvertently made the dollar stronger with respect to European currencies. To permit expansion of the money supply via inflation, Franklin Roosevelt closed the gold window for domestic payments and made the possession of gold by Americans illegal. This permitted America to fight a deflationary depression and a world war by printing massive amounts of money.

For Rand, this moment in 1933 was an abomination. Real money had not merely been withdrawn from circulation, but outlawed entirely. It was an unfortunate product of Keynes, who had prophesied that debasement of the currency was the first step on the path to the destruction of capitalism. From Rand's perspective, no government that engaged in such looting of wealth could be considered legitimate.

The Bretton Woods Agreement of 1944 made the US Dollar the world's reserve currency linked to gold at the 1934 price. This functioned well until Lyndon Johnson's disastrous "guns and butter" decision of 1965, which led to the London Gold Pool as an attempt to support the dollar by suppressing the gold price. Charles de Gaulle put an end to that by demanding payment in gold for France, which prompted Richard Nixon to close the gold window to foreign payments, which in turn set off the double-digit inflation of the Seventies. In 1975 Americans again were permitted to possess gold as a result. Fed Chairman Paul Volcker pushed interest rates above 20%, thus ending the inflation of consumer prices, but the liquidity spigot was never turned off, which led to the inflation of asset prices in the 1982-2007 bull market in stocks and real estate.

Fiat currencies can be very messy and full of unintended consequences. But so can gold.

Discussion Topics

- The word "give" is banned in Galt's Gulch. How does an Objectivist society demand the redefinition of the concept of charity?

- We've seen Rand's ideal Objectivist society operating in Galt's Gulch. How well would it work in the real world?

- Dr. Hendricks, one of America's best surgeons, left the profession because the government nationalized the health care system. What is the cautionary tale here?

Chapter II: The Utopia of Greed

Synopsis

Dagny is a prisoner in Galt's Gulch courtesy of her uninvited arrival, which the reader finds is rather against the founding premise of the community. Galt acknowledges that. He has made up the rule on the spot and admits it; its enforcement is simply the threat of coercion, and if put to it, Galt would be incapable of actually chaining her to the wall, although what we know of Dagny's sexuality leads us to suspect that she might not find that altogether disagreeable. In any case Dagny isn't eager to leave the confines of this fascinating place and the company of this fascinating man. She's there for a month, that same set of dates that circumscribes the annual vacations of the founders. Galt wants her to be a guest at his expense. But that also seems to contradict the social contract, a point that Dagny realizes immediately. Her clever response takes Galt entirely by surprise.

"I propose to earn my room and board."

"By what means?"

"By working."

"In what capacity?"

"In the capacity of your cook and housemaid."

She has him very neatly. After all, if Akston can sling hash and Daniels can sweep floors, why can't she cook his breakfast and sew his buttons? She'll be staying there at least until her ankle and ribs heal, in any case. He surrenders, laughing. Room and board and ten dollars a month. In gold. He even gives her a $5 advance on her salary.

They make coins differently in Galt's Gulch, but one of the last US denominations of the sort was the Half Eagle, a truly beautiful piece of work with an eagle on one side and a woman wearing what appears to be a French Revolutionary "Phrygian cap" on the obverse. The cap has "Liberty" printed on it. Five dollars worth of gold these days would fit under Dagny's thumbnail. We have come to that.

It is an interesting domestic arrangement: prisoner, then servant, and even that is a thin veneer under which a good deal more is going on.

That special pleasure she had felt in watching him eat the food she had prepared...it had been the pleasure of knowing that she had provided him with a sensual enjoyment, that one form of his body's satisfaction had come from her...but what have they made of it, the preachers of woman's duty? The castrated performance of a sickening drudgery was held to be a woman's proper virtue – while that which gave it meaning and sanction was held as a shameful sin...the work of dealing with grease, steam, and slimy peelings in a reeking kitchen was held to be a spiritual matter, an act of compliance with her moral duty – while the meeting of two bodies in a bedroom was held to be physical indulgence...

That's actually a little harsh by Rand's own standards. Whatever happened to *"There is no such thing as a lousy job, only lousy men who don't care to do it"*? Her point is that it is irrational to consider the one a duty and the other mere animal pleasure, which is fine as far as it goes. One can, of course, consider both a duty – Lillian Rearden comes to mind here, although it is doubtful that she ever held a potato peeler in her life. Or both a pleasure, if not quite of the same sort. Both propositions are equally rational and utterly beside the point. Nor, even in the Fifties, was sex within marriage considered a mere physical indulgence, especially by anyone who had actually tried it. Because we actually are talking about marriage here. Somewhat later Dagny has to admit it to herself.

His wife – she thought, letting herself hear consciously the word Dr. Akston had not pronounced, the word she had long since felt, but never named – for three weeks she had been his wife in every sense but one, and that final one was still to be earned...

174

Earned, how? What must she yet achieve in order to be worthy? We shall see.

The first visitor that pops in, a slender, golden-haired male of ethereal beauty, is none other than the ferocious pirate Ragnar Danneskjøld, who is as threatening as a schoolboy and far more interesting. We saw him once in a brief meeting with Hank Rearden, but now we get to see him at home, in the valley that is the refuge and the abode of his wife, another self-exile, the actress Kay Ludlow. His month's vacation is a month with his beloved, and we begrudge them even the few minutes it took for breakfast at Galt's, a custom of some twelve years' tenure. The third at that traditional breakfast, Francisco d'Anconia, is nowhere in sight for the first time in all those years, and no one really knows why until the next arrival, Owen Kellogg, breaks the news that Dagny's disappearance has caused a sensation and that the mountains of Colorado are being combed for her, or her remains. We know before we're told where Francisco is, and it comes as no surprise when we learn later that Hank is searching for her as well.

No communication with the outside is permitted, of course, although Galt will allow her at least to ask for an exception. It's a test; practically everything that Dagny encounters for the next few weeks is a test, and if she strangled the lot of them for their presumption in that regard no rational reader would vote to convict. Nevertheless, Francisco does show up and declares his love for her, suspecting but not knowing that his love is fated to be unrequited, suspecting her preference to be Rearden and not knowing that it is now, inevitably, Galt. It is a love declared, a love undying, and we admire Francisco for his loyalty if not altogether for his common sense.

Galt drops a statement that indicates he is fully aware of what is going on: that of all of them, Francisco has given up more than any, meaning, we are to presume, not only his fortune and his reputation, but his love as well. And yet here he is, his love intact for the woman he declares he has deserted. It is she, in fact, who has deserted him.

"Francisco, I've hurt you in so many different ways – "

175

"No! No, you haven't hurt me – and he [Rearden] hasn't either, don't say anything about it, it's he who's hurt, but we'll save him and he'll come here, too, where he belongs… Dagny, I didn't expect you to wait…if it had to be anyone, I'm glad it's he."

She closed her eyes, pressing her lips together not to moan.

"Darling, don't! Don't you see that I've accepted it?"

But it isn't – she thought – it isn't he, and I can't tell you the truth because it's a man who might never hear it from me and whom I might never have…

It is Galt, of course, and Galt knows it. Yet Galt will not have her, for as a "scab," an apostate, she and he have not yet reached that intellectual convergence that is Rand's *sine qua non* for a lubricious roll in the hay. She is unworthy. We are exasperated.

It is, after all, a rather exacting and impossible standard that Rand has set for her mating of thoroughbreds. This business of "only the ultimate may be chosen" is not one she followed in her own personal life; apparently the rules applying to Rearden, Francisco, Galt and Dagny did not apply to Ayn Rand, Frank O'Connor, and Barbara and Nathaniel Branden. Nor did they apply to Branden when later he threw both Rand and Barbara over for a young actress and was tossed from Rand's circle as a consequence.

The romance in the novel is nearly as painful for the principals as it is for the reader. Galt won't make a move until he is certain that his best friend Francisco has had every chance, but both he and Dagny acknowledge that were she to favor Francisco as a consequence of that chance, they would be living a lie. Rearden hovers over that calculus like an orphaned cherub.

We are on much firmer ground, which the reader is tempted to kiss, when we leave the romantic entanglements for the chapter's exposition. Each of a succession of persons whom Dagny meets explains to her the reasons why he or she chose the refuge of Galt's Gulch. First is the composer Richard Halley:

"There's only one passion in most artists more violent than their desire for admiration: their fear of identifying the nature of such admiration as they do receive."

That's actually pretty good, but it's safe to say that many of our own artists are not quite so discriminating in taste as he: fame is its own intoxicant, after all. But Halley is refreshingly old school about art – it is as much a pursuit of truth as any philosopher's.

"The sacred fire which is said to burn within musicians and poets... An intransigent devotion to the pursuit of truth, Miss Taggart? Have you heard the moralists and the art lovers of the centuries talk about the artist's intransigent devotion to the pursuit of truth?"

Not lately, to be honest. Where art consists of lumps of excrement thrown upon a canvas, one suspects that the truth thereby illuminated is of the same nature as the medium. The debasement of art in our age is that it no longer seeks truth, but celebrity. Those artists still in it for the truth had better have another gig for the rent or they'll starve; they've always starved, and yet their art, and the truth it describes, remains inviolate. Halley knows this, and he knows as well that the same pursuit of truth drives scientist and – yes – businessman.

"Name me a greater example of such devotion than the act of a man who says that the earth does turn...who says that an alloy of steel and copper has certain properties which enable it to do certain things, that it IS and DOES – and let the world rack him or ruin him, he will not bear false witness to the evidence of his mind!"

Here is a composer who writes with mathematical precision, a firm grasp of tonal relationships, statement, recursion, and within that rule set a desperate and successful drive to express the lyrical, and he is doomed to disappointment when his listener feels he has grasped the whole thing merely by feeling. That's not what Halley wants. That's the reason he has fled to the valley.

The actress Kay Ludlow gives her testimony, a somewhat peculiar one, truth be told. She is tired of acting in films where her beauty – and her acting ability, this much is left unsaid – make her out to be the eternal villain, forever losing out to the mediocrity of the girl next door. One might understand that frustration if one could recall a single movie of that type, but this is fiction, after all. Ludlow then walks off with her Ragnar, two paragons of physical beauty and moral clarity. One wonders what their children will be like.

A young woman with children, two little boys, is next to explain herself.

"They represent my particular career, Miss Taggart...you know, of course, that there can be no collective commitments in this valley and that families or relatives are not allowed to come here, unless each person takes the striker's oath by his own independent conviction... I came here to bring up my sons as human beings..."

Galt's Gulch is a perfectly formed community in the sense that the inhabitants are actually able to assent to or reject the social contract personally. For their children, as Edmund Burke pointed out, there are difficulties. The boys, of course, have taken no such oath, nor are they yet capable of comprehending it. Rand does not explain at what point they will have to, but it is a seminal matter in the formation of this new society, this utopia, because once it attempts to reform the ruins of the outside world there will need to be continuity if it isn't to be only one generation long. Certain details of how the phoenix will be made to rise from the ashes have been left unattended in the dramatic narrative, and this is one of them. Rand seems to feel that children raised under a strict regimen of rationality will be incapable of behaving otherwise. It is a notion not borne out by the actual history of any utopian revolution.

We now attend a dinner party thrown by Dr. Akston to which only the elite of the elite are invited – Galt, of course, Francisco, Ragnar and his wife, and Dagny. She is now explicitly one of the group and yet has not joined them, a daughter in the sense that the three men are Akston's sons. It is not clear that her own personal achievements, however prodigious, are the entire explanation. There is obviously a paternal relationship between Akston and his former students. In one charming moment he barks at Ragnar for the "danger" he subjects himself to by sitting on the bare ground; this is a fellow who dodges the world's navies on a daily basis. It is a rather sweet touch, one indication that despite her Spartan devotion to her moral argument and her attempt to paint a novel onto a billboard with a giant brush, Rand is striving to draw her main characters as people.

Dagny and John explore Francisco's copper mine in the hills above the valley. Quickly becoming the consummate railroad professional, she suggests that Francisco stop using mule power and build a railroad to get his copper out. She asks for a pencil and paper and draws what she has in mind: a short narrow-gauge line with a tunnel and some trestles. But she stops in midstream as she realizes that she can't give up her transcontinental railroad for this. Galt has warned her that her commitment must be total; if she stays, she will have to hear about every wreck and disaster on her railroad as it dies. One cannot, in his words, *"fake reality."*

The outside world intrudes once again the next day in the form of Hank Rearden's plane nearly touching down in the valley but departing. It is a metaphor for his life and a reminder to Dagny that the outside world will not be easy to discard. And yet it is Francisco who wishes to communicate with Rearden that she is alive. They deride it as *"pity"*, but it is in fact compassion, not necessarily an indicator of a lack of intellectual discipline, but a check against proceeding according to the dictates of a reason that is based on faulty premises. When one deifies Reason, one had better be sure that his idol doesn't have feet of clay.

And so we have reached Dagny's crisis of conscience. Will she renounce the decaying world and stay in the valley? She has two days to decide. To return will be to become their acknowledged enemy, for her abilities are what stand between the strikers and their victory. It is clear that Rand understands just how very difficult that will be, for opposed to the undeniable moral rectitude of the strikers is Dagny's veneration for the achievements of her predecessors and the price they paid to achieve them. She is caught between two betrayals, and our hearts go out to her. Galt, for his part, has not committed to staying either, but if they catch him and find out who he is and what he means, his death is a certainty. It is Midas Mulligan who tries to make them aware of the danger.

"You know the cities will be hit worst of all. The cities were made by the railroads and will go with them."

"That's right."

"When the rails are cut, the city of New York will starve in two days. That's all the supply of food they've got...they'll go through the whole of the agony – through the shrinking, the shortages, the hunger riots, the stampeding violence in the midst of the growing stillness."

"They will."

"They'll lose their airplanes first, then their automobiles, then their trucks, then their horsecarts...their factories will stop, then their furnaces and their radios. Then their electric system will go... There's only a worn thread holding that continent together. There will be one train a day, then one train a week – then the Taggart Bridge will collapse and – "

"No, it won't!"

It was her voice and they whirled to her. Her face was white... Slowly, Galt rose to his feet and inclined his head, as in acceptance of a verdict. "You've made your decision," he said.

Yes, she has. It is for all the achievers who have gone before her that she'll fight, not necessarily all the people who will suffer if she doesn't. It was the railroad tunnel, after all, and not the people who perished in it for which Dagny returned to the world after her last abortive exile. Dagny honors the achievement – the Taggart

Bridge – and ignores the purpose that it now serves. There are many literary valleys in *Atlas Shrugged*, and here we have one of the peaks. Rand has led us carefully to this moment, and it is critical in the novel. The strikers aren't simply walking away from their tools, they are giving up that which is most precious to them except for their own souls. It is a wrenching, agonizing commitment. Francisco has made it, and we see what it has cost him. What will it cost Dagny if in the end she does summon the courage to make it?

Galt leaves her with a souvenir, the balance of her month's wages, a single five-dollar gold piece. And she knows that it is she whom he will be following, and why.

"Don't look for me out there," he said. "You will not find me – until you want me for what I am. And when you'll want me, I'll be the easiest man to find."

She watched [his plane] like a star in the process of extinction, while it shrank from cross to dot to a burning spark which she was no longer certain of seeing. When she saw that the spread of the sky was strewn with such sparks all over, she knew that the plane was gone.

The road to Atlantis is paved with human bones, and they hurt the feet when they're trodden upon. Perhaps Dagny will walk it despite that. Perhaps not.

Greed

The title of the chapter is Rand's derisive reference to the erroneous premise that profit is greed. It is an easy enough accusation to make – as she pointed out in the previous chapter, the Sign of the Dollar is plastered on the ample waistcoats of sundry cartoon businessmen in order to connote an insatiable desire for more, a characterization that, repeated often enough, need not prove its case. Let us take a moment to examine it.

What is greed, after all, but the desire for more of something than one needs? Naturally the question "needs as measured by whom?" arises immediately, generally being answered by "needs as defined by an onlooker with tender feelings and lofty moral pretensions, unlike that greedy fellow over there," a moral proposition perfect only in its circularity. One would hear that a lot at one of Lillian Rearden's cocktail parties. "Needs for what?" is another question that comes to mind. One of these "whats" might be the accumulation of surplus, profit, for the funding of other economic enterprises. Such surplus is termed "capital", and the system under which one successful economic enterprise is used for the springboard to another is called Capitalism. The objection socialists have to that system is the faulty premise that the accumulation of such surplus is morally reprehensible, "greed." It's one reason there are so few successful new businesses under socialism. Legal ones, anyway.

Rand shows us that whole line of reasoning won't do, because in fact what has happened with that formulation of the term "greed" is to accept need as the arbiter of value. Rand regards this as a fundamental error and through Jeff Allen's grim tale, told us why, and it took us precisely one sentence, one false premise, to fall into it.

And it is a fundamental error. It is startlingly evident in the case of the possession of firearms in the United States, wherein the prohibitionist demand, "Why do you need a firearm?" forces a faulty premise, that the determinative factor in the sanctity of one's personal possessions is some else's perception of need. Why do you need a raise? Why a large, comfortable, and presumably wasteful automobile? Why do you need anything at all when others have needs that may be judged more pressing? This is central to Rand's philosophy – this criterion requires one to live for someone else and empowers the judge of need with the power of life and death. It is a power that may only be sanctioned by the victim, in the beginning. In the end it is claimed by pure, brute force.

A utopia, though, is this place where Dagny finds herself, this place we will come to refer to, as do all its inhabitants save one, as Galt's Gulch. It is a place of the mind, constructed around a moral premise that is a social contract: Galt's Oath. Now we understand this oath a little better: *"I swear by my life and my love of it that I will never live for the sake of another man, nor ask another man to live for mine."*

Richard Halley and Contemporary Composers

Rand's composer Halley is a man of Spartan devotion to his craft, a man whom we could readily see starving, as he nearly did, for the sake of that perfect expression of truth in music. Celebrity, for Halley, became ashes in his hands when at last he achieved it. He disappeared shortly thereafter.

By contrast we cite the real-world case of Richard Wagner. Wagner spent much of his time soliciting funds from wealthy Germans to subsidize him while he wrote great German "music dramas", and he was not shy about describing his operas that way. Once someone gave Wagner money, he treated the donor shabbily, and the more the donor gave, the more contemptuous Wagner was. He had an attitude of absolute entitlement.

In *My Favorite Intermissions*, Victor Borge had a wonderfully droll, but absolutely accurate, view of Wagner.

"'I cannot live like a dog,' he wrote to Franz Liszt, 'I must be soothed and flattered in my soul if I am to succeed at this horribly difficult task of creating a new world out of nothing.' Well, I don't know about his soul, but Wagner did all right for his body. He imported lilac curtains and satin quilts and silk ribbons. He ordered huge quantities of exotic powders and delicate cold creams and perfumed bath salts. He installed soft lights and hung brocaded tapestries and put up Chinese incense burners and kept his music scores in red velvet folders. He filled his house with golden cherubim and ivory figurines and hand-decorated porcelains. After that, composing was a snap."

In justice we must acknowledge that Wagner delivered on his promises. He not only reformed German opera, gone dissolute after Mozart and Beethoven, but completely reformed the art of opera *in toto*, influencing Verdi among his contemporaries, and those who came after.

Clearly Halley was no Wagner. Some have suggested that the model for Halley was the Finnish composer Jean Sibelius. But Halley's profanity-laced lecture points more to the brilliant and irascible American composer Charles Ives, who had finally reached acclaim before his death in 1954 at age 79.

During the Thirties, Ives attended a concert of modern classical music in New York when he sat in front of a man who complained during the intermission that the music didn't have any melodies he could hum. In this we hear an echo of Rand's character Mort Liddy, who so corrupted Halley's Fourth Concerto. Ives turned around and hissed, "You goddamn sissy!" That, we find easy to believe, is the voice of Richard Halley.

Discussion Topic

- Mulligan traces the coming collapse of New York, which will no doubt parallel the collapse of Starnesville but on a much grander scale. He also anticipates that the collapse of New York will take down the looters' regime in America; even Dagny sees this. What will this collapse be like for the average citizen? What will he or she witness?

Chapter III: Anti-Greed

Synopsis

As Dr. Robert Stadler sits in a grandstand in Iowa on a hot day, he complains to Dr. Floyd Ferris about being dragged halfway across the continent – for what? Ferris treats him with slight deference barely concealing contempt. He knows this day will usher in a new era, and the business of today is government.

Stadler examines with some trepidation a building that looks like a giant mushroom, a ruined farm with a herd of goats, and a steel trestle that goes nowhere. The mushroom-shaped building is the laboratory for Project Xylophone. This project, so named because it is about the use of sound, is a weapon of mass destruction. If once again we cringe a little at Rand's invocation of "sound rays," at least something of the sort is imaginable even if certain laws of physics have to be suspended in order for it to have the effects described.

A two mile area has been cleared for the test, but Xylophone in its present incarnation can handle a distance of one hundred miles. As the weapon is activated, the goats go into convulsions and die, the farmhouse collapses and the trestle disintegrates. Dr. Stadler discovers to his horror that this invention is based on theoretical work he had done years ago while accepting the looters' coin at the Institute. What is its purpose?

"It is an invaluable instrument of public security. No enemy would attack the possessor of such a weapon...it will promote peace, stability, and...harmony. It will eliminate all danger of war."

"What war? With the whole world starving and all those People's States barely subsisting on handouts from this country – where do you see any danger of war? Do you expect those ragged savages to attack you?"

We chuckle a little at Stadler's naivete.

Dr. Ferris looked straight into his eyes. "Internal enemies can be as great a danger to the people as external ones," he answered. "Perhaps greater."

He goes on to describe Project X, without a hint of irony, as a purely virtuous mass-murdering device.   It was, after all, produced without the idea of making a penny of profit.   We chuckle at his own misguided morals, but not at the result – what it is demonstrated here is the malevolent power of the collective when it expropriates and concentrates the surplus given it by the productive individuals within it.   It is not the morality of its production, but the morality of its use, that properly describes such devices.

Ferris hands Stadler his speech, and the old scientist is both horrified and paralyzed.   It took a good deal of convincing the powers that be to get them to invest in such a thing, and Dr. Stadler's reputation was the clincher.   And he will grant its use, or else.

Ferris spoke again… "It would be unfortunate if anything were to happen to jeopardize the State Science Institute…or if any one of us were to be forced to leave it.   Where would we go?   Are you thinking, perhaps of universities?   They are in the same position. If anyone wished to oppose a government policy, how would he make himself heard?   Through these gentlemen of the press, Dr. Stadler?   Is there an independent newspaper left in the country? An uncontrolled radio station?"

Fortunately this is only fiction.   The bulwark of freedom in the United States, we are frequently informed, is a fearless press that is not beholden to the government, respects truth above all, and does not attempt to become a tool of party for the manipulation of public opinion.   Unfortunately, that is fiction as well.

There is a dissenting voice, of course – Rand places it into a young newsman's mouth:

"Dr. Stadler!   Tell them you had nothing to do with it!   Tell them what sort of infernal machine it is and for what purpose it's

186

intended to be used! Tell the country what sort of people are trying to rule it! Tell them the truth! Save us! You're the only one who can!"

Dr. Ferris whirled upon the young man and snapped, his face out of control, distorted by rage... "Give me your press card and your work permit!"

So much for a press that has sold its soul for the trappings of power. It has earned the yoke it bears. But what does Ferris mean? The Unification Board controls the ability of an individual to find employment. Rand saw this in Russia before she fled, her own father having had his business establishments twice expropriated by the State. What is "unified" in this sense is very real: work, the ability to find it, and the power to withhold it. The young man has just been sentenced to slow starvation. As the State progresses, there will be ration cards and the starvation even quicker.

That lifeless lump of fur that once was a goat could have been Stadler, and it *will* be unless he obeys his masters. His worth to them now is his name, not his mind. His thirst, like that of the composer Halley, is for the praise of those capable of appreciating his achievements. He has lost his soul but praise he has. Not, alas, on that basis; the praise is hollow, and he is now a hollow man.

Dagny arrives in Manhattan by way of the airport bus. She had been dropped off near Watsonville, Nebraska, and had taken a train and plane back to New York. Reading the newspaper, she had seen her brother's statement that she had died in a plane crash, not deserted. She had identified herself to a reporter at the airport to report that she was still alive.

At her apartment she tries to reach Hank at the mill but reaches his secretary Gwen Ives instead. Dagny calls Hank at his hotel in Colorado. He is relieved that Dagny is alive, and she is necessarily somewhat evasive in telling Hank what happened. Hank will fly back and see her in the evening. Dagny goes to work.

There she is greeted by Eddie Willers, who has managed somehow to hold Taggart Transcontinental together for the last two months, and her brother James, who explains to her that all the railroads in the country are now to be consolidated under a Railroad Unification Plan. Cuffy Meigs, an armed paramilitary representative from the Unification Board, is running the operations side of Taggart Transcontinental; Clem Weatherby is apparently out of the managerial loop. Eddie explains that Meigs is rerouting motive power so that the Smather brothers in Arizona can get their grapefruit hauled; they had pull in Washington. There is a pretense that trains are given their priorities for reasons of public welfare, but everybody knows that Meigs, the *"Unificator"*, makes his decisions based on pull.

Jim sits down with Meigs, Dagny and Eddie in her office. Jim explains the Railroad Unification Plan: all railroads have pooled their resources with their gross revenue managed by the Railroad Pool Board in Washington. Revenue is parceled out by the board according to need, by the mileage of track owned. Taggart Transcontinental is now using the tracks of the Atlantic Southern for transcontinental traffic. It's perfectly all right. Taggart, being the largest, has the right to anyone else's track and the lion's share of the proceeds – not profits, of course, that would be greed.

[Dagny] "We run our trains without charge for the use of the [Atlantic Southern] track? Has anybody calculated how long the Atlantic Southern is expected to be able to remain in business?"

"That's no skin off your – " started [Cuffy] Meigs.

"The president of the Atlantic Southern," said Eddie impassively, "has committed suicide."

As well he might, given that all railroads are now relieved of the necessity of competition by the simple virtue of being owned by the same entity. Not The People, not even The State, except in the persons of that ruling class that has assumed power over them both. And those persons have their own agenda. As always, the "good of the people" turns out to be the good of a very small and influential subset. The rest need merely be placated by soothing and inspiring propaganda campaigns, such as the one to which Dr. Stadler found his name attached, to his horror.

Jim begs for understanding from Dagny, and she realizes there is nothing to be gained from using reason with Jim and Meigs. Meigs gets up and leaves, ordering Dagny to do something about *"all those train wrecks."*

Jim tells Dagny that she is booked on Bertram Scudder's radio show that evening for a morale-building speech; this has been mandated by Thompson and Mouch. She recognizes the telltale sign of the sanction of the victim, and she refuses to cooperate, ordering Jim out of her office.

Lillian Rearden drops in on Dagny to tell her that she *will* appear on Scudder's show. Lillian explains to Dagny why Hank signed the Gift Certificate, and that it was *she* who informed the authorities and took Rearden Metal away from Hank. Although Dagny must have guessed, this is confirmation for the first time that Hank had given over his life's achievement in order to shield her from public opprobrium. Dagny agrees to appear on the show.

On the Bertram Scudder Show, Dagny tells the nation that she has been Hank Rearden's mistress for the past two years and is proud of it. As Jim, Lillian and Scudder sit paralyzed, Dagny explains that it was blackmail concerning this relationship that caused Hank to sign over Rearden Metal, blackmail emanating from the national government. Scudder terminates the broadcast as Dagny laughs; the air goes dead.

Hank hears the broadcast and with remarkable perception realizes that she is referring to their affair in the past tense. She has found a new love. Just as noble as Francisco was under identical circumstances, he is actually happy for her. Rand's male heroes are apparently incapable of the jealousy that Dagny herself has felt and are capable of a sacrifice of their own feelings that seems entirely contrary to Rand's philosophy. This, one is tempted to conclude, may be the sort of contradiction that should impel Rand to check her own premises concerning human relationships.

Dagny can tell Hank nothing of Atlantis, of Galt's Gulch. He can't help himself from pressing her, but she dodges all but one of his questions.

"Who is he?"

Her chuckle of desperate amusement was involuntary. "Who is John Galt?"

"So there is a John Galt?" he asked slowly.

"Oh yes! There's one thing I can tell you about him, because I discovered it earlier, without promise of secrecy: he is the man who invented the motor we found."

"Oh!" He smiled, as if he should have known it. Then he said softly, with a glance that was almost compassion, "He's the destroyer, isn't he?" He saw her look of shock, and added, "No, don't answer me, if you can't. I think I know where you were...Good God, Dagny! – does such a place really exist? Are they all alive? Is there...? I'm sorry. Don't answer."

She smiled. "It does exist."

He remained silent for a long time.

"Hank, could you give up Rearden Steel?"

"No!" The answer was fiercely immediate, but he added, with the first sound of hopelessness in his voice, "Not yet."

Nor Dagny her beloved Taggart Transcontinental. Not yet.

The American Experiment with Railroad Nationalization

Rand did not originate the idea of the nationalization of railroads. The US entry into World War I in 1917 found America's railroads unable to keep up with the war effort. This was primarily due to over-regulation by the Interstate Commerce Commission, whose refusal to grant rate hikes deprived railroads of necessary capital. Another problem was over-expansion, which had pushed a number of railroads into bankruptcy on the eve of the war. Added to this toxic brew was labor strife, which was averted only when Woodrow Wilson forced an eight-hour day on the railroads, thus adding to labor costs.

The railroads did their best to coordinate during the war, but competition still reigned. The government began asking for priority shipping, with each government agency chivvying the other out of freight capacity on the rails. The result was congestion everywhere; some heavily used rail lines saw freight trains stacked up one behind another for weeks.

In late 1917 the ICC recommended that Congress nationalize the operations of the railroads, so Congress created the United States Railroad Administration in early 1918. Competition was curtailed by fiat. Standardized locomotives were ordered as designed by a government committee and paid for by the government.

The USRA was moderately successful, and a number of high-end infrastructure improvements came out of the exercise, all paid for by government. This influx of taxpayer money, and equipment and infrastructure paid for by it, permitted the nation's railroads to go into the Twenties with their balance sheets restored.

While the experiment worked, it was horribly expensive, in the long run being an exercise in corporate welfare. When World War II broke out, the experiment wasn't repeated, and the railroads performed in an exemplary manner.

Discussion Topic

- During the Fifties, the idea of using "X" to represent government secrecy was already a cliche. Pulp writers of the era would name a character "Secret Agent X" with little sense of shame; in fact, one suspects that it is with tongue in cheek that Rand blandly explains that "X" stands for "Xylophone". Here we see government using science as a tool of official state terror. This implies that the bonds of popular sovereignty have been severed completely, no doubt in the name of a national emergency. Where do we see hints of this today?

Chapter IV: Anti-Life

Synopsis

Jim Taggart hands a hundred dollar bill to a bum on the street, and the bum contemptuously takes no notice of the denomination.

Under the Railroad Unification Plan, the machine of industry has run down further. There are ripples.

- In North Dakota, a short line has gone bankrupt, relegating the state to a *"blighted area"*. The local banker has killed his family and then himself.

- A single freight train has been taken off the roster in Tennessee, shutting down a factory that had been dependent upon it. The owner's son quit college and is now awaiting execution for a murder committed with a gang of raiders.

- A Taggart station in Kansas has shut down, and the station agent gave up his dream of becoming a scientist for the more mundane profession of dishwasher.

Jim Taggart has been busy. His day began with a meeting with the Argentine ambassador where he discovered that Argentina was to be declared a people's state in two weeks. It was followed by a cocktail party at Orren Boyle's where it was decided to loan $4 billion to Argentina and Chile. That was followed by a party given by Jim at the cellar-like bar on the 60th floor of a skyscraper, in which was formed the Interneighborly Amity and Development Corporation, an outfit presided over by Orren Boyle that would possess exclusive rights to run the industrial concerns of the various people's states of South America. The final event was held at the home of the Chilean ambassador, who appeared to be nothing more than a gangster. Here Jim learned that on September 2, all d'Anconia Cooper properties would be nationalized. Jim made a mental note: sell d'Anconia, buy Interneighborly. He felt no pleasure in this because he was not thinking about money any longer, and that bothered him. In his mind he was traveling down a fogbound alley holding things he preferred not to think about.

Arriving home, Jim senses in Cherryl that things are no better here. He brags that he has closed a big deal today, and she seems neutral in her reaction. Something has changed. Cherryl is asking questions she wouldn't have asked before, and it's making Jim very nervous. She knows something she didn't before, and the tenor of the questions hints that she suspects he isn't the railroad magnate she worshiped after all.

He asks for champagne while he brags that he and a group of men will control the nationalized properties of South America to help the underprivileged. She doesn't appear all that impressed with Jim's coup. He complains that slum dwellers like Cherryl have no humanitarian spirit, something that can be felt only by those born to wealth. Cherryl has no sympathy for the welfare philosophy; having come from the slums, she knows that most of the poor want something for nothing. She tells Jim straightforwardly that he doesn't care about the humanitarian spirit either. He brags that he will end up one of the richest men in the world, and she indicates that even if he does, she wants nothing from him. She tells Jim that she respects Hank Rearden even as Jim brags about having beaten him.

Cherryl is proud of what Dagny did on the radio and has noticed that the government never answered her charges. Jim explains that Bertram Scudder took the fall for that disaster. It was better for the nation – and Jim – that Scudder become the scapegoat. Scudder's fatal mistake was his membership in the Tinky Holloway faction; its rival, the Chick Morrison faction, won, and Holloway traded Scudder for some favors. Cherryl is horrified that this is the kind of victory her husband is pursuing. Jim complains that he did not create this world, he only lives in it. In Jim's words Cherryl hears the echo of her drunken father.

Cherryl had worked hard to be Mrs. James Taggart, approaching the task as would a military cadet, but Jim was never satisfied. She could not understand the intellectual scum that formed Jim's orbit. She perceived that men like Simon Pritchett and Balph Eubank were phonies, and her worst discovery was that her husband was also a phony. The only true thing Jim had said was that he was surrounded by enemies. Conversations with people within the railroad revealed to Cherryl that his enemies did in fact work there – and he had earned their hatred. It develops that Cherryl has done some research of her own, some simple inquiries that led her to the office of Eddie Willers. It was Eddie who told her the whole truth. Everything she thought she married in Jim resided, in fact, in Dagny instead. *"Thank you, Mr. Willers,"* was all she said when he finished.

When she confronts Jim about it, he turns ugly and accuses her of ingratitude. He can't put into words what he wants; it can only be felt. Cherryl can't accept this and says that what she loved about him wasn't real. Cherryl now feels something – and it is fear. Jim accuses her of being a gold-digger who trades love, but can't just give it. Jim feels that loving a man for his virtues is cold justice; it's unearned love that matters. Cherryl explodes. Jim is a charlatan like the welfare pimps, wanting unearned love and unearned admiration. He wants to be like Hank Rearden without working for it.

The champagne arrives, and Jim mockingly proposes a toast to Francisco, which Cherryl refuses. Jim becomes enraged and leaves the room.

At her apartment, Dagny yearns to be back in Galt's Gulch and hopes to spot John on the street in New York. The doorbell rings – it is Cherryl. She is there to pay a debt; she apologizes for everything she had said at the wedding. She admits that she now knows the truth about who really runs the railroad and that she knows Jim for what he is.

It is interesting that we have not seen Dagny in interaction with other women to this point, except for the contemptible Lillian Rearden. Cherryl is Lillian's opposite in every respect. Dagny understands that she has met something clean, brave and struggling to live.

Dagny admits that when people say she is hard and unfeeling, it is true – because she is being *just*. Dagny has held herself above the terrible world Jim inhabits by one rule, to place nothing above the verdict of her own mind. This connects with something Cherryl had felt in her poor youth in Buffalo, something people around her had wanted to destroy. That attempt to destroy is *"anti-life"* as Rand has come to make us understand it, that one's life is not one's own, but that someone else has the ultimate claim on it. It is that proposition that Galt's Oath defies.

A premonition tells Dagny to suggest that Cherryl stay with her tonight, but Cherryl decides to go home. She looks broken.

Moments after Cherryl has left Jim, Lillian Rearden shows up. Lillian is unhappy about the quality of the new class of looters, who are not *"our crowd"*. She has come to her own crisis of confidence. She is to be made destitute by a divorce that to her dismay, she cannot stop, even with the sort of connections she thought she had made by presenting her husband and his life's work to the looters. Jim needles her about how she always said she didn't care about money, but she says she cares about *poverty*. Bertram Scudder can no longer help, but if Jim could get Wesley Mouch to intervene... Jim explains that the channels of pull have become so convoluted that it is impossible to get favors from the right people anymore.

Jim and Lillian drink champagne. Lillian says that Hank thinks little of Jim, and Jim wants just once to beat him. And in a sense he does in the next few minutes, as he beds Lillian Rearden.

Cherryl comes home in time to catch them after the act. She confronts Jim who becomes enraged and then brags about it. She asks why he married her; Jim tells her she was a cheap little guttersnipe from Buffalo who had no choice but to love him as he was – because she was worthless. She now understands that their marriage was always a matter of his desperate need to find someone to whom he could feel superior. The balls at which he paraded her, incorrectly dressed and fumbling, the social affairs at which he smirked in the background as others smirked at her in the foreground, the entire elevation of a lower class girl to the social heights for the purpose of degradation and humiliation, all of that was his highest expression of being. She shares Jim Taggart's fogbound alley, and the illumination she now finds in it is that of an oncoming headlight.

The cover has been torn off Jim Taggart, and what we see underneath are the writhing worms of mental and emotional pathology. He has married Cherryl because he felt both that she was worthless and that she was committed to a hopeless struggle to find worth. It was the hopelessness on which Jim was feeding, an image that is disturbing because it rings so very true. The chapter title is here – *"anti-life,"* and Jim Taggart is Rand's pitch-black psychological masterpiece.

Cheryl flees the sordidness of the apartment for the sordidness of the street, now rejected in low society for what her clothing makes her appear, just as she was rejected by high society for what she actually was, and by both for what she was trying to become. Cheryl now thinks she has nowhere to turn – more accurately, she forgets that she does. She forgets her promise to Dagny to come and see her, the only person she knows who might have the strength to pour into the wreckage of her life. She forgets everything but flight.

Then she ran, ran by the sudden propulsion of a burst of power, the power of a creature running for its life, she ran straight down the street that ended at the river – and in a single streak of speed, with no break, no moment of doubt, with full consciousness of acting in self-preservation, she kept running till the parapet barred her way and, not stopping, went over into space.

A creature running for its life that kills itself out of a sense of self-preservation – it is the contradiction that is *"anti-life."* It is death by cognitive dissonance. It is also a tacit recognition of soul, for what other aspect of self could Cheryl possibly hope to preserve at the cost of her life? Rand's philosophy might not be leading us there, but her narrative is.

Anti-Life and Sexuality

They[James Taggart and Lilian Rearden] did not speak. They knew each other's motive. Only two words were pronounced between them. "Mrs. Rearden," he said... Afterward, it did not disappoint him that what he had possessed was an inanimate body without resistance or response. It was not a woman that he had wanted to possess. It was not an act in celebration of life that he had wanted to perform, but an act in celebration of the triumph of impotence.

This is *"anti-life"* in the matter of procreation. Rand is once again silent and perhaps well so. But this notion of sex as possession is not restricted to those for whom its expression is toward an inanimate object – Rand's term for Lillian, and we believe it – but in fact it permeates her descriptions of the actual terms of sex between the *übermenschen* as well. It explains Dagny's serial monogamy, surely. But it risks the conclusion that one's self is not only one's own most precious possession, but may be given to another unreservedly, at least for the time, and yet simultaneously is a commitment that may be withdrawn at a whim, just as Dagny's was from Rearden. She had certainly given herself to him to the degree that when he discovered her antecedents with Francisco, she resigned herself literally to being beaten to death by him. That is a very peculiar frame of mind for someone who considers her own life her highest value. And yet when Galt comes along that commitment evaporates as if it had never been.

One may, of course, regard this behavior as a retreat from the ideal that someone under stress, and with less than true moral enlightenment, would make, and that once all is resolved, Dagny will be better adjusted. But Rand does not take that way out of the conundrum. Rand is tapping a deep appreciation of human sexuality that does not correlate very well to her ethical theories, and she describes it accurately. In so doing, Dagny becomes something more than a pasteboard figure behind which Rand's mouth is moving; in a literary sense she is now her own person.

This is a wonderful thing to discover in a novel, and it places Rand the story-teller in opposition to Rand the theoretician. It pits the inner logic of her narrative against the inner logic of her philosophy. Both are strong enough to make their case, and it's up to the reader to reconcile them or to choose between them. This is one reason why despite its many failings *Atlas Shrugged* is a novel that must be taken very seriously indeed.

Discussion Topics

- The bum who accepts Jim Taggart's largesse, a one hundred dollar bill, does so contemptuously – and he doesn't even know Jim!   What in New York and American society at this juncture might explain this attitude?

- Jim has always preached about virtue, humanitarianism and how money is not important.   However, this has never stopped him from trying to profit from any number of enterprises, ethical or otherwise.   Now he has stopped caring.   What has changed?

- The fogbound alley and the oncoming headlight are two images Rand has created to represent the revelatory developments of Jim's and Cherryl's relationship.   Rand the screenwriter has come up with two intense visual metaphors.   What do they mean?

- Cherryl has always been the fly in the *Dom Perignon* for Jim's friends, and she has been too innocent to see it.   Now the veil is lifted.   Jim expects Cherryl to love him as he is – morally diseased – because of her own worthlessness. Rand suggests that Cherryl killed herself out of a sense of survival.   What sense of worth was it that Cherryl died to preserve?

Chapter V: Their Brothers' Keepers

Synopsis

In California a copper wire breaks on a Taggart phone line. The last replacement wire has been sold to black marketers with government connections, and no one will report anything because of possible repercussions from those with pull. An employee calls Dagny in New York to report the break, and Dagny asks Eddie to have their Montana people ship copper wire to California. Jim comments cryptically that there soon won't be any problems with copper.

Jim complains about an uncoordinated transportation policy. Dagny judges that the Rail Unification Plan has failed, but Jim sees it as an act of sabotage by the bankers who won't carry their fair share. He rambles; Dagny senses Jim is stalling her in his office, and she notes he has changed since Cherryl's suicide, and not necessarily for the better.

Dagny knows that there are issues with a lack of transportation, but the friends of Cuffy Meigs don't have this problem – or the friends of Orren Boyle, or the friends of others with pull. Pull now has been compartmentalized into people with specific pull in specific areas. Dagny won't give Jim the reassurance he wants with respect to the future of rail; she said all she had to say three years ago. When Jim asks for a solution, Dagny tells him to get out of the way and let those who can fix the problems do so, but Jim wants her to accept the reality of the current system. He *wants* to be president of the railroad and insists that Dagny has an obligation to supply his wants; Jim has the right accorded him by weakness. Dagny begins to walk out in revulsion, but Jim holds her back to hear a radio news broadcast; it's the reason he's been stalling her.

The legislature of the People's State of Chile voted to nationalize d'Anconia Copper's properties in cooperation with the People's State of Argentina. This is what Jim expected to hear – but not what follows. As the vote concluded, explosions were heard at the harbor. Not only were the d'Anconia properties in Chile blown up, but every d'Anconia property all over the world.

Even the d'Anconia ore ships have been scuttled, and every employee was paid a half hour before the destruction. All the key personnel of the company have disappeared – including Francisco.

Jim calls the Chilean ambassador and screams at him on one phone while he screams at Orren Boyle on another. For Jim the loss of the looted assets is financial disaster. Dagny now perceives Jim's game and the money he and his friends had committed to it.

Dagny and Hank dine out, and Hank understands that Francisco did in fact keep his oath to him: Francisco acted in the defense of his friends. He tells Dagny of his meeting with Ragnar, but she already knows. Hank now understands that Ragnar was an agent of The Destroyer, and Dagny makes it clear that so was Francisco. Hank realizes that he was being recruited.

Hank regrets that he is not going to be able to deliver much more industrial output to Dagny; he is selling black market Rearden Metal to various sections of the country to stave off total collapse. Of course, whatever Hank saves this year, the looters will devour next year. Hank wishes he could go to Francisco and apologize.

At an adjoining table, a diner reacts violently to the d'Anconia Copper destruction:

"We can't permit it to be true."

A government worker says it was just a series of accidents, all coincidental, and it is unpatriotic to believe otherwise. Then the calendar display on the office building flashes a message, *"Brother, you asked for it!"* signed by Francisco with his full Spanish name. Hank cheers while the diners degenerate into hysterics.

The dance of d'Anconia's copper continues. In Montana, a copper wire breaks, idling a copper mine adjoining a Taggart spur. The station agent strips out the station's wiring and puts the mine back to work. Dagny tells Eddie to send Minnesota's wire to Montana. Jim has procured every piece of government paperwork to get wire requisitioned to the railroad, but he hasn't been able to get the actual wire.

California passes a confiscatory tax to help the unemployed, causing oil companies in the state to go out of business. Washington assures Hank that this legislative insurrection will be taken care of in short order, and Rearden Steel has absolute top priority in the rationing of oil. Hank can't believe that the bureaucrats are actually trying to placate him.

Philip shows up at the mill asking again for a job because he needs one. He can't perform any real tasks, but he is entitled to a livelihood. Hank throws him out.

Hank's divorce from Lillian goes without a hitch. It's too easy, and his lawyer thinks the Aristocracy of Pull wants something from him.

At the plant, the Wet Nurse asks for a job – a real job at the mill; he is tired of being a leech. Hank would happily offer him a job, but the Unification Board would never allow it. The Wet Nurse thinks that something is up: the government is bringing in goons to fill empty employment slots, and he thinks they are going to pull something.

In Minnesota a copper wire breaks at a grain elevator. Dagny has Eddie send the Taggart Terminal's stock of wire to Minnesota – and nails, paint, light bulbs and tools. People are scavenging railroad hardware to sell on the black market.

Dagny receives a phone call from Minnesota. The rail cars set to haul that state's wheat crop have not shown up, and the massive harvest will rot in its silos. The caller says that once he hangs up, he is going to become a deserter. Dagny's investigation within the railroad shows that every necessary form has been filled out, but the grain cars are not going to Minnesota. She finds that the paperwork has been falsified, and Cuffy Meigs is sending the cars to Louisiana to carry Emma Chalmers' soybeans, now deemed more important by the government bureaucracy than wheat.

Minnesotans riot and burn down government and railroad buildings while the press clamps a lid on the story. The railroad rounds up every kind of car imaginable and sends them all to Minnesota, and grain slowly begins to move. When Minnesotans take matters into their own hands, the State Chief Executive asks for the Army to intervene, and the Aristocracy of Pull finally gives Minnesota a higher priority than Emma Chalmers. But it's too late; the cars are in California where the soybean processing plant is located. Minnesota degenerates into civil war as the wheat rots, and the soybeans turn out to be unfit for human consumption.

Dagny dines with Wesley Mouch, Eugene Lawson, Dr. Floyd Ferris, Clem Weatherby, her brother Jim, and Cuffy Meigs. The Aristocracy of Pull now wants to abandon the rest of America's rail service to serve Minnesota. Dagny tries to bring reality into the discussion by asking that Taggart save the eastern US while other carriers handle their own areas. Let the Atlantic Southern handle transcontinental traffic. They don't listen. California's threat to secede has them flummoxed. Ferris and Lawson suggest abandoning America's industrial plant and becoming more like India: it's time for some serious privation. Meigs thinks it's time for a North American Union by conquering Canada and Mexico: it's time for some serious looting.

In the bowels of the Taggart Terminal a copper wire breaks, choking traffic. Dagny receives a call about the wire and leaves the meeting in relief. Her employees are clueless as to what to do, so Dagny calls her counterpart at the Atlantic Southern and asks to have their Chicago terminal signal engineer fly to New York. She sends out a crew to recover whatever copper is available on the Hudson Line despite not having the permission of the Unification Board to abandon it. She asks that all available laborers come to the terminal to operate the switches and signals manually. And one of the men is John Galt!

After giving the orders, Dagny walks down the tunnel near the vault where the motor is stored, knowing that John will follow her. He does, and when at last they are alone, they take each other brutally on a pile of sandbags. In the afterglow, Dagny learns that Galt was the mysterious person who visited her at the John Galt Line's offices that night. He tells her he knew about her affair with Hank, and he admits he has been an anonymous track worker at the terminal for the past twelve years, ever since leaving Twentieth Century Motors.

Dagny and Galt state their love for each other. She intends to stay because she thinks the looters are cracking. Galt knows they aren't, but she needs to see that for herself. He asks her not to search him out, but when she is ready to leave for Galt's Gulch, she should chalk the Sign of the Dollar on the pedestal of Nat Taggart's statue. He will be there for her within 24 hours. John leaves to become a human lamppost in the warrens of the Taggart Terminal.

Looting and the Mechanics of Collapse

The decline of the nation's economy accelerates under the benevolent guidance of the Unification Board, whose members have arrogated themselves the right to dispose of the wealth of the entire country. Here we have a fictional version of the end game of socialism. It began with a false premise – that profit was greed and that the capitalist class was exploiting the people for its own gain. That class was dispossessed of its wealth by a political class that took over the direction of their enterprises in the name of the people, and turned that profit, not into further economic investment, but into their own pockets just as they had assumed the original owners did. To the looters it's baffling – everything is being done for the noblest and most politically correct of reasons, and still the enterprises are failing. The original premise remains unchecked – it cannot be checked, for to do so is to undermine the entire world view that defines the political class.

Jim Taggart can't figure it out.

"Things are, it seems to me, going wrong," he said. There appears to exist a state...of confusion tending toward an uncoordinated, unbalanced policy. What I mean is, there's a tremendous national demand for transportation, yet we're losing money."

They're losing more than that. The entire system, cobbled together from theft and fraud, is failing. A single strand of copper wire failing has taken the Taggart Pacific Line out of communication. The last decent machine tool operation in the country has had the shipment that would have kept it staggering along expropriated and diverted to a well-connected and incompetent competitor. Both close their doors.

The people of [the town supported by that company] had been placed on national relief, but no food could be found for them in the empty granaries of the nation at the frantic call of the moment – so the seed grain of the farmers of Nebraska had been seized by order of the Unification Board – and Train Number 194 had carried the unplanted harvest and the future of the people of Nebraska to be consumed by the people of Illinois. "In this enlightened age," Eugene Lawson had said in a radio broadcast, "we have come, at last to realize that each one of us is his brother's keeper."

There is a quiet horror in that paragraph that may not be readily apparent to those who have never known anything but agricultural plenty, an unending surplus that takes us through bad harvest years as if nothing had ever happened. It is a tiny pinpoint in human history. For most of that history a bad harvest meant universal hunger for a year or more, one reason men were willing to fight to possess productive land before they had taught themselves to read. But if the seed grain is gone, the game is over. There will be no planting, no harvest, no food, and no amount of wishful thinking or political haranguing can stave off starvation.

But the seed grain can be stolen back; in fact, that's the only real recourse. And this applies to more than seed grain. As long as the bag of loot stays full, the thieves may indulge in an obsession over the social justice involved in ensuring that each has his proper share. The bag had better not empty. And unfortunately, it isn't being replenished.

But as long as the thieves can find an additional victim, the game may continue. And that's what Jim Taggart and the rest of the Aristocracy of Pull have up their collective sleeve. Copper is scarce? Seize it!

And so the plan comes to fruition. D'Anconia Copper is to be nationalized worldwide, its assets to replenish that bag of loot and be squabbled over by the political class. Jim makes certain that Dagny is listening to the radio broadcast of the event, but his triumph is short-lived. Francisco has finally liquidated, but on his terms, not on theirs.

...the sound of a tremendous explosion rocked the [legislators of the People's State of Argentina] hall. It came from the harbor...the chairman averted panic and called the session to order. The act of nationalization was read to the assembly, to the sound of fire-alarm sirens...the explosion had broken an electric transmitter – so that the assembly voted on the measure by the light of candles...every property of d'Anconia Copper on the face of the globe had been blown up and swept away.

It is a haunting image that frames an astounding feat of destruction, accomplished with an actuarial precision: no one hurt, everyone paid off, and the authorities unable to find the cream of Francisco's people, who seem to have disappeared mysteriously. Those who sought to profit from the inside knowledge of the theft are left drastically overexposed, Jim Taggart numbering high among them. The shock wave circles the planet.

Looting and the Mechanics of Famine

Starvation looms, but after two difficult years Minnesota has a bumper crop of grain that might just save the day. Rand was an expatriate city girl, a New Yorker by passion and conviction, and occasionally it shows in minor details such as this, as well as the typically modest New Yorker conviction that the city is *"the world's motor"*. Minnesota is, in fact, tenth among the fifty states in wheat production at roughly 18% of the production of the largest, which is Kansas. Rand has Nebraska, ninth highest and the next one up the list, plundered even of its seed grain in order to feed another state's hungry. But this year Minnesota is the country's granary. All it will take to bring it to market and to give the country's ruling class the time it needs to retain power for one more year is transportation. Rail transportation.

And that's really too bad, because the Unification Board has other priorities. The worst of these priorities is a real character study in self-appointed expertise, the mother of the political figure who died in the Taggart Tunnel disaster.

Emma Chalmers…was an old sociologist who had hung about Washington for years, as other women of her age and type hang about barrooms. "The soybean is a much more sturdy, nutritious, and economical plant than all the extravagant foods which our wasteful, self-indulgent diet has conditioned us to expect…an excellent substitute for bread, meat, cereals, and coffee – and if all of us were compelled to adopt soybeans as our staple diet, it would solve the national food crisis…"

Compelled, indeed. We are all acquainted with ostensibly well-meaning nutrition tyrants who would happily dictate our diets for our own good. Emma – *"Kip's Ma"* after the late and unlamented political martyr – is one of these and has decided with all of the agricultural expertise that a degree in sociology can confer that her Louisiana soybean fields are the dietary future of the country. And that's where nearly half of the rail cars necessary to transport the Minnesota harvest have been sent. It is a disaster.

"Every shed, silo, elevator, warehouse, garage and dance hall along the track is filled with wheat. At the Sherman elevators there's a line of farmers' trucks and wagons two miles long…"

But there is no transport. City people often forget this, but Rand is aware, possibly from the horrors of the Ukraine in the Thirties, that there is little storage space on the farms for the wheat they have harvested. It is milled, or it is lost. Dagny's desperate effort to load the stuff into coal cars contaminates the crop. Loading it into passenger cars sends it reeling off the tracks when those cars, never designed for such a use, fail. There is rioting, and the crop ends up rotting or in flames. At last Dagny pounds the seriousness of the situation into the dense heads in Washington:

But by that time, it was too late. Kip's Ma's freight cars were in California, where the soybeans had been sent to a progressive concern made up of sociologists preaching the cult of Oriental austerity, and of businessmen formerly in the numbers racket…the

*harvest of soybeans did not reach the markets of the country: it had
been reaped prematurely, it was moldy and unfit for consumption.*

And so will Minnesota starve? No, it will not. Where there
is grain there are flour mills enough to support local demand.
Kansas, North Dakota, Montana, Oklahoma, Washington, Texas,
South Dakota, Colorado, Idaho – the top wheat producing states
will have bread for themselves. Nebraska will starve unless
somehow it can get seed grain from the others, and one suspects
that even in the current state of total systemic breakdown that will
happen just as Rearden found men to sell him coal. But the cities
will starve. New York, the country's motor, will starve.

Dagny demands that the government retrench, pulling back
like a retreating army around the defense lines of the industrial east.
The Aristocracy of Pull decides, on the contrary, to expand in the
face of even worse destitution elsewhere. It is madness.

Dagny's Sexuality and the Coupling with John Galt

It takes place on a pile of sandbags in an abandoned granite
vault, evening clothes torn off, and as we have known for 900
pages, Dagny likes it rough.

*...then she felt her teeth sinking into the flesh of his arm, she
felt the sweep of his elbow knocking her head aside and his mouth
seizing her lips with a pressure more viciously painful than hers...*

And so on. At this point it is hardly over-imaginative to
conclude that Rand's sexuality was as kinky as anything in Fifties
literature: the chain on Dagny's wrist, the submission, half-naked
vulnerability in a room full of men in tuxedos, possession,
servitude in Galt's house, an acceptance of Rearden's violence, and
now taken at last, her evening clothes scattered among the filthy
canvas sandbags in her own railway tunnels. *"We are not
animals,"* Dagny stated some chapters ago. Apparently we are.

It is a wonderful contrast to consider Rand's pious asseveration
that sexual intercourse is the highest expression of intellect with
the consummation of her principals' relationship: bloody, violent

and covered with dust in the primordial dirt of a man-made cave. On a theoretical level it is not necessarily a contradiction; on a level at which A really is A, we know perfectly well that Rand has been putting us on. Her astringent theorizing has failed there in the cries echoing through the granite tunnel, and we thank God it did.

Discussion Topics

- Steel for a company in Nebraska is diverted to Illinois because the Nebraska company is doing well, while the Illinois company is a failing concern in a failing town. The town is too important to fail, and thus so is the company. As a result, both companies fail. Discuss contemporary examples of this misplacement of priorities.

- People were at first content to seize just a little of the wealth of the rich. Now they want it all. Cuffy Meigs wants to go all the way and seize Canada and Mexico. What in this chapter explains why dying nations become predatory when the money runs out?

- The diners in the restaurant reacted to Francisco's destruction of d'Anconia Copper by trying to deny its reality. Dr. Simon Pritchett might have added, "Can you be sure that Francisco d'Anconia ever existed?" How is this sort of defense mechanism useful? Is it common?

- Emma Chalmers believes in soybeans and the wisdom of Asians in eating them, in preference to wheat, claiming that it will lead to a more sustainable lifestyle. As a government bureaucrat, she is imposing this decision on America and risking the destruction of the Minnesota wheat crop as a result. In the end the soybeans are inedible and both are lost. How are believers in pseudo-science with power leading us down this path today?

- The Aristocracy of Pull considers shutting down America's industries to become an agricultural society like India. Would it be rational to de-industrialize a country, and if so, why? What could possibly justify such a decision?

- Minnesota degenerates into civil war. California threatens to secede. Would the bonds of Union sunder due to a central government that cannot perform its functions or intimidate its member states, and if so, what would be lost or gained?

Chapter VI: The Concerto of Deliverance

Synopsis

The union at Rearden Steel demands a raise without bothering to ask Hank, and the impetus comes from the new workers inserted by the Unification Board and spotted by the Wet Nurse. The Unification Board rejects the raise petition, but the media run stories in favor of the union and against Hank. Then the workers attack managers and disable critical equipment. The IRS attaches Hank's assets due to a delinquency in paying income taxes that had never occurred. A bureaucrat calls Hank to apologize, claiming it was all a mistake. Then Tinky Holloway calls and asks Hank to attend an evening meeting in New York. Hank agrees to attend although Holloway's insistence on a specific time has his guard up.

Holloway and Claude Slagenhop are working on intelligence provided by Philip Rearden, who is afraid that if Holloway pulls off a power play, Hank will desert. That would mean the mills will be confiscated and that Philip can't inherit them.

At home Hank takes a call from his mother; she wants to meet with him at his old home. Present are his mother, Philip – and Lillian. They are there to beg for forgiveness and mercy; the money they have isn't enough to live on since Hank's assets were attached. Hank doesn't care. He perceives that his family is terrified that he will desert and that the government will come after *them*. Philip tells Hank that he can't desert without money – and a piece of the puzzle falls into place. So *that* was what the attachment order was about! And his family were to be hostages! Enraged, Lillian tells Hank that she was bedded by Jim Taggart; she pauses in her tirade as Hank watches her deflate. Hank tells them he could have forgiven them had they urged him to desert.

Hank arrives at the Wayne-Falkland suite that had previously been occupied by Francisco. Present are Wesley Mouch, Eugene Lawson, Jim Taggart, Dr. Floyd Ferris and Tinky Holloway. They want to know what policies Hank wants changed – while Lawson checks his watch frequently. They have a plan that will give Hank a five percent price increase for steel; this will ripple on to price increases elsewhere. But there will be no pay raises. Jim tells

Hank about the success of the Rail Unification Plan, and Mouch tells Hank there is now going to be a Steel Unification Plan. Every operator will be allowed to make as much steel as he can, but revenues will be pooled and distributed by the number of blast furnaces each company possesses. Hank quickly does the math and realizes that this is a plan to bail out Orren Boyle. Eugene Lawson says that it's Hank's duty to comply and suffer because Boyle is simply too big to be allowed to fail. Hank suggests that they junk all their regulations, let Boyle fail and let him buy Boyle's assets; they balk. He suggests they simply expropriate his mills, and they recoil in horror. He asks how he can produce if he produces at a loss; Ferris says he will produce because he can't help himself. Jim says that Hank will do *something* to fix the problem – and the last piece fits. Francisco was right – he is the guiltiest man in the room because he had accepted the reality that these men had created. Hank walks out.

Hank arrives at his mill to find it on fire and hears gunshots; there is a mob storming the mill, and open war has broken out. Hank turns around to head for the east gate and discovers the Wet Nurse lying wounded in the dirt. He had tried to stop the rioters, and in return they shot him and dumped him on the slag heap. The riot was ordered from Washington as grounds for introducing the Steel Unification Plan; the meeting in New York had been a decoy. Hank carries the Wet Nurse in his arms, but he dies along the way.

Hank enters via the east gate and heads for the infirmary still carrying the dead youth. His loyal employees are winning the war with the rioters, but the front gate is the scene of a major battle. A man on the roof of a building by the gate fires into the crowd and doesn't waste a bullet. Two rioters club Hank to the ground, and someone shoots and kills the attackers; Hank awakes on the couch in his office. The new furnace foreman, Frank Adams, had killed his attackers and was instrumental in organizing the battle for the mill – and Frank Adams turns out to be Francisco d'Anconia! Francisco now consummates the long-delayed recruitment of Hank Rearden.

Lillian Rearden and the Looters' World View

We have questioned Rand's understanding of her own heroes, which is a backhanded tribute to her power as a novelist – the very questions wouldn't be possible if her characters weren't drawn finely enough to be able to measure their observed behavior against Rand's theoretical explanation of it. We cannot question her supreme understanding of her villains. This, for instance, concerning Lillian:

The lust that drives others to enslave an empire, had become, in her limits, a passion for power over him. She had set out to break him, as if, unable to equal his value, she could surpass it by destroying it, as if the measure of his greatness would thus become the measure of hers, as if – he thought with a shudder – as if the vandal who smashed a statue were greater than the artist who had made it...

This is a glaring parallel to Jim Taggart's outburst at Cherryl in an earlier chapter where he had destroyed an antique vase. Jim and Lillian are mental twins.

Lillian had set out to break Hank like a horse she intended to ride, just as the looters imagine all of society to be, a powerful but brute animal saddled for guidance by the clever. They're in charge because they're clever, and the measure of that cleverness is the fact that they're in charge. It's a nice, tidy, self-consistent world view untroubled by circularity or, for that matter, by results. The media can spin results, after all, at least for a time, but they can't spin facts as fundamental as an empty granary.

The Battle of Rearden Steel

We have come to the shooting at last. The first shot was fired into the Wet Nurse, who was unceremoniously dumped onto a slag heap. He wasn't quite finished, however, and Rearden finds him after he has dragged himself some one hundred vertical feet to the edge of a ravine near the roadway.

A scum of cotton was swimming against the moon, he could see the white of a hand and the shape of an arm lying stretched in the weeds, but the body was still...

It might have been better to remain that way, for over the course of the next four pages we are treated to the bathos of a death scene right out of Italian opera. The young man is at last conferred the dignity of a name – it is Tony – and a kiss from the belatedly paternal Rearden as he breathes his last. Of course Tony has achieved his moral epiphany, but we knew that two chapters ago. He is, as Cherryl before him, an innocent playing a game far beyond his capacity, who pays for it with his life.

And the game is afoot. Gunfire in the background reminds us that we are at war, and as he drops the cooling corpse off at the dispensary, Hank spies the lynchpin of the factory's defense.

On the roof of a structure above the gate, he saw, as he came closer, the slim silhouette of a man who held a gun in each hand and, from behind the protection of a chimney, kept firing at intervals down into the mob, firing swiftly and, it seemed, in two directions at once, like a sentinel protecting the approaches to the gate. The confident skill of his movements, his manner of firing, with no time wasted to take aim, but with the kind of casual abruptness that never misses a target, made him look like a hero of Western legend...

We wince. Rand, who has taken the trouble to inform herself of the minutiae of railroads and steel mills, is on considerably shakier ground with regard to firearms, and this won't be the only time. While it is conceivable that a two-gun hero of movie westerns might attempt to hip-shoot from an elevated position into an oncoming mob in two separate directions at once, it is not recommended combat procedure. Even a paragon of accuracy must encounter the necessity to reload, a two-handed process that in real life tends to happen at the most inconvenient moments.

But this fellow is also good enough to intercept a direct attempt on Rearden's life some moments later and carry him from the fray.

"That was that new furnace foreman of ours. Been here two months. Best man I've ever had. He's the one who got wise to what the gravy boys were planning... Told me to arm our men... Frank Adams is his name – who organized our defense, ran the whole battle, and stood on a roof, picking off the scum who came too close to the gate. Boy, what a marksman!"

It's Francisco, of course – who sought out the man he described as his *"greatest conquest."* And so Hank is, for at last they sit down for the conversation that precedes the disappearance into Galt's Gulch.

Discussion Topics

- It was common in European history for a man accused of a crime to have his entire family brought to trial with him. This was known by the legal term *attainder* – "corruption of the blood" – which is explicitly banned by the Constitution. It was observed in the Soviet Union when Stalin went after a Politburo member, like his faithful servant Molotov, by going after his wife. Are we seeing attainder in America today, and if so, where?

- Union violence has a long and honored history in America. The Kohler plumbing fixture concern in Wisconsin has experienced 75 years of labor violence, the worst of it in the Fifties, and most of it abetted by government officials. The Florida East Coast Railroad strike in the Sixties saw trains blown off the tracks and union members serving prison terms in excess of twenty years. Rand did not invent the Battle of Rearden Steel. Where are hints of explicit violence, or violence implied through political action, emanating from unions today?

Warning! Reading John Galt's Objectivism Speech

The next chapter contains the long radio speech by John Galt that is Rand's philosophical treatise on Objectivism. It's important because Rand regarded it as the centerpiece of her book, but it stops the action absolutely cold and launches the reader from a novel into an angry polemic. Attempting to read the entire speech in one session is a recipe for non-comprehension.

Chapter VII: "This is John Galt Speaking"

Synopsis

A sleeping Dagny is awakened by Jim, who barges in with terrifying news. Having had his fill with the attempted takeover of his steel mill by murderous thugs, Hank has disappeared, taking his top people with him. In Jim Taggart's panicked opinion, it is desertion, a fatal blow to the country's morale, or at least to the ability of the ruling class to maintain control, which to him is one and the same. We know where Rearden has gone, and so does Dagny, who will not move to bring him back.

The media take a series of positions, all obviously directed by the government. First they declare Hank to be a traitor. Then they say that the loss of one person is unimportant because the individual is of no significance to society. Then the party line changes to Hank dying in a car crash.

A week after Hank's disappearance, Dagny receives a letter with no return address mailed from a small town in Colorado. It is from Hank.

I have met him. I don't blame you. H.R.

The reference is to Galt, of course. Dagny has avoided the terminal tunnels, but her examination of the payroll records shows that a John Galt has been working under her very nose for the past twelve years. She sees his home address in the records and struggles not to go to him. His presence in the tunnels had been her motor through those days, just as his presence in the city had been her motor through the months of that summer, just as his presence somewhere in the world had been her motor through the years before she ever heard his name. Now she feels as if her motor, too, has stopped.

America has degenerated into anarchy with each rebellion ending only in further destruction. Trains are attacked in four western states. There are rebellions where local officials are overthrown and tax collectors are murdered. There are warlords, chaos. States secede and collectivize everything in sight, only to fail within a week; the Army is hardly forced to fire a shot to restore order. The media refuse to report any of it. Orren Boyle suffers a nervous breakdown and goes into seclusion.

The only thing that can save them now is – a radio broadcast? Even if the Aristocracy of Pull no longer controls the country, they *do* control the media, and it's the best shot they have. Head of State Thompson decides to address the nation. Every radio and TV station and poster in America advises the people to listen to this most important speech on the national crisis.

Jim tells Dagny that Thompson wants her to go to the New York studio to attend a conference that will precede his speech. For the third time in the book, Dagny's presence is commanded, this time accompanied by a large police officer to act as her *"bodyguard."* Dagny, with Eddie and Jim in attendance, goes to the studio where she sees Thompson, Wesley Mouch, Eugene Lawson, Chick Morrison, Tinky Holloway, Dr. Floyd Ferris, Dr. Simon Pritchett, Emma Chalmers, Fred Kinnan, Mr. Mowen and Dr. Robert Stadler. The old academic's face now reflects his history, seamed with guilt that has congealed into hatred. In fact there is no conference. As the radio plays military marches, the attendees take their places for a propaganda photo to show the solidarity of science, business, labor and industry behind the government. Dagny tells Thompson she will not participate in this farce. They are at least bright enough not to stick a microphone in her face this time.

A technician informs the men that something has gone horribly wrong; they are off the air all over the country. They are being jammed, and he can't identify the source.

Precisely at 8 PM, the voice of John Galt takes over the nation's airwaves as he begins The Speech. Dagny recognizes the voice, and so does a horrified Eddie Willers – he knows that voice all too well from his meals in the Taggart corporate cafeteria.

"For twelve years, you have been asking: Who is John Galt? This is John Galt speaking… I am the man who has deprived you of victims and thus has destroyed your world, and if you wish to know why you are perishing, I am the man who will now tell you."

The Speech

We and the listening country – Thompson, like our own detestable autocrats, has pre-empted regular programming – are now the rapt audience for a 60 page rant against the sitting government and a disquisition on a new moral philosophy. It is decidedly not the general run of evening entertainment, and if the country had, as is likely, responded with a collective turn of the power switch, the novel would have ended rather abruptly. It did not, possibly out of curiosity, possibly out of desperation, possibly because there wasn't a beer and a good book within handy reach. In any case, it is time to consider the contents of The Speech.

It is certainly an odd thing to pop up in the middle of a novel, a gigantic boulder against which the dramatic flow breaks and ebbs, an enormous pothole into which the little train of the narrative descends with a crash, a joyless, aggravating, self-righteous, angry denunciation wherein the speaker informs his audience that it is starving because it is unworthy of his standards. It is also, however, a statement of first principles and an ethical manifesto. It is, at last, Galt's turn before the proscenium. He's waited long enough.

We are grateful to Dr. David Kelley for his invaluable outline of the speech, available for perusal on the Objectivist Center website (www.objectivistcenter.org). It is, frankly, not an easy thing to find the structure, and if certain critics have treated it as a stream-of-consciousness blast against the *status quo*, that isn't entirely unjustified. That is not to say that Rand simply tossed it off in a single evening of passionate writing – far from it, she originally budgeted three months for the construction of Galt's speech and it ended up taking her two years. That is an awfully long time in which to produce 60 pages of text, and the result is tightly structured enough to offer considerable resistance to being pulled apart into its constituent components.

Galt speaks about moralities – what he terms the Morality of Death, which is, under various descriptions and interpretations, the moral code, ages old, that has led the country to disaster; the Morality of Life, which is that of free men and women interacting in transaction, value for given value, an approach that is equally

219

old but has been ruthlessly suppressed for reasons that Galt will detail; and at last What is to Come, life under a new moral code that will provide the structure under which the phoenix will rise from the ashes of a shattered and ruined society.

Each of these is worthy subject matter for an analysis far more reaching than the limitations of this guide will allow, and so we will not attempt any categorical criticism of the philosophy behind it but attempt to stick to principal themes and try to pin them to the shoulders of the giants that Rand disdained to stand upon. As we have complained in the past, none of these things, either the principles or the difficulties, are unprecedented in the annals of Western philosophy, and as one might expect, Rand is led down a few false paths in her machete-work through the jungle in search of a clearing.

It's a manifesto, to begin with. Karl Marx began his with "A specter is haunting Europe," and the specter that is haunting America in *Atlas Shrugged* is along those same lines: starvation, exploitation, a breakdown of a societal model that has run its course, those in charge of it having subverted it to their own ends and now clutching at the disintegrating fabric with an iron hand. And from its wreckage a new one is to be born, predicated on new moral propositions, a new ideology. Rand is not a conservative in any real sense; she is a revolutionary, utopian radical, and the difference between her and Marx and Engels, whom she despised, is the nature of the moral code that is to build her new society. Let us first examine the Morality of Life.

The Morality of Life

Galt presents the foundational philosophical propositions for this moral code. These, as we have seen in the titles of the main sections of *Atlas Shrugged*, are taken from Aristotle: non-contradiction, the exclusion of the middle ("either-or"), and identity ("A is A"). Rand's philosophical foundation rests on an objective reality, a "something" that is out there, and that it is the function of man's mind to apprehend. *"Existence exists,"* is her pungent summation. In fact, Leonard Peikoff stated that she would have preferred "existentialism" to "objectivism" as a descriptive term but that it was "already taken." Rand's moral code, then, rests on the propositions that (1) there is something independent of man's existence that it is the function of his mind to apprehend and order, and that (2) it is reason that is the specific function of the mind that offers a provable, consensual view of the universe, and that (3) the rules of relations between people – morality – depend on an agreement on facts that is only attainable by reason; morality is therefore dependent on man's mind, and that any system that denies that mind is either falsely moral or openly immoral.

Galt states, *"You have heard no concepts of morality but the mystical or the social,"* i.e., Church and State, respectively, and his is a third way, Reason. Each of the two former is based on the concept of sacrifice, the notion that an individual life is not only measurable merely in the context of its relation with God or fellow men, but necessarily subordinate to them and ultimately to be discarded in their favor. That it is to be discarded at all – sacrificed – is the proposition Rand challenges.

A moment for an important point – it is, in theory, the God of Adam or the god of Marx, the Collective, that makes this demand, but in fact it is men who make that demand in their names, and in doing so spread the corruption that has plagued the world. The underlying morality is of Death, and its proponents are murderers.

Underneath this flow of verbiage is an attempt to reprise a good deal of Western philosophy, and the result is dense enough to make for difficult reading. Rand's definitions now pelt us like hail, terms are tossed about like straws in a tornado – and are just about as easy to catch – and the real-world reader becomes as impatient as the fictional radio listener must have been. Within the short space of ten pages we are told that reason, purpose and self-esteem are three fundamental values that imply the virtues of rationality, independence, integrity, honesty, justice, productiveness and pride. All of these abstractions are so heavily dependent on definition that they become nonsense in its absence and obsessive in its presence. What, for example, are we to make of such over-polished gems as, *"the law of causality is the law of identity applied to action"*? That sort of thing is more at home in a graduate philosophical seminar than on a radio broadcast to a seething nation.

221

There are two classic requirements of any logical system – first, that it is self-consistent or free of internal contradiction; and second, that it succeeds in mapping its logical propositions to observed reality, that it fits the evidence. Rand's ethical system here is long on internal consistency, and depends strictly on her narrative to represent its mapping to the real world; that is the consequence of attempting to present a philosophy in novel form. What is most fascinating about *Atlas Shrugged* is that there are times when the narrative, finely developed as it is, isn't particularly cooperative. It is no act of postmodern textual deconstruction, but of simple observation, to point out once more that there is a distinct tension between narrative and philosophical system, and that any serious consideration of Rand's opus either must resolve these or conclude that by her own standards that one or the other of these, her premises, is in error.

We will delve a little deeper into the Morality of Life when we come to consider Galt's way forward out of all of this mess. Let us now consider his characterization of the morality that gave rise to the Twentieth Century Motor Company debacle and to the looters rioting at Rearden's gates: the Morality of Death.

The Morality of Death

This consists of two parts, which we shall consider separately – that of the social, the State, and that of the mystical, the Church, exemplified by Marxist socialism and Christian theology respectively. In brief we suggest that her understanding of the former was exquisitely precise, both from theoretical study and up-close observation of a Marxist revolution; and that her appreciation of the latter is somewhat less so for similar reasons, lack of close observation. Let us attempt to show why.

"...there are two kinds of teachers of the Morality of Death: the mystics of spirit and the mystics of muscle... The good, say the mystics of spirit, is God, a being whose only definition is that he beyond man's power to conceive – definition that invalidates man's consciousness and nullifies his concepts of existence. The good, say the mystics of muscle, is Society – a thing which they define as

an organism that possesses no physical form, a super-being embodied in no one in particular and everyone in general except yourself. Man's mind, say the mystics of spirit, must be subordinated to the will of God. Man's mind, say the mystics of muscle, must be subordinated to the will of Society."

The Mystics of Muscle

Galt's, and Rand's, objections to the socialist approach are illustrated in the story of the Twentieth Century Motor Company's fall from a state of capitalist grace to the depths of envy-soaked socialist hell, through the precept of "from each according to his ability, to each according to his need," a precept that even practicing Marxists gave up after Lenin nearly lost control of the nascent Soviet Union by attempting its practice. As we have cited elsewhere, Trotsky evaded the issue by explaining that the people simply weren't ready for that yet, not in an advanced enough state of class consciousness, his form of a state of grace. That would require a New Soviet Man, raised in a state of superior education toward class consciousness. It is a signature problem of utopian systems, Plato's to Marx's, and Rand's itself is no exception: the system turns out to be a fairyland that may only be populated by fairies, the existence of either being contingent on the existence of the other. We may wish to recall this stipulation when we come to consider the world as Galt's Gulch writ large.

The moral foundation of collectivism means this to Galt:

"...your code hands out, as its version of the absolute, the following rule of moral conduct: If you wish it, it's evil; of others wish it, it's good...this double-jointed, double-standard morality...splits mankind into two enemy camps: one is you, the other is all the rest of humanity. You are the only outcast who has no right to wish or live. You are the only servant, the rest are the masters, you are the only giver, the rest are the takers, you are the eternal debtor, the rest are the creditors never to be paid off. Their right is conferred upon them by a negative, by the fact that they are non-you."

The answer of the classical socialist, that it's all right because everyone is in this position, does not resolve the objection at all. It is in this sense that collectivism cannot allow the individual; Rand, the radical individualist, is very clear and very persuasive on this point. The demand on the part of others that one live one's life for their benefit does, in every final analysis, demand the death of the individual, and that is why Rand thunderously rejects it.

And, in practice, the Collective, the State, always turns out to be an abstract concept populated by concrete individuals – the elite, the cadre, the New Class – who are in it for themselves despite whatever rhetoric they employ to the contrary. So it was at the Twentieth Century Motor Company, so it is under socialism – the individual does not die, he simply becomes crippled, paranoid, petty, and eventually destructive of everyone's interests including his own. He does not die; he simply turns into something contemptible.

"A morality that holds need as a claim, holds emptiness – non-existence – as its standard of value; it rewards an absence, a defect: weakness, inability, incompetence, suffering, disease, disaster, the lack, the fault, the flaw – the zero."

The less than zero, technically, although we'll cede Rand the point. It is the social manifestation of the Morality of Death. Let us now examine the second one, the Church, or rather Rand's conception of it.

The Mystics of Spirit

Rand was a celebrated atheist, having set the terms of reality such that to be considered real, any of its manifestations, whether a pebble or God, must be observable by multiple individuals and logically testable in the sense that the earlier Logical Positivists had termed "falsifiability". God fails to meet these standards. As someone positing that the highest standard of life is an individual's own reason, this for Rand was conclusive. That there might be tests outside reason was an argument she spent a great deal of energy refuting – true or not, it led to observable abuses that meant that the manipulative non-producers, the clergy, could deny reason altogether and consolidate power in the pursuit of the mystical. It was her conception of the Church. In some important respects it was John Calvin's as well: that its undeniable spiritual virtues had been subordinated to the demands of temporal power by men unworthy of either. It is Calvin's view of Original Sin that Rand has appeared to adopt as categorical, a topic we will address momentarily.

But from there their paths diverged sharply – Calvin's path toward predestination, Rand's toward free will, and to maintain the supremacy of free will she was willing to discard God Himself. Rand must have free will; it is a basic Objectivist axiom without which her system does not work. And so she must present fate as a construct, an illusion.

"That which you call your soul or spirit is your consciousness, and that which you call 'free will' is your mind's freedom to think or not, the only will you have, your only freedom, the choice that controls all the choices you make and determines your life and your character...thinking is man's only basic virtue, from which all the others proceed. And his basic vice, the source of all his evils, is that nameless act which all of you practice, but struggle never to admit: the act of blanking out, the willful suspension of one's consciousness, the refusal to think – not blindness, but the refusal to see; not ignorance but the refusal to know..."

But where from there? For this does not disprove, but merely denies, the proposition that all acts of men are fated, that we all are trapped into a fabric previously woven and only think that we have the ability to move, warp to weft. It is in that context that Rand expresses *Atlas Shrugged*'s single instance of what she conceives of as formal Christian doctrine:

"Your code begins by damning man as evil, then demanding that he practice a good which it defines as impossible for him to practice. It demands, as his first proof of virtue, that he accept his own depravity without proof... The name of this monstrous absurdity is Original Sin. A sin without volition is a slap at

225

morality and an insolent contradiction in terms: that which is outside the possibility of choice is outside the province of morality. To hold, as man's sin, a fact not open to his choice is a mockery of morality. To hold man's nature as his sin is a mockery of nature. To punish him for a crime he committed before he was born is a mockery of justice. To hold him guilty in a matter where no innocence exists is a mockery of reason. To destroy morality, nature, justice, and reason by means of a single concept is a feat of evil hardly to be matched. Yet that is the root of your code."

It is a masterly summary of one of the greatest and earliest schisms of the Christian church, one that was pivotal in Western history for nearly fifteen hundred years. Rand is walking in the pathway trod by the great before her. Her words could have been spoken, and something very like them were, by an individual named Pelagius in the Fourth Century AD, an early Church father whose most influential rival in theory was Augustine of Hippo, a converted Manichean who insisted that Original Sin meant that man was inherently imperfectible (in this life) due to the transmission of the sin of Adam – the partaking of the knowledge of good and evil – through his descendants. Rand, and everyone else who reads that passage, considers what was gained through that act of disobedience to describe the very essence of man. Galt continues:

"The evils for which they damn [man] are reason, morality, creativeness, joy – all the cardinal values of his existence. It is not his vices that their myth of man's fall is designed to explain and condemn, but the essence of his nature as man. Whatever he was – that robot in the Garden of Eden, who existed without mind, without values, without labor, without love – he was not man."

One might think from this that Rand has refuted Genesis; in fact, it is only an indication that she appreciates the issues therein. She isn't the first by far. Is this idea of Original Sin a condemnation of man, or merely a description? An image, or an act of justice? The key is what she terms volition – free will.

226

And the degree to which it is instrumental in the description of man is the topic that set Pelagius and Augustine at one another's throats.

The two men did not settle it between them, although Augustine came out on top for a time. And yet by the time of the Reformation there had slowly evolved a general consensus within the Church that, in fact, the doctrine of Original Sin meant not that man was inherently sinful but that he was inclined that way, not that he was guilty of anything by the mere act of being born, but that the possibility of sin was open to him. Certain of the Church fathers – Origen, Ignatius, Justin Martyr – came to a position perfectly compatible with Rand's, if only her philosophical studies had brought her to that realization.

Certain others did not. The interpretation that Galt identifies as *"yours"* is, in fact, that of Calvin, who embraced the doctrine of Original Sin after what to him seemed centuries of desuetude. For him it is that inherent nature that required the redemption of Christ. But it is, for Rand, an offense against free will, impermissible because it implies that volition is illusory, that man is, in fact, what she termed derisively a robot.

Here Rand is retracing a truly critical path in Western philosophy. Did she realize it? Certainly the classes she took in Petrograd under N. O. Lossky should have given her the necessary background. She graduated from her studies in 1924, which places her in a front-row seat to observe the advent of Soviet communism and its immediate effects, which she painted for us in miniature in Starnesville, Wisconsin. But possibly she did not – most philosophy curricula then and today avoid a thorough assessment of ground covered by the Church fathers mentioned here who are known collectively as the Medieval Schoolmen, whose defense has been made most loudly by, of all people, that unrepentant old atheist Bertrand Russell, for whose guidance in the matter we are profoundly grateful. It is very fertile ground indeed. Aristotle reached us through these men, and one wonders if Rand completely appreciated that. Perhaps not – there are indications that Rand's grasp on history was not quite up to her grasp on philosophy. For example:

"The infamous times you call the Dark Ages were an era of intelligence on strike, when men of ability went underground and lived undiscovered, studying in secret, and died, destroying the works of their mind, when only the bravest of martyrs remained to keep the human race alive."

This is, actually, nonsense. The giants of intellect that were the Schoolmen struggled over the same issues that outraged Rand during this specific period, men whom she disparaged as "mystics" for their faith in a God she cannot reach by reason. One reason the formal philosophical community has offered Objectivism less respect than perhaps it might deserve is Rand's dismissal of this monumental intellectual progress without understanding it. It cost her a great deal of time, effort and credibility.

Reformation, Counter-Reformation – Sixteenth Century Europe seethed with this controversy. Seventeenth Century Europe burnt nearly to the ground over it. Then came the Enlightenment and a fellow named Immanuel Kant who bears a considerable resemblance to Rand in terms of the philosophical issues with which he came to grips, with whose work she was very familiar and whose conclusions she rejected. If one wishes to place Rand's philosophy in real-world chronological terms, this might not be a bad place for it. It is at the birth of capitalism, the emergence of the individual – new economies, new political philosophies are about to create a New World. The only sense in which we may call Rand a conservative is that these precepts are hers, and the social revolution she advocates will, she hopes, bring us back into accordance with them.

Rand takes her place in the rise of individualist thought that has continued to this day. Enlightenment political philosopher John Locke's basic premise is that the proper repository of political rights is within the individual, which is, for Rand, the proper repository of morality as well. Economist Ludwig von Mises later proposed that the individual is the proper repository of economic activity. These three facets of individualism constitute the core of Rand's approach to her new society. This is very serious business, and despite the length of Galt's speech, Rand touches on it fairly lightly. Those seemingly interminable 60 pages turn out to be too short for the subject.

Did this foundation of Objectivism really belong here in a work of fiction? One is tempted to state that the novel could have done very well without it – most of these principles have already been stated in one form or another by one or another of her characters, hero and villain. The narrative flows around it quite satisfactorily. In fact, it is there because without it the rest of the novel wouldn't have existed.

What is to Come

To finish Galt's speech – What is to Come, the necessary conclusion of any political manifesto. Lenin's *What is to be Done?* finishes Marx – it delineates the steps by which a core of ideological leaders must take control of the inchoate and unshaped forces of revolution. Rand could have slipped so very easily into this model – after all, she has an elite, already fiery-eyed with moral certitude, a core, a cadre – why not make them the new ruling class? Galt as Philosopher-King, Dagny as his Queen – it is, in fact, precisely what Mr. Thompson and the rest of the present ruling class will expect after the last echoes of this speech reverberate across the country.

Well, it isn't going to work like that – first, because the rules are going to change. No more of the model of producers and leeches, vampires and victims. The sanction of the victim has been withdrawn in favor of objective truth. Freedom starts there.

"Just as man can't succeed by defying reality, so a nation can't, or a country, or a globe. A is A. The rest is a matter of time..."

C. S. Lewis agrees: "The very idea of freedom presupposes some objective moral law which overarches rulers and ruled alike... Unless we return to the crude and nursery-like belief in objective values, we perish."

"So long as men, in the era of savagery, had no concept of objective reality and believed that physical nature was ruled by the

229

whim of unknowable demons – no thought, no science, no production were possible. Only when men discovered that nature was a firm, predictable absolute were they able to rely on their knowledge, to choose their course, to plan their future, and slowly, to rise from the cave..."

"Such was the service we had given you and were glad and willing to give. What did we ask in return? Nothing but freedom...free to think and to work as we choose – free to take our own risks and to bear our own losses – free to earn our own profits and to make our own fortunes – free to gamble on your rationality, to submit our products to your judgment for the purpose of a voluntary trade, to rely on the objective value of our work and on your mind's ability to see it..."

And no less, and no more, will be demanded in the new world to rise from the ashes of the old.

"I am speaking to those who desire to live and to recapture the honor of their soul. Now that you know the truth about your world, stop supporting your own destroyers. Withdraw your support. Do not try to live on your enemies' terms or to win at a game where they're setting the rules... Do not attempt to rise on the looters' terms... Go on strike – in the manner I did. Do not try to produce a fortune, with a looter riding on your back. Do not help them to fake reality..."

"The honor of their soul" – we know exactly what Rand means, although one is led to wonder what would happen to her rhetoric should she subject the existence of that soul to the same scrutiny she accords the existence of God. Such a proof would at best be inferential, "self-evident," and her villain, the nihilist Pritchett, doesn't find it so. Man is, we recall him stating, merely a collection of chemicals. And yet man is a collection of chemicals that spans chasms with bridges, continents with railroad tracks. That is Rand's evidence for the existence of soul. The Schoolmen called it a teleological argument.

Galt concludes with his vision of the future:

"When the looters' state collapses, deprived of the best of its slaves, when it...dissolves into starving robber gangs fighting to rob one another – when the advocates of the morality of sacrifice perish with their final ideal – then and on that day we will return. We will open the gates of our city to those who deserve to enter, a city of smokestacks, pipelines, orchards, markets and inviolate homes... With the sign of the dollar as our symbol – the sign of free trade and free minds – we will move to reclaim this country once more from the impotent savages who never discovered its nature, its meaning, its splendor."

In short, the strike is to continue, only now it will include the entire country. Here for the first time we understand that not only industrial magnates and persons of outstanding entrepreneurial ability are capable of this sort of moral conduct, but that everyone is – Rand calls this *"the best that is within you."* Galt's Gulch is a gated community in a literal sense – the world to come will not be.

"You will win when you are ready to pronounce the oath I have taken at the start of my battle: I swear – by my life and my love of it – that I will never live for the sake of another man, nor ask another man to live for mine."

And now the real import of that oath is clear: that it is the individual, not the collective or the mystical, neither State nor Church; it is the individual who is Atlas, who will shrug, who will pick up the shattered pieces of the world once it hits the hard surface of reality, who will assemble them once again into the world that is to come. It is a nation of individuals, and not a collective, that will emerge.

Discussion Topic: Dissecting The Speech

- *"You have sacrificed justice to mercy. You have sacrificed independence to unity. You have sacrificed reason to faith. You have sacrificed wealth to need. You have sacrificed self-esteem to self-denial. You have sacrificed happiness to duty."* To Rand, self-esteem was something quite different from the current Cult of Self-Esteem in that it had to be earned; it was, in fact, a result of one's status as a moral human being and not a precursor. It is interesting to note that her lover and follower Nathaniel Branden carved a career in psychotherapy out of this important aspect of human personality. Rand would find it characteristic to see that twisted into a false meaning in popularization in the same way that she portrayed Richard Halley's concerto twisted and cheapened into film music by Mort Liddy. Discuss each of these sacrifices in the light of Rand's exposition of philosophy, the concept of these as opposing poles, whether compromise is possible and how it may be attained.

• *"For centuries, the battle of morality was fought between those who claimed that your life belongs to God and those who claimed that it belongs to your neighbors – between those who preached that the good is self-sacrifice for the sake of ghosts in heaven and those who preached that the good is self-sacrifice for the sake of incompetents on earth. And no one came to say that your life belongs to you and that the good is to live it."* Once more, Rand has described her belief that the false doctrines of Church and State leave no room for the individual. To what extent is this a fair characterization?

• [from the mystics of spirit and the mystics of muscle] *"**Selfishness** – say both – is man's evil... **Sacrifice** – cry both – is the essence of morality, the highest virtue within man's reach... 'Sacrifice' does not mean the rejection of the worthless, but of the precious. 'Sacrifice' does not mean the rejection of the evil for the sake of the good, but of the good for the sake of the evil. 'Sacrifice' is the surrender of that which you value in favor of that which you don't... A sacrifice is the surrender of value. Full sacrifice is full surrender of all values."* This is, to say the least, a rather exceptional definition of "sacrifice." For Rand, the

232

exchange of something one values for something one values more does not qualify as sacrifice – a mother's exchange of her life for her child's, for example, a soldier's for his country. True to her individualist tendencies, she argues that it is the individual's decision as to what constitutes sacrifice. Discuss whether this definition is too restrictive, whether the sacrifice is invalidated at the behest of a third party instead of an individual's decision, and whether the definition of sacrifice is even valid.

- *"Walk into any college classroom and you will hear your professors teaching your children that man can be certain of nothing..."* This, outside of the confines of a course in philosophy, seems a bit dated. On the contrary, the modern problem is one of unwarranted certainty – to paraphrase Ronald Reagan, "It isn't what you don't know that is the problem, it's what you do know that isn't so." The modern classroom is plagued, not by a firm adherence to uncertainty as a principle, but unquestioning adherence to principles that suffer from a lack of uncertainty, from a lack of serious questioning. Unquestioned, these constitute a body of knowledge Rand would not differentiate from religious faith: multiculturalism, diversity, sustainability, to give three contemporary examples. Suggest others – patriotism, globalism, environmentalism – and discuss them in the light of Rand's insistence on objective truth.

- *"They proclaim that every man born is entitled to exist without labor and, the laws of reality to the contrary notwithstanding, is entitled to receive 'minimum sustenance' – his food, his clothes, his shelter – with no effort on his part, as his due and birthright."* This seems embarrassingly similar to the modern belief in entitlements. What are the foundations of an individual's call on society for any of these basics?

- *"There are two sides to every issue: one side is right and the other is wrong, but the middle is always evil."* Does Rand really mean "issue" here, or "logical proposition"? Discuss the difference between the two.

- *"...[L]earn to treat as the mark of a cannibal any man's **demand** for your help. To demand it is to claim that your life is **his** property – and loathsome as such a claim might be, there's something still more loathsome: your agreement."* Here Rand appears to reject the demand made by one individual upon another individual by virtue of their mutual membership in some sort of common collective. Was John Donne wrong, then, when he wrote that "No man is an island"? What are the limits of any individual's demand on another? At what point must that aid demanded be refused on principle?

- *"The doctrine that 'human rights' are superior to 'property rights' simply means that some human beings have the right to make property out of others..."* Where is there a conflict between property rights and human rights? What might it look like? To what degree are property rights, in fact, human rights?

- *"The only proper purpose of a government is to protect man's rights, which means: to protect him from physical violence... The only proper functions of a government: the police, to protect you from criminals; the army, to protect you from foreign invaders; and the courts, to settle disputes by rational rules, according to **objective** law."* Here perhaps we notice a similarity to the Preamble of the Constitution: "to ensure domestic tranquility, to provide for the common defense." But what does Rand mean by "objective" law?

- *"But a government that **initiates** the employment of force against men who had forced no one, the employment of armed compulsion against disarmed victims, is a*

234

nightmare infernal machine designed to annihilate morality... Such a government substitutes for morality the following rule of social conduct: you may do whatever you please to your neighbor, provided your gang is bigger than his." Gang, tribe...class? Political party? How close is this to a fair statement of the "politics of identity"? Is this the inevitable consequence of the source of political rights being vested in the collective rather than in the individual? Why should this be so?

- *"A country's political system is based upon its code of morality. We will rebuild America's system on the moral premise which had been its foundation..."* Here is the basis on which Rand has been labeled a conservative. Is it, in fact, accurate? Or is Rand simply using this to disguise her utopian scheme for the future under a mythical past? Is there even a difference, and if so, what is it?

- Had you been listening to the radio when all this happened, would you have listened to the entire speech, or would you have tuned out at some point? Would you have acted upon The Speech? What could you have done?

Chapter VIII: The Egoist

Synopsis

The reaction of the men in the studio is one of disbelief.

"It wasn't real, was it?"

"We seem to have heard it."

"We couldn't help it."

"We don't have to believe it, do we?"

Each question is a challenge to reality, not to the facts of The Speech. There is the panicked moment when Wesley Mouch fears that the playing of a march to fill dead air will lead people to believe that they authorized The Speech; Mr. Thompson, quicker than Mouch, counters:

"You damn fool!... Would you rather have the public think that we didn't?"

It's a point, actually – the issue now is control of a country roiling with revolution, and it's fairly clear that the current bunch isn't up to it. Thompson demands the return of normal broadcasting and no mention of The Speech. Chick Morrison orders a lock on the story in the press.

Eugene Lawson sobs in rage at what he has just heard.

"It's the most vicious speech ever made!"

Morrison doesn't think that people of refined spirit will listen to Galt's message. Tinky Holloway, who can't speak for labor, says that the workingman won't buy it. Emma Chalmers, who really can't speak for women, says it's no sale for women. Dr. Simon Pritchett, the nihilist philosopher who can't speak for science, says scientists won't accept it. Mouch thinks that Galt may be a friend of big business, and that prospect terrifies Mr. Mowen, both that Galt may be an inconvenient friend and the notion that big business could be characterized as having any friends at all. Dr. Floyd Ferris thinks that people are too dumb to understand it; he is, of course, assuming that people must understand the finer points of deontological ethics before they'll be affected by Galt's diatribe. It isn't the case. Unstable, even nonsense words, timed correctly, can be the pebbles that start landslides.

It is Fred Kinnan who brings them all back to earth with his statement about people not wanting to starve. But he will not help them by telling them what to do. The man who once demanded full control of the Equalization Board was after power, not the opportunity to lead. They are two very different things.

Dagny tells them they have no choice but to surrender because their future is one of total destruction. Thompson stalls Dagny, telling her he and the men need to evaluate the situation first.

But Dr. Stadler understands the situation, and after Dagny departs with Eddie, he urges them to murder Galt. They are taken aback, because despite Dagny's explanations, they really don't understand Galt at all. But they – Thompson, especially – do know a potential asset when they see one, someone who might be bribed to be a figurehead, someone who might act as a fall guy, someone who might even have an idea they'd consider worth trying. Thompson is correct, but not in the way he thinks. Will Galt deal? Yes, of course – but on his terms. And unfortunately for the Aristocracy of Pull, those terms specify its dissolution.

Stadler advises Thompson to follow Dagny; she has to be in league with Galt and his deserters. Thompson tells Mouch to put a tail on Dagny, and if she leads them to Galt, they must bring him in *alive*.

As Dagny and Eddie walk on empty sidewalks past abandoned shops through a city where the lights in buildings above the 25th floor are turned off, he tells her that he recognized the voice of John Galt as his Anonymous Rail Worker friend. She tells him not to seek Galt if he values the life of his friend. She promises him she won't desert. Things are falling apart rapidly now, and she is sure that the men of government will soon throw in the towel.

The media ask people not to be alarmed by The Speech but to see it as just one opinion. The country is silent until:

- Homes and factories are set ablaze by owners who disappear.

- A speaker at a political meeting in Cleveland is beaten by a mob when he accuses them of selfishness.

- A layabout brother accuses his working brother of selfishness and is beaten to a pulp.

- A woman who orders her child to give his best toy to the children of neighbors has her jaw broken by a bystander.

- Chick Morrison's whistle stop tour ends with his train being stoned by the populace.

- Thompson has the government sending continuous radio messages to John Galt without effect.

- The Unification Board tries to fill management jobs with little success.

- Official broadcasts tell the nation that the government will soon work with John Galt, and stories are spread by Morrison that Galt is already in Washington conferring with government leaders.

- America's industrial base grinds toward collapse.

- Hyperinflation erupts.

- Covered wagons travel by night to avoid gangs of raiders, lights appear in distant buildings not known to exist, but soldiers don't dare investigate.

- The Sign of the Dollar begins to appear on abandoned buildings and government installations.

Rearden Steel is nationalized as the property of a deserter. People from the Boyle faction and Meigs faction fail to get the plant to produce, so they settle for looting the company and shipping its physical plant to friends in Europe and Latin America. An old and loyal worker who remembers Hank Rearden finally burns the plant to the ground to avenge his boss.

Thompson asks Dagny what to do; she tells him to start the process of decontrolling people and removing taxes. Thompson balks and tells Dagny he hopes that Galt is still alive. The government is breaking into factions, and one faction wants to introduce official state terror and mass murder in order to force the people's obedience.

In a fantastically irresponsible lapse of self-discipline, Dagny seeks Galt herself. It is actually a little out of character, but smart people sometimes do disastrously stupid things, and this is very, very stupid indeed. At least Eddie Willers, for all his lack of discretion, did not know to whom he was betraying them all. Dagny does, and as a conspirator Dagny Taggart must now rank among the most hapless amateurs in all of modern literature. Rand offers us no real explanation for this other than her loneliness. She lasted only ten days. One sympathizes, but in truth it is quite simply her worst moment in the novel.

So Dagny takes a 4 AM walk through a Manhattan that looks like Starnesville to find the apartment of John Galt. Based on the Taggart personnel records, she knocks on the registered address of John Galt, an apartment in a run-down building. He answers, sweeps her in and kisses her longingly. Dagny thinks they are safe, but John disabuses her of that notion; they have about thirty minutes before the midnight knock on the door. They will torture her in his presence if they realize the link between them, and he'd rather commit suicide than place her in that kind of jeopardy. Dagny must feign sympathy with the government, and John gives her the alibi she must use as she turns him in for the reward. He gives her a tour of the apartment he has lived in for the past twelve years, including his lab, run by his motor.

Their brief moment of happiness is interrupted by the knock. Three soldiers and a bureaucrat enter, and Dagny turns Galt in to the authorities. But the civilian says his job is to greet Galt in the name of the people and convey him to the national leadership. Their attempt to get into Galt's lab reveals a room full of white dust; his self-destruct mechanism has done its job.

Galt is ensconced in the Wayne-Falkland, guarded by troops and government agents; there are public statements that he has joined the government. Thompson assures Galt he is not a prisoner, although he can't leave, and offers him Wesley Mouch's job. Galt says that if Thompson is serious, he will abolish all income taxes immediately. Thompson bridles at this, and Galt tells him that he cannot function as economic czar, telling people to be free at the point of a gun. If Thompson wants him to sit at a desk and issue directives drawn up by the Head of State, he will comply, but he doesn't have any ideas on how to fix the current system other than to abolish it.

Chick Morrison notes that the people are not reacting to promises that John Galt will deliver prosperity; they no longer believe anything the government says. Mouch, Morrison and Kinnan fail to make any headway with Galt, although Kinnan understands him perfectly. Eugene Lawson screams that he can't talk to Galt.

"I don't want to have to believe it!"

Ferris subtly suggests torture, and Thompson shuts him up.

Although the government has announced the John Galt Plan, things are deteriorating rapidly.

- South Dakota farmers are burning government buildings and the homes of the wealthy.

- California has degenerated into civil war between Emma Chalmers' People's Party and the Back to God Party.

- War has broken out between Georgia and Alabama over a factory.

Thompson asks Dagny for advice, and she plays along with Galt's strategy of making Thompson believe she is on the government's side. What Galt wants, she explains, is the whole earth; those are the stakes. She convinces Thompson to let Galt see the confidential reports on how the nation is crumbling. It is two-edged advice: Thompson thinks it will impel Galt to help them, she knows it will only steel his resolve.

Arriving at her apartment, Dagny receives a note from Francisco giving her instructions on how to help and a phone number by which to reach him. We are as relieved as Dagny that a competent conspirator has finally come along to take charge, and Francisco is both a master dissimulator and a man of action. The time for dissimulation is almost over; soon it will be the time for force.

Galt meets with Thompson and Jim Taggart, who gives a long lecture on selfishness and accuses Galt of egoism. Morrison hands Galt petitions from schoolchildren, cripples, ministers and mothers begging Galt to tell the country what to do. Dr. Ferris lectures Galt on moral responsibility, suggesting that the government may order children and the elderly to be put to death for lack of food; this so enrages Thompson that he ejects Ferris from the room. Galt asks to speak to Dr. Stadler.

Twice in the novel Galt has been described as an *"egoist,"* hence the chapter title, and Rand does so with a precision of meaning that sends us to the dictionary to discover the difference between the term and its more prevalent cousin, "egotist." An egoist is, in this sense, an individual for whom self-interest, rational or otherwise, is the basis for morality, which perfectly encapsulates the Objectivist ideal. An egotist is someone with an exaggerated sense of self who expresses it by self-aggrandizement. Although the two terms overlap there are subtle shades of difference. Rand's code demands the former and sees the latter as a weakness. That's quite a bit of mileage to get out of a single letter of the alphabet.

Eddie tells Dagny that a failed attack by raiders on the Taggart Bridge over the Mississippi is not the only problem; a faction in the California civil war is holding Taggart trains for ransom in San Francisco. Eddie decides to fly to San Francisco on an Army plane to take charge of the effort to resolve the crisis. He finally admits his feelings to Dagny, and she tells him she has known for years.

We come at last to a climactic meeting – philosophically speaking – between Galt and his old teacher, Dr. Robert Stadler. The old academic delivers an apologia that is rife with self-justification and hostility toward the man who has held to the standards that Stadler taught and betrayed. Galt doesn't have to say a word to leave Stadler a trembling puddle of self-realization and self-loathing.

Galt's voice had the same unbending austerity as his eyes: "You have said everything I wanted to say to you."

Mr. Thompson tries one last time to create a propaganda vehicle that will quell the rising violence. It is a plot device that Rand has used three times now for dramatic effect, and frankly it's getting a bit well-worn: first Dagny, in her abortive debate with Bertram Scudder over the merits of Rearden Metal, then the radio broadcast in which she declared her affair with Hank, and then the broadcast that ended up as *"This Is John Galt Speaking."* Now there is this one, in which the country's new savior, John Galt himself, is to be introduced as the figurehead of a new government.

Morrison arrives with a valet to get Galt prepared for an official dinner in formal attire. At the ballroom, to the applause of hundreds, Galt sits at the center of the official table; even Dagny is there, although Stadler is absent. The event is covered live on radio and television, and a newsman announces the inauguration of the John Galt Plan for Peace, Prosperity and Profit. The government men make speeches in praise of Galt and the plan, but when it's Galt's turn to speak, he has one simple message:

"Get the hell out of my way!"

It's not the message Mr. Thompson was looking for, but anyone who heard Galt's polemic on the radio knows exactly what he means, whether they understood deontological ethics or not. He isn't playing along. They're on their own. And at long last, the main course for the hungry looters will be the government itself.

Discussion Topics

- Only Eugene Lawson attacks the content of The Speech, and he does so hysterically. The others don't question the content, but the nature of reality itself. What is going on here, and how did supposedly rational men reach this pass?

- Dr. Ferris has no problem with mass murder to get people to obey or to eliminate the "useless eaters" of society when food gets scarce. What kind of government would allow such things to be discussed in a civilized century?

- In the absence of the people's ability to affect government policy, they resort to "politics by other means", i.e., assassination, insurrection, secession and civil war. Since 1865 the national government has insisted on the last word as to the means of violence. Vainglorious chest-beating aside, how can the people resist a government with modern armed forces, weapons of mass destruction, drones, and the will to use them against its own citizens?

Chapter IX: The Generator

Synopsis

Dr. Robert Stadler flees New York by car, listening to the broadcast from the Wayne-Falkland Hotel. Following John Galt's one sentence, the air goes dead, and every radio station on the dial is off the air. Stadler has taken all of four days to reach Iowa, an indication that travel is now next to impossible in a disintegrating country. Where before we've had travel impossibly compressed in time – aircraft, for example, appear to display supersonic speed over the great white areas on the map that compose the American Midwest – here we have a bit of reality, and for Stadler it isn't pretty.

The Aristocracy of Pull isn't having much luck convincing their prisoner Galt to save the country, or rather to do so on their terms, which leave the present ruling class in place. They don't understand Galt, but they *do* understand how to get people to do what they wish, and they know that Stadler means something to Galt. By the time they find out what that is, Stadler realizes they will kill him, hence his panicked dash for the power that possession of his invention will confer.

The motive? His mind had repeated insistently that his motive was terror of Mr. Thompson's gang, that he was not safe among them any longer, that his plan was a practical necessity... To seize control, to rule...there is no other way to live on earth...

He isn't the only one to think that way.

Harmony City, the home of Project X, is a beehive of activity, populated by armed men and armored trucks. He is challenged at the gate by a guard who wants to know if Stadler is one of the old or one of the new. Stadler blusters his way past the guards into the mushroom-shaped building and finds that discipline is in short supply among the paramilitary group holding the site. An officer asks if Stadler is a Friend of the People, and he says he is he best friend the people have ever had. Identifying himself as the inventor of the Xylophone, he is taken through the building – and realizes that somebody has already put his plan into motion. His overbearing manner gets him in to see *"The Boss"*, who turns out to be Cuffy Meigs!

Drunk, sweating and pacing restlessly, Meigs issues orders to establish the People's Commonwealth in Harmony City, now to be known as Meigsville. He is going to hold the region for ransom to the tune of half a million dollars for every five thousand people. If the money is not delivered by the next morning, he will activate the Xylophone.

Meigs is delighted to find that Stadler, who says he is going to take control, has come with neither weapons nor soldiers to back him up. The notion of such a thug in possession of his brainchild rouses Stadler's last scrap of self-deception.

"Do you think I'll let you cash in on my life? Do you think it's for you that I...that I sold – " He did not finish...

But he did. Sold, indeed. Only in his world one doesn't get value received for value offered. That's only true where the terms of exchange are Galt's, not Meigs'. In the world Stadler has chosen there are only looters who have, at last, run out of things to steal.

And Stadler himself has run out of time. Project Xylophone turns out to be a formidable weapon indeed, and in an effort to demonstrate that he is as good a man as any of those *"dime-a-dozen"* technicians, Meigs throws the wrong lever. It destroys the entire site. Every standing structure within a radius of a hundred miles disintegrates. It also slices the Taggart Bridge in half, which is decidedly inconvenient for the first six cars of a passenger train that end up in the Mississippi as a result. Quite a swan song for the weapon of mass destruction that takes with it, in its death throes, both its creator and its usurper.

The significance of this is not lost on the reader. That bridge was the one thing that had kept Dagny from shrugging herself. It's gone now, in the blink of an eye, destroyed by a jackbooted ignoramus pulling a lever, a fitting end for Stadler who has, in the final analysis, sold out to precisely such a man.

At the Wayne-Falkland, Mr. Thompson orders Galt back to his room under heavy guard. Chick Morrison resigns and flees.

"He [Chick Morrison] has a hide-out all stocked for himself in Tennessee," said Tinky Holloway reflectively, as if he, too, had taken a similar precaution and were now wondering whether the time had come...

It has come – and passed. They're trapped unless Ferris can buy them some breathing space. Ferris suggests that the State Science Institute has a tool that just might help – the Ferris Persuader. What is it that they intend to persuade Galt to do?

"We've got to...MAKE HIM...take over... We've got to force him to rule," said Mouch in the tone of a sleepwalker.

The notion of a shackled Philosopher-King is nearly too ridiculous for fiction were it not for the fact that Rand understands her villains very well, and what Mouch has in mind actually does make twisted sense.

"He has to...take over...and save the system."

Galt is to perpetuate the very system that keeps them in power despite the fact that they can create nothing, produce nothing, but merely confiscate and redistribute all the efforts of men and women greater than themselves. At last the parasites realize their peril: in all the world, this host is the last one, and when it perishes, so do they. Mouch still clings desperately to their original faulty premise: given that all of capitalism is theft, who would not want to take his place as the Prince of Thieves?

Ferris, however, has fewer illusions. Galt will be a cooperative figurehead for as long as he's useful. He tells Eugene Lawson to get the nation's broadcast stations ready for a speech by John Galt in three hours.

Dagny leaves the hotel, runs to a phone booth and calls Francisco, updating him on the government's plans. She is relieved to hear a reasonable voice after the madness she has heard in the mouths of the teetering ruling class. They have been indiscreet enough to declare their intentions in front of her, and she wastes no time informing Galt's friends. We are as relieved as Dagny to hear Francisco, at last, become what he really is. Francisco tells her to go home, change her clothes, pack, and meet him in forty minutes two blocks east of the Taggart Terminal.

She drops by the office just in time to hear that the Taggart Bridge has collapsed.

"Miss Taggart!" cried the chief engineer. "We don't know what to do!"

Dagny leaps to her desk like a prizefighter at the sound of the bell, picks up the phone – and then stops.

The receiver clicked softly back into its cradle. "I don't, either," she answered. In a moment, she knew it was over.

It is the moment: Dagny has finally shrugged. But there is one final bit of symbolism she expresses defiantly before the statue of her heroic ancestor. Seizing her lipstick and...

...smiling at the marble face of [Nat Taggart], the man who would have understood, she drew a large sign of the dollar on the pedestal under his feet.

It is the signal, now useless, that she agreed upon to mark her final break.

As she reaches the rendezvous point, she notices that New York is in a state of panic. Francisco reaches her on foot, and she recites Galt's Oath: *"I swear – by my life and my love of it – that I will never live for the sake of another man, nor ask another man to live for mine."* They leave together.

The home of Project F is a small building, most of whose space is underground, that sits away from the State Science Institute's main building in New Hampshire. Sixteen men guard the building, oblivious to what is going on in the basement. Wesley Mouch, Jim Taggart and Dr. Floyd Ferris sit while a naked John

Galt is strapped and wired to a mechanism much like a generator, the Ferris Persuader.

Ferris orders Galt to become dictator and take control of the present system; Galt's response is silence. Ferris orders the mechanic to turn up the current, and Galt arches in pain. They torture him in various combinations of current applied in different ways to sundry places. Wesley Mouch breaks, begging for it to end, lest Galt's death end in their own deaths. Ferris wants more than obedience, he wants *acceptance*.

Then the generator breaks down. No one knows how to fix it – except Galt. The mechanic flees the room in horror as Galt laughs. Jim leaps to the generator and attempts to fix it; it is at that moment that James Taggart falls apart – because he sees what lies at the end of that fogbound alley, his hatred of existence. Jim turns catatonic, and his friends remove him from the room. They tell Galt they intend to come back.

The Torture of John Galt

This is the strangest scene in the entire novel. It is at once the consummation of Rand's view of sexuality among the elite as a form of power exchange, an expression of the supremacy of mind over flesh, and a reformulation of one of the oldest jokes about engineers in the entire body of human comedy.

Nothing is spared Galt in the way of modesty, although modesty is, one suspects, a quality more desirable in lesser men. He is stripped naked and spread-eagled on a leather-covered table, and Rand's single concession to decency is that electrodes are attached to wrists, shoulders and ankles instead of the more customary locations. We are treated to a two-page description of his physical circumstances that for the era borders on the pornographic. Rand here is very much on the edge of outrage and reveling in it.

One is tempted to caution the reader not to try this at home. The Ferris Persuader runs electrical current through, as Rand describes it, the lungs, which is in real application across the heart as well. *"Safe voltages"* only, according to her, although there is in fact no such thing, and it is amperage and not voltage that kills in

248

any case. That aside, Galt is in for a remarkably unpleasant few minutes, spurred on by Jim Taggart in a rather disturbing sadistic frenzy. Even Wesley Mouch is alarmed.

"What's the matter with you?" gasped Mouch, catching a glimpse of Taggart's face while a current was twisting Galt's body: Taggart was staring at in intently, yet his eyes seemed glazed and dead, but around that inanimate stare the muscles of his face were pulled into an obscene caricature of enjoyment...

Even by modern standards this is pretty strong stuff. The room reeks of sweat, sadism and homoeroticism. Jim is revealed as finally having crossed the line into the insanity whose borders he has spent the novel exploring. One must wonder what the recently deceased Cherryl would have thought of her husband and conclude that her watery grave constituted a kindness of sorts.

We are relieved – and the novel remains publishable – by the fortunate malfunctioning of the device, specifically its generator, reminding us once again of the chapter title.

And so to the joke. One must wonder if Rand had heard it, or something like it, or simply came across its expression of irony all by herself. It is simply that a true engineer – and Galt is certainly that – reacts to this situation in character, which is to see it as a technical challenge. One early version of it had an engineer condemned to the guillotine watch two of his predecessors released by a malfunction in the dropping of the blade, and when his turn came, he pointed and said, "Oh, there, I see what the problem is!"

And so Galt tells them in cold detail how to fix the instrument of torture to which he is affixed. What results isn't laughter, it is flight on the part of the crew and the final descent on the part of Jim Taggart into madness. He has, at last, noticed the monster in the mirror.

"No..." he moaned, staring at that vision, shaking his head to escape it. "No...no..."

"Yes," said Galt.

So much for Jim. While they escort his quivering remnants from the room they caution the guards to guard carefully,

...the living generator [that] was left tied by the side of the dead one.

That is Galt, of course. He remains, bound, naked – Rand has taken considerable trouble to remind us of the point – and triumphant. And his friends are on the way.

Discussion Topics

- In Starnesville, there were no thugs on horseback to claim the town as a fiefdom. Now Cuffy Meigs attempts to claim anything within a hundred miles of the Xylophone as his fiefdom, beating Dr. Stadler, who had the same idea. What can we expect along these lines as economic and societal disintegration progress, and from which quarter?

- Dagny's act of shrugging is the key moment of the novel. What was the tipping point that made her finally take Galt's Oath?

- Dr. Ferris wants more than the mechanics of John Galt working for the looters' government, he wants acceptance. He wants the Sanction of the Victim. Why?

Chapter X: In the Name of the Best Within Us

Synopsis

Dagny arrives at the Project F building, silencer-equipped automatic in hand. She engages in a battle of wits with a rather unintelligent guard who appears to be more of an insensate bipedal mammal than a reasoning human being. He knows who she is, knows she is a friend of Head of State Thompson, but refuses to admit her to the building because Dr. Ferris has ordered that no one be admitted. She answers by pulling out a gun. The guard is caught between two masters, the Head of State and the Executive Director, and he can't decide which one to follow. She puts him out of his misery by firing a bullet from the silenced gun into his heart.

Calmly and impersonally, she, who would have hesitated to fire at an animal, pulled the trigger and fired straight at the heart of a man who had wanted to exist without the responsibility of consciousness.

It does seem a bit harsh, inasmuch as three of the four guards are bound and gagged in the nearby bushes, courtesy of Francisco's raiding party. Nor does Francisco need to kill the next guard who challenges them, drawing his own silenced pistol and shooting the guard's gun out of his hand like a hero in a Forties Hollywood western. The firearms-familiar reader now risks ocular damage from rolling his eyes, but the worst of it is still before us.

Hank Rearden joins them, and once again they attempt to talk their way past guards who are as befuddled as the reader at the vision of three industrialists – the guards do recognize them – attempting to bludgeon them with logic. The guards are no match for the brilliant repartee of our heroes, but unfortunately the latter are no closer to their goal despite a clear rhetorical victory. In the ensuing gunplay, force guided by reason prevails, aided by the third of the Four Musketeers, Ragnar Danneskjøld, who swings like the buccaneer he is on a rope tied to a conveniently sited tree limb, crashes through a nearby plate glass window without a

251

scratch and then shoots one of the guards as another guard shoots his own chief. In the melee Rearden has received a bullet to his shoulder that is bleeding heroically, but – what else would it be? – is merely a flesh wound.

This, to modern sensibilities, is painful to read. If there is a single mid-century Hollywood cliché that Rand has kept out of this weird, bloodlessly homicidal scene, it is a singing cowboy and a dancing horse. To recapitulate, despite the presence of a small army of armed men waiting outside, we have four philosopher generals with side-arms executing a raid on a fortified enemy camp, whose occupants unaccountably decline to treat their hostage as a hostage or at least to put a merciful bullet into his recumbent figure.

Galt is unharmed, more or less, and Rand has one last opportunity to remind the reader that he is naked before they dress him. And off he goes, assisted by Francisco and Dagny, to the refuge of Francisco's airplane, which takes its place in a formation of airplanes, Galt's rescuing army, all headed back to Colorado with their chief safely in hand.

Galt saw the thin red trickle running from Rearden's shoulder down his chest.

"Thank you, Hank," he said.

Rearden smiled. "I will repeat what you said when I thanked you on our first meeting: 'If you understand that I acted for my own sake, you will know that no gratitude is required.'"

"I will repeat," said Galt, "the answer you gave me: 'That is why I thank you.'"

This dialogue, given the circumstances, is worse than implausible; it is mind-numbingly awful. In simple point of fact, Rand is out of her element, and here it shows. This would have been reparable had the hard-nosed editor she did *not* employ sent it back blue-penciled with a peremptory demand for a rewrite. That did not happen, and readers already skeptical of Rand's work are left with a bad taste in their mouths that is unjustified by the preceding 1100 pages of strong and occasionally brilliant writing.

Fortunately, we are not done, lest this difficult interlude threaten to drag the entire novel down with it. They speak of a time of peace to come. Danneskjøld has hidden his warship, which is to be converted to an ocean liner when circumstances permit, stating that this was his last act of violence. His men are building homes in Galt's Gulch where they will wait out the coming storm. For a storm there will be, and all is a very long way yet from the utopia to come.

There were not many lights on the earth below. The countryside was an empty black sheet, with a few occasional flickers in the windows of some government structures, and the trembling glow of candles in the windows of thriftless homes. Most of the rural population had long since been reduced to the life of those ages when artificial light was an exorbitant luxury, and a sunset put an end to human activity. The towns were like scattered puddles, left behind by a receding tide, still holding some precious drops of electricity, but drying out in a desert of rations, quotas, controls, and power-conservation rules.

And just that quickly Rand's writing is once again not merely competent, but prescient. It is a vision of our own "sustainable" future under our own looters and moochers.

It took them a moment to realize that the panic had reached the power stations – and that the lights of New York had gone out.

Dagny gasped. "Don't look down!" Galt ordered sharply.

She turned to Galt. He was watching her face, as if he had been following her thoughts. She saw the reflection of her smile in his. "It's the end," she said. "It's the beginning," he answered.

Had Rand written "The End" at that point, no one would have faulted her. It is closure of sorts, the logical end to the narrative, a

253

finish and the promise of a new beginning. But it isn't going to be quite that easy. There is one more thing, one final tying of a loose thread that saves the consummation of the novel from treacly embarrassment and reignites the philosophical and emotional struggle she has taken so much trouble to stir in the minds of her readers. There is, at the last, not exactly an answer to the question posed so many chapters ago concerning whether there are innocent victims in the act of Atlas shrugging, but an image that suggests an answer. There is the fate of Eddie Willers.

A civilization is collapsing, and the lights of New York are darkened. The people fleeing the dead cities on foot, or using the last drops of gasoline in their empty tanks, abandon the useless hulks of industrial civilization as they draw their last gasps by the side of the road and re-enter the pre-industrial world that is the penance men must pay for permitting the parasites to ruin them. Galt and Francisco were right, and Dagny was wrong – she and Rearden did not, in the end, *"hold out to the last wheel and the last syllogism."*

But Eddie Willers did. While the others were experiencing moral epiphanies and waving firearms around like magic wands, Eddie was plugging away doggedly at keeping Taggart Transcontinental, the *"artery of the country,"* pulsing feebly. He had fixed the problem in San Francisco, obtaining immunity for the railroad from three different factions in the civil war tearing California apart. Now, without warning, the eastbound *Comet* stops abruptly in the middle of the Arizona desert as the locomotive fails.

To everyone's shock, a train of covered wagons appears out of the night. It had left California's Imperial Valley due to the civil war and the seizure of crops, and had headed east by night to avoid the government's minions. The wagon master offers to take the train's passengers on board for a fee and informs Eddie that the bridge over the Mississippi is gone. Eddie watches as the train's passengers and crew leave the *Comet* for the wagon train. And there he sits on a dead train headed for New York over a bridge that no longer exists. It's over. The artery is severed, the continent with it. Yet, unbelievably, courageously, Eddie will not give up.

Dagny! – he was crying to a twelve-year-old girl in a sunlit clearing of the woods – in the name of the best within us, I must now start this train!

When he found that he had collapsed on the floor of the cab and knew that there was nothing he could do here any longer, he rose and he climbed down the ladder... He stood still and, in the enormous silence, he heard the rustle of tumbleweeds stirring in the darkness, like the chuckle of an invisible army made free to move when the Comet was not. He heard a sharper rustle close by – and he saw the small gray shape of a rabbit rise on its haunches to sniff at the steps of a car of the Taggart Comet. With a jolt of murderous fury, he lunged in the direction of the rabbit, as if he could defeat the advance of the enemy in the person of that tiny gray form. The rabbit darted off into the darkness – but he knew that the advance was not to be defeated.

Then he collapsed across the rail and lay sobbing at the foot of the engine, with the beam of a motionless headlight above him going off into a limitless night.

This piece of lyrical, desolate beauty is from the same pen that thrashed so clumsily in the beginning of the chapter. That is all we know of the fate of Eddie Willers.

At the collapse of d'Anconia Copper, Francisco took his best people off to Galt's Gulch. At the end of Rearden Steel, Hank did the same. Ragnar Danneskjøld's crewmembers are building their own homes there in the shelter of the valley. But Dagny's very best lies abandoned on the rails in the Arizona desert. It is a jarring, tragic and enigmatic image. Its place here as the final chord of this monolithic novel is far from accidental. Eddie's last, desperate cry is, after all, the title of Rand's final chapter.

What are we to make of this? Rand and her interpreters have not provided a satisfactory answer. That may lie in the duality of Eddie's last decision. It was at once a gesture of stubborn courage – *"don't let it go!"* – and an act of surrender, a decision not to fight the next battle. It was both an invocation of self – *"in the name of the best within us"* – and a denial. Eddie was, throughout, living

255

for the woman and the railroad he loved and not for himself; to Rand that is a cardinal sin. If there were a character flaw in Eddie sufficient to account for his abandonment, perhaps it is that. What is clear is that Rand is suggesting the inevitable fate of the second-tier producers in the absence of their betters. These too are the innocent who must suffer when Atlas shrugs.

Nevertheless, the more romantic among us must hope for that speck on the horizon that grows steadily into the shape of Dagny's airplane, touching down on the sand to lift her loyal and loving childhood friend to safety, to that place down at the second table in Valhalla that he has earned in blood. For the sound of that distant engine we wait in vain. And we think the less of Dagny and yes, of Rand herself, for the silence.

There is a coda to this as there is to all works of such a titanic construction. It is in the echoes of Richard Halley's Fifth Concerto, the Concerto of Deliverance, through the winter landscape of Galt's Gulch.

The lights of the valley fell in glowing patches on the snow still covering the ground. There were shelves of snow on the granite ledges and on the heavy limbs of the pines. But the naked branches of the birch trees had a faintly upward thrust, as if in confident promise of the coming leaves of spring.

The principals are in a similar state: Mulligan working on a plan of investments to make the phoenix rise from the ashes, Kay Ludlow contemplating a battered case of film makeup, Ragnar Danneskjøld poring over his Aristotle, Francisco and Hank and Ellis Wyatt chortling over the prospect of bargaining with Dagny for transportation in the world to come. In his library, Judge Narragansett is amending the Constitution, excising those contradictions *"that had once been the cause of its destruction."* And in their place he adds a new clause that might be the topic for a furious controversy:

"Congress shall make no law abridging the freedom of production and trade..."

It is a parting gift from Ayn Rand, a grateful immigrant, and were something like it to be enacted in reality, the world would indeed look very different. Rand, the radical, the rabble-rouser, the arrogant, difficult, infuriating author, has dropped one last mind-bomb. And she has, to close, one last cheery expression of defiance.

They could not see the world beyond the mountains, there was only a void of darkness and rock, but the darkness was hiding the ruins of a continent... But far in the distance, on the edge of the earth, a small flame was waving in the wind, the defiantly stubborn flame of Wyatt's Torch, twisting, being torn and regaining its hold, not to be uprooted or extinguished...

"The road is cleared," said Galt. "We are going back to the world."

He raised his hand and over the desolate earth he traced in space the sign of the dollar.

Are they, then, headed back so soon? Is this the next winter or a dozen winters later? We do not know, and we are left to wonder just how bad it has gotten in the world beyond the mountains, and for how long, to make it possible for a world-wide renaissance to be born from a hidden valley in the mountains of Colorado. But seeds do turn into forests, after all. In fact, they are the only things that do. And these are just the people to plant them.

Discussion Topics

- Catholics and Orthodox Christians cross themselves at the beginning of prayer in a ritual known as the Sign of the Cross; the Cross is the preeminent symbol of all branches of Christianity. So it is with Rand. The Sign of the Dollar appears on their cigarettes. It appears in solid gold at Galt's Gulch. It is scrawled by guerrilla warriors on government buildings as America frays and falls apart. At the very end, John Galt, as the founder of the new religion of Objectivism, makes the Sign of the Dollar as a benediction as he prepares with his saints to return to earth in a second coming. Rand, the atheist, has certainly not shrunk from religious symbolism in the body of *Atlas Shrugged*: soul, virtue, sin, temptation, fall and redemption. To what degree is the novel dependent on these theological concepts? To what degree is Rand's philosophy?

- What will happen after the book ends? Will America accept the new paradigm and remodel itself on Objectivist principles? Will there be a second civil war? Can the disintegration be stopped? *Should* it be stopped? Will Galt win? What will America look like, and how will it get there?

Coda: Ten Years After

What does happen after Atlas shrugs? Ayn Rand preferred not to advance the story much beyond Galt's ceremonial drawing of the Sign of the Dollar, probably wisely, inasmuch as post-apocalyptic fiction was as yet a sparsely populated field. Narrative in *Atlas Shrugged* was only a secondary object anyway.

We can speculate, but exact models turn out to be surprisingly few. The collapse of central government in post-Shrug America suggests the fall of the Western Roman Empire, and Rand herself alluded to the Dark Ages during Galt's speech, although hers was a screenwriter's understanding of history, his an engineer's, and their apparent conception of the Dark Ages bore very little resemblance to the real thing.

There are significant differences, however, between the two scenarios. For one thing, technology in the real world is more pervasive and persistent than we are given to believe in the novel; for another, the Roman Empire exhibited nothing like the capitalist infrastructure of pre-Shrug America, and that is likely to show a persistence of its own. Banking, credit, deficit spending and widespread economic depression had to wait until the Renaissance to take a form that would be recognizable to a banker such as Midas Mulligan. That infrastructure will be far easier to rebuild than it was to invent in the first place. Pieces of it – local banks, for example – might not disappear at all.

More contemporary models of collapse are not without their own difficulties. That of Rhodesia/Zimbabwe, for example, offers insights into survival among the ruins of a people dependent on a past surplus no longer being generated in the present. It is a useful enough model but for the fact that its continuation is now entirely dependent on outside sources that serve to prevent, or cushion, complete economic collapse. No such outside agency will be available to a post-Shrug America; about that Rand is quite specific. Short of an invasion by wealthy and benevolent extraterrestrials, we'd be on our own.

The Day After

Let us start, then, by listing the things we have been told in the novel and extrapolating from there. The security doors on Galt's Gulch have clanged shut, and we may assume that there is very little in the way of ingress and egress. New York fell quickly. The rest of the country has been pretty much picked clean of potential Gulchers. For a time, the Gulch lies inert, developing inwardly like a chick in an egg, presenting an egg's blank face to the outside world.

Central government collapsed within the novel. Government, the economy, the raising of food – and children, a topic Rand avoids with the assiduity of a vampire to garlic – transportation and education: all these things localize in the sense that electricity did in one of the last chapter's lovelier metaphors. Rand likened it to a stream stopped and turned stagnant, evaporating and leaving little puddles here and there. She actually can write like that when she cares to make the effort.

So what we have is a constellation of little communities more or less self-sufficient, stuck in a pre-industrial state of technology and relating to their neighbors very little. We saw this in Starnesville, Wisconsin. As far as they are able, they will subsist on the surplus created by their industrial antecedents; we are reminded, comically, of the mayor of Rome's possession of a particularly luxurious shower stall culled from the ruins of the Twentieth Century Motor Company. They will not use electricity unless situated at some sort of natural source: a waterfall, perhaps, or a coal mine, and there only until the generators fail. Replacement parts are no longer being produced.

They will not use cash. Rand described the likely devolution of exchange toward a barter economy in Starnesville. It is not fantasy. Paper money is, after all, no better than a promise. Even when it is backed by gold, it is only good insofar as the guarantor's promise of exchange for precious metal is to be trusted. Backed by nothing at all, it is quickly meaningless, printed in whatever amount the printer thinks can be a temporarily convincing illusion of value. In Zimbabwe we have seen this classic progression from trusted currency to toilet paper, a slide based on the slow realization that no central bank would exchange it for anything of value but would happily continue generating the joke. It wasn't even very good toilet paper.

It is the fact of backing, and not sentiment toward the backers, that is critical. Certainly the bulk of communities would retain a commitment to the dollar not only out of nostalgia but out of sheer necessity for some medium of exchange. Sentiment and custom are, however, insufficient to run an economy in the long run, as holders of Confederate dollars finally came to concede.

However, the necessity for a medium of exchange would not simply evaporate. Local currencies would arise, just as they did during the early days of America, each backed by the issuers' physical possession of gold. The micro-economy of Galt's Gulch works on this literal physical presence, although the notion of making a financial transaction of the magnitude its denizens are accustomed to by hauling sacks of the stuff around is as impractical in fiction as it proved in fact. There is, by all reports, a small forklift moving weighty piles of gold from one alcove to another within the bowels of the New York Fed to reflect financial transactions between countries. That has an atavistic charm to it, but one can quickly discern that it probably would be outside the capabilities of the common investor.

And thus there is no central government and no central currency. That would be high on the "to do" list of the nascent federal government on that debatably happy day when it once again coalesces around the political ambitions of its sovereign states. In the new federal government presumptive, the currency would most certainly be backed by gold if Rand's entire thesis is to be followed. The opportunities for thievery inherent will not be new, but they will at least be different.

But for now we have the Dark Ages, the real ones, not the Randian caricature. Civilization will contract to the limits of lamplight and torch, of horse and oxcart. And incidentally, we have seen covered wagons emptying towns at the close of *Atlas Shrugged*, but where, one wonders, did the drovers and the teamsters find the necessary livestock? One does not simply harness a riding animal and expect magic to happen. If the farming economy is bereft of the internal combustion engine, who or what will pull the plows?   This has starvation written all over it, and it is one additional reason why the farming areas will produce only that which is sufficient to their own needs.   They won't have a choice until Wyatt's wells start producing again and Hammond's engines roar to life once more.

There is the difficulty of Galt's motor.   For Rand it was merely a plot device, a contrivance intended to prove Galt's competence as an engineer and to symbolize the benefit withheld from the world as a consequence of his strike.   However, it is, in addition, a rather prodigious piece of technology, and we must do our best to make allowance for its likely influence on the post-Shrug world.

What little we know of the actual workings of the motor implies essentially free, unlimited energy for its possessors.   Lest we get too carried away with the implications we must remind ourselves of the promises made for nuclear energy in its nascent stages: "Electricity too cheap to meter," to give but one overstated example.   Taken literally, the notion of infinite free energy forever would be transformational, to say the least.   It would be less on the order of the transition of steam to electricity and more on the order of the discovery of fire.   There Galt might be regarded as Prometheus indeed.

But Rand was not writing hard science fiction, and hence we must apply a brake of skepticism if we are accurately to anticipate the direction of the post-Shrug world that Rand would have us believe is informed more by a new moral code than by technology. Let us propose, therefore, that there are reasonable limitations on Galt's motor, at the very least the notion that such static electricity as we are accustomed to observe striking the earth in the form of lightning must be produced by some sort of atmospheric dynamic – one does not expect to see lightning out of a clear, blue sky. Rather than supplanting all other known sources of power, Galt's motor will take its rightful place as an honorable competitor.   That seems more in keeping with Rand's sentiments in any case.

But we may be certain that the Galt motor will play in the events to come.   For now the Gulchers have sole possession.   It is to be remembered, though, that once this technology becomes public, the days of sole possession are likely to be numbered, especially in the absence of any sort of intellectual property protection that was formerly supplied by the federal government. We recall that one of the last acts of that government was to expropriate everything formerly protected by patent law. That government is no more.

Thus the state of the country after Atlas shrugs. It isn't, nor does Rand intend it to be, markedly different from that of the United States of 1840 or so. It is to be remembered that the real-life Taggart Bridge, the Rock Island Mississippi River bridge, was not constructed until 1856. Up to that point even the railroads were necessarily regional. And regional political and economic structures are the most likely pattern one might expect from a post-Shrug America.

Would these independent communities retain a loyalty to the government of Mr. Thompson and Cuffy Meigs? Hardly. Would they retain a loyalty toward that social contract that is the Constitution, buttressed by the memory of the past prosperity it accorded? That is very likely. But the Constitution is, after all, a blueprint for federal, and not local, government. Would the people surge forward united, based on a universal acceptance of that garbled, borderline incoherent statement of principle that was Galt's radio broadcast? It seems, to be charitable, unlikely. They would, as people do in that situation, abide.

One might construct an entire body of fiction around this alternate world. It is a pity that Rand declined to do so.

Where from Here?

We must assume that the inhabitants of Galt's Gulch have been assured by some sort of benchmark or omen that their return is likely to succeed. It seems rather implausible that it could have been in the spring following the collapse that is detailed in Rand's final chapter. How long before the warehouses run out? How long before the population gives up its sentimental attachment to Central Park and begins to migrate to where the food is? How long before the last gasoline pump runs dry and the last automobile's riders take to horseback? Our society is, at the test, quite a bit more resilient than one might think, a bounty offered a thankless people by the capitalists it affects to disdain. Let us say ten years.

Even this may be a bit abrupt. One annoying thing about Rand's social model is that it posits helplessness on the part of the ordinary citizen in the absence of guidance from the super-producers, something that is not borne out empirically. When that last gas pump runs dry, are we really to believe that no one in this country is capable of figuring out how to make a refinery work? Given that the technical manuals are still there and a hundred year old process is not in fact lost, is it not perfectly accessible to anyone who wishes to try? And in the absence of a stifling, confiscatory government, there will be profit to be had. There will be opportunity, and there will be free men and women to grasp it. And there will be capitalism, because that is the natural recourse of the unfettered.

The single suspension of disbelief necessary to make *Atlas Shrugged* work as a novel is that the genuine producers are so tiny in number that a single individual and a handful of friends may convince the lot of them to strike; that there even exists a super-elite whose absence is sufficient to make the entire system come crashing down. It may be a contrivance necessary for fiction, or it may be that Rand believed this with all her heart. The authors do not.

But let us remain within the boundaries of fiction. A decade later, let us imagine Galt's people finally ready to emerge from their bastion. They have wealth, they have expertise, and they have a moral code that enables the trust necessary for large scale economic transactions. What they don't have is a foothold, a necessary consequence of sequestration. Where do they start?

Colorado, of course.

Consider its advantages. First, there is physical proximity to Galt's Gulch in a time when travel has become highly unreliable. Second, there reside the remnants of the last, and presumably the most modern, of America's industrial development. Wyatt's wells are still there, and so are the numerous concerns whose needs were to have been met by the John Galt Line. The latter is, of course, torn up for its rail, but the most important part is that the roadbed still exists, the routes cleared, the rights-of-way established, and the human spirit that has produced it has not been extinguished.   Given resources, Dagny will have it operating again in weeks, not years.

Third, it's close to where the food is grown.   The existence of railroads was originally to move resources to consumers, wheat to the granaries and timber to the mills.   Kansas and Nebraska aren't starving, but they are only producing that which is sufficient to their local needs.   The cities are at the end of this logistics chain, not at its beginning.   That chain will be re-forged, extended once again to the hollow and empty concrete canyons of New York. But it starts in Colorado.

It will start with the re-occupation of the Wyatt fields, the re-population of the factories that produce necessities first, and luxuries only later when the economic surplus necessary to afford them is once again in place.   There will be tractors before there will be limousines, all paid for in product, financed in gold by the Mulligan Bank.

Towns and villages that have earned a hardscrabble existence from the land itself will find that they too have product to trade, wealth to earn, but only if they agree to trade with Colorado on Galtian terms.   Some with brute strength may be tempted to try to acquire that wealth by force, not trade.   The Coloradans will have to devise a means of collective security: force, as Rand proposed, guided by intelligence.   The ability to produce will not confer a magical safety; the Gulchers will find they have to fight for their freedom.   These things are not a function of talent or economics, they are inherent in the human condition.

They will likely prevail, not just because force guided by intelligence really does beat brute strength, but also because freedom is impossibly seductive, and that too is inherent in the human condition.   Even a brute knows it, envies it and will, given the chance, embrace it rather than destroy it.   Freedom is an intoxicant, an elixir, a permanent addiction.   A half-century of relentless propaganda could not stamp out its attraction even in the New Soviet Man.   Galt flashes gold, he propounds morality, but what he actually offers is freedom.   Prosperity is only a necessary consequence.

What a story it might be! Towns in Colorado, Kansas and Wyoming re-establish industry, technology and education, lit by the electricity that is a product of their own labor, the light beating back the darkness without. It will be a clarion call for the honest and a siren song for the looters who will still be practicing their bullying, lies and theft, and who will see in the new towns a new host for their parasitism. Danneskjøld has stated that he has committed his last act of violence. Poor fellow, he is impossibly naïve. Reason will prevail, yes, but reason alone and unarmed will not.

Galt's motor will play its part in presenting its possessors with a tremendous advantage in the beginning. In time it will be reverse-engineered – stolen – and cheap clones will be placed in the service of the looters just as Orren Boyle managed with Rearden Metal until a timely salvo from Ragnar Danneskjøld brought that process to a well deserved halt. Galt had better hope that the magic that turned his motor into dust upon unauthorized examination still works.

And at last it will be worth someone's while to rebuild the Taggart Bridge. It may be Dagny or her granddaughter, if Rand will allow her the blessing of offspring. And so to a new utopia? Probably not. For however excellent it is in the beginning, the rot will take hold from within once again if all of human history is any guide. Galt will be acclaimed a moral genius for a generation, two, perhaps ten, but that part of the human condition that is not *"the best that is within us"* will find its voice once more, and the conflict between producer, moocher and looter will once again rage. We are not, nor despite Rand's or Nietzsche's fondest fantasy, will we ever become, super-beings. Neither are we animals, but we are men and women. We learn, we enjoy, we grow complacent, we forget, and we pay for the lesson once again in blood. It isn't fiction, it is history.

The New Characters of the Post-Shrug World

Who will accomplish this act of economic and cultural sporulation? Unfortunately Rand does not give us a great number of clues in that direction. One of her major weaknesses as a

266

novelist is a distressing tendency toward static main characters; very few of them are a whit different at the novel's end than they were at the beginning. Francisco's character is revealed slowly but does not evolve. Galt's is a very rock of permanence. Dagny's only real change is in the identity of her lover of the moment, and Rearden at the end is the same as Rearden at the beginning, only happier because his external circumstances have changed. It is as if Rand is presenting a Galtian philosophical epiphany as an end state, an attainment of perfection.

Worse, those characters that do develop in the novel – Cherryl Taggart, Eddie Willers, Tony the Wet Nurse, even Jim Taggart after a fashion – all come to a rather unhappy end as a consequence. And so beyond the certainty that Francisco will mine in the diaspora to come, Wyatt drill, Galt engineer, and Dagny build railroads, we are left with very little to populate a cast of characters that must fill the roles that an expanding civilization will inevitably find wanting.

And so we'll have to find new characters or develop old ones into new roles. Perhaps Quentin Daniels will finish his tutelage under Galt's hand and find a talent for building radio sets and firearms. Perhaps Owen Kellogg will find a direction in life – he's a natural leader – and so one of those newborn towns will have him as its mayor, or its defender. Perhaps another will be led by a mysterious character named Floyd Kennedy, who is Fred Kinnan under a new identity. Perhaps Jeff Allen will make the transition from hobo to patriarch.

And maybe, just maybe, one night in Stockton, Colorado, before the gates of the town walls slam shut, a stranger with a backpack and a staff will stagger in out of the storm, and Francisco will take him into the shelter of a clapboard tavern lit by bare electric bulbs, sit him down, thrust a mug of ale into his hand and say, "Good to see you, Eddie. Welcome home."

Stranger things have happened.

Summary

Where does Rand leave us at the conclusion of this monumental work? Atlas has shrugged. The leadership of the revolution has filtered down from its progenitor, John Galt, through his closest circle of friends, through a class of achievers that encompasses the fields of science, engineering, construction, transportation, art and philosophy, to settle at last on the shoulders of the common citizen, who must bear the ultimate responsibility for choosing a life of mind or a life of "fake reality." That choice is still very much up in the air as the novel ends. The country is in chaos as the result of the strike of the men and women of the mind, and the resolution is to be found only through the adoption of a new moral code based on objective truth and rational dealings between men and women.

Galt is so certain of his victory in the last scene that he announces the return of the strikers. The denouement of the novel took place at the beginning of winter and the coda in the spring, but which spring? We cannot tell.

It's time then for a broader perspective on *Atlas Shrugged*. The structure of the novel is straightforward. There are three sections of ten chapters each. The arc of the plot ascends through a desperate effort of the industrialists to reignite the country's production, countered by moves on the part of the established powers in academia, bureaucracy and culture, descending in the final third of the book to the ravaging of the country and the escape of its creative elements. Let us recapitulate both Rand's narrative and the philosophy that it is intended to illuminate.

Part I: Non-Contradiction

The first third of the novel contains an introduction to characters, both protagonists and villains, and a description of the dynamic that exists between industrialist and bureaucrat, between objective philosopher and nihilist pretender. The world it describes is very much a creation of the latter in each case. We learn this from set-piece speeches at formal parties, from radio broadcasts and the other manifestations of popular culture, and from the mouths of the principals Rand casts as villains.

This section introduces us to our heroes, Dagny Taggart and Hank Rearden, and elaborates on their struggle to construct a railway that will support the last, best hope of the country with respect to industrial progress, resisted with an inexplicable stubbornness by those who, it would seem, would be its principal beneficiaries. It ends in triumph. Finding one another's arms and handing the Colorado industrialists their lifeline, Hank and Dagny obtain a victory that is known to be hollow even as it is accomplished. The section ends with the dissolution of the Colorado industrialists and the last, defiant, fiery gesture of Wyatt's Torch.

Within this section Rand defines the philosophical case of the looters. Economic inequities, which seem the result of achievement, are, in fact, the result of theft. Profit is immoral, extra value squeezed out of the consumer of goods and services beyond the latter's "natural" cost. This profit exists to feed the demands of greed and arrogance, and it is the rightful role of the State to control the greedy and arrogant in the interest of the collective. It is society – the collective – that has the ultimate claim on the fruits of the individual's labor, a claim it makes in the name of all. This culture is maintained by its promoters' control of the bureaucracy, academia, journalism and popular culture, through which a steady stream of propaganda beats the citizen into acceptance.

Within this set of premises is the notion that individuals who are achievers compose a class of their own, whose interests, motivated by greed, are inimical to the collective. Opposed to them is a ruling class whose task it is to rectify the theoretical theft by means of a real theft, and to redistribute the wealth to its source, the collective, taking a generous cut off the top for itself.

This is the case of the looters. Their methods are persuasion, law and naked force. They are secure in the knowledge that their enemies are law-abiding. They flatter themselves that they are equal in virtue to the producers as all are merely thieves. They feel superior to the producers as they are the more successful thieves. In a world where all economic activity is theft, success in

269

thievery is the logical summit of society and the rightful task of those who sit there.

We learn in this section that Rand regards human sexuality to be as much an expression of the mind as a steel bridge or a railroad track, the rightful property of the creative that has been suppressed and misrepresented in an effort to exercise power over them. In this sense, economic liberation is sexual liberation as well. Here Dagny becomes not simply Rand's protagonist, but her surrogate, and to a remarkable degree their own sexual lives run in parallel.

Part II: Either-Or

In the second section we are shown the philosophy of the looters in action as it methodically takes the country into its grip.

Dagny and Hank discover that, just as in Colorado, the entire country is beginning to crumble under the rapacious onslaught of the ever-hungry looters. And most remarkably, the producers who could be counted on to feed the parasites for the good of all are beginning to disappear. The host is weakening, and the parasites are growing apprehensive. They will do what they can to maintain the system, even at the cost of eliminating some of their fellow parasites and by inviting the hosts to share in their power – by feeding upon themselves.

But there is organized resistance to the conspiracy of looting. It is underground and its perpetrators are damned as agents of greed. Yet it is the parasites, the looters, who truly are the greedy ones. They will not stop until they control all production so that they may redistribute its fruits in places other than the pockets of those who actually earned them. That turns out to be their own pockets, the reward of cleverness and the righteousness of promoting social justice.

The philosophies of both looter and producer are based on self-interest, but that does not make them equivalent, nor is actual theft the equivalent of accused theft. One critical difference is that the thief must have the producer, but the converse is not true. The producer must create or there will be nothing to steal – he must live for the sake of the thief. For the code of theft that is this twisted social contract to function, he actually owes this to the thief on behalf of the collective of which they both are a part. That social contract requires the sanction of the victim. It will have no difficulty in procuring the sanction of the thief.

We understand in this section that someone, The Destroyer, is acting to break this social contract by withdrawing not only the sanction, but the physical presence of the victim. The section ends when the principals are about to meet The Destroyer.

Part III: A is A

In this section we learn at last Rand's conception of an ideal social contract, first by observing the activities of its proponents in a mini-utopia named Galt's Gulch, and later through an exhaustive rhetorical presentation. The main dramatic conflict arrives when the principals, Dagny and Hank, must run to completion the course that has caused the rest of the creative class to go on strike. The agonizing conclusion requires the abnegation of all that has kept them producing under the existing system. It is clear at last that it is the creators and producers who are the exploited and the ones who claim the exploited status, their oppressors. The things that have been earned – material wealth, family, social status, and most vital of all, the opportunity to create – must be rejected for the strike to have any chance of success.

In the end, they are. Dagny is admitted into the company of the strikers as the alpha female to Galt's alpha male. The rest accept comfortably subordinate positions. It is not, in the end, an egalitarian society even though predicated sternly on equal rights. It is a hierarchy built on relative technical excellence and moral virtue, and its citizens compete fiercely for primacy within their chosen fields.

This, then, is the case of Rand's heroes, and the foundation of a new philosophical approach to morality she termed Objectivism. We have examined its particulars in some detail, but briefly the idea is that human existence is based on reason and the recognition of the part of reason in the dealings of men and women with one another. The repository of both rights and responsibilities is within the individual, and no valid moral code may be based on one individual's right to demand that another live for his or her benefit.   There are no group rights; indeed, class identification is essentially a curiosity, and social mobility is unhindered by it, driven only by individual merit.

As we have seen, these are ideas developed during the philosophical period labeled the Enlightenment, and Rand is only to be considered a conservative in that she wishes to base her new utopia upon these old ideas.

As John Galt traces the Sign of the Dollar in the air, we leave the novel with the knowledge that a new world is to be built upon *laissez-faire* capitalism and human rights, based on reason and focused on the individual.   Rand's case is that it is the only system ever to have developed a surplus that offers the luxury of being second-guessed, scorned and looted.   For her that is its greatest testament.

Rand's Sources

We have stated that Rand has attempted to reconstruct the body of modern Western philosophy from first principles, which is broadly, but not entirely, the case.   She had a formal philosophical education in Russia before emigrating to the United States, and not only acknowledges, but pays open tribute, to Aristotle as her principal intellectual model.

Here we see the divergence between Rand's philosophy and the tremendous body of fictional narrative that is *Atlas Shrugged*, for her narrative runs very much along the lines of another philosopher, Nietzsche, with his insistence that human excellence creates a defense against nihilism and that the superior man or woman has, within certain limits, the right to make his or her own rules.   This dynamic between philosophy and narrative, between reason and passion, between Aristotle and Nietzsche, runs the entire length of the novel, and in the end it is up to the reader to resolve it – or not. It is that demand which takes the novel out of the category of popular fiction and into the realm of serious intellectual consideration.

Rand's Style

Ayn Rand was the adult identity of the Russian girl named Alisa Zinov'yevna Rosenbaum, for whom English was not a native language. It is a testament to her linguistic abilities that she mastered English to the point at which she could support herself as a professional screenwriter and playwright in the depths of the Great Depression. This was a signal accomplishment, and by the time she began writing *Atlas Shrugged* she already had one best-selling novel, *The Fountainhead*, to her credit. For this reason we must search for another source for those odd quirks that catch the modern reader's eye, such as the use of the formal "one" for the vernacular "you" in the mouths of her least educated characters, a fondness for the formal "perish" in place of the more common "die", and a correct, but somewhat strained, insistence on "you'll" in the place of "you" in informal conversation. Further, that even her least educated and most despicable villains tend to present their ideas in the form of logical propositions that would not be out of place at an Oxford formal dinner.

These are not fatal flaws; they are scarcely to be considered flaws at all, but stamps of the author's fiercely analytical approach to human intercourse. That analytical approach is not always happily applied, especially when it comes to the description of the vagaries of human sexual relations. Here the conflict between narrative and philosophy is most sharply defined – we rejoice that Dagny and Galt have found one another but are dismayed at the strange rationalizations that attempt to bring their joyful and vigorous sexual attraction within the realm of analytical reason. Rand's narrative describes the lovers with convincing verisimilitude; her philosophy struggles to account for them. If, in the end, we suspect that there is something more than reason going on here, we have Rand the story-teller to thank and leave Rand the philosopher to be furious about it.

The Faults of *Atlas Shrugged*

It's too long, for one thing. Each of the protagonists has his turn before the podium, but because they are of an identical philosophical stance, their various expressions of it tend to blend into one another. In fiction there is no need to hear the same idea expressed in many different ways in the mouths of sundry proponents. In philosophy, or more accurately in the teaching of philosophy, there is.

Lest we lose sight of Rand's objective here, it is not simply to give the reader a rousing adventure ride, but didactic: to teach. If the same philosophical or moral point takes various shapes, it is the teacher's hope that the student will apprehend one of them. For a novelist this is wasteful; for a didact it is indispensable.

There is, of course, the matter of The Speech. As a literary construction it is disastrous, an enormous, immobile rock of idea placed in the middle of a stream of plot. Despite Rand's best effort to make it accessible, it is dense, complicated and challenging. It does not advance the plot, it stalls it, but it is the reason for the plot's existence.

The Speech is the finish of the novel of ideas; the ensuing three chapters compose the resolution of the narrative. It is a unique and somewhat clumsy construction, but it does appear to serve its purpose.

We have mentioned Rand's tendency to present her protagonists as having achieved a degree of philosophical enlightenment that prevents their characters from developing much in the novel. Her heroes are far more static than her villains, who undergo a relentless and pitiless exposition, but who in the end must appear more finely drawn as a result.

Like many novelists, Rand has been accused of being cruel to her minor characters. We have seen the Wet Nurse mocked nearly up to his last breath, Cherryl Taggart hounded over a precipice and into a watery grave, and most poignant of all, the abandonment of the loyal, able and virtuous Eddie Willers along a deserted track in the Arizona desert. The elite protagonists bask in their perfection and seem to shade their eyes against the glare of a glorious future while standing on a mountain of bones of those who did not live to make the journey. One understands that such a monumental project will have its victims; one waits in vain for the heroes of the piece to acknowledge them.

Atlas Shrugged's Place in Modern Literature

Flawed as it is, *Atlas Shrugged* succeeds brilliantly as a novel of ideas. It has an acknowledged appeal to young people in that it presents a clean, workable system of ideals on which to base a moral approach to the world. Its coherence, certitude and outrageous political incorrectness appeal to the rebel in young and old. In it the complications of parenthood do not arise; the difficulties in accommodating ideals that in practical application, eventually conflict, are nowhere to be found. It is not necessarily a young person's novel, but it is an idealist's novel.

If *Atlas Shrugged*'s critics tend to accentuate its flaws and ignore its message, they do so at the risk of echoing the absurdities of Rand's villains: the collectivist, the nihilist, the person whose education and reputation exceed his or her actual intelligence. Most timeless about *Atlas Shrugged* are the culture and character of its villains. Five decades after its publication, their voices still sound in the mouths of its detractors and of public servants who solemnly repeat the platitudes without considering their sources. They need to check their premises.

15 August 2009

Suggested Reading

For its time, *Atlas Shrugged* was a unique admixture of philosophy and politics, and it is difficult to begin an understanding of Rand's great work of synthesis by going straight to the original sources. Fortunately there is a more graduated approach available, for many of the same issues and influences that crystallized in *Atlas Shrugged* were the topic of one of the great philosophical popularizers of the late 20th Century, Mortimer Adler. Through a lengthy career he touched on nearly all of the constituents of Rand's magnum opus.

By Adler and recommended in the area of philosophy:

* *Aristotle for Everybody: Difficult Thought Made Easy* (1978)

* *Ten Philosophical Mistakes* (1985)

Economics:

* *The Capitalist Manifesto* (introduction for Louis Kelso's work) (1958)

* *Haves Without Have-Nots: Essays for the 21st Century on Democracy and Socialism* (1991)

Political science:

* *We Hold These Truths: Understanding the Ideas and Ideals of the Constitution* (1987)

And toward religion:

* *How To Think About God: A Guide for the 20th-Century Pagan* (1980)

For the reader already acquainted with the ideas illuminated by Adler:

- *Knowledge and Decisions* and *Marxism*, both by Thomas Sowell. Capitalism versus Communism, in contention for the soul of the 20th Century, by a genius who understands both.

- *Animal Farm* – George Orwell. Sweet and succinct, this novella speaks directly to the inevitable corruption of a ruling class and the fate of those trusting enough to place it in a position of authority.

- *A History of Western Philosophy* – Bertrand Russell. A work of stunning brilliance and the ruthless application of common sense in the pursuit of truth, this encapsulates all of Rand's intellectual sources and quite a bit more.

These can also form a foundation for the consideration of Rand's primary sources:

- *Metaphysics* – Aristotle. Rand got a good deal more than her section titles from this seminal work.

- *Thus Spake Zarathustra* – Friedrich Nietzsche. Surprisingly readable given its occasionally jarring content, but often indirect and allusive. Christians are as shocked by his repudiation of God as socialists are by his repudiation of egalitarianism. The latter, however, seem to recover rather more quickly once that inconvenient principle is dispensed with.

- *Groundwork for the Metaphysics of Morals* – Immanuel Kant. Not Kant's best-known work – which would be the *Critique of Pure Reason*, also recommended – but the one in which he derives his own system of ethics after a pattern that readers of *Atlas Shrugged* may find familiar. Rand rejected Kant's conclusions, but they seem similar enough to hers to lead certain of her followers at the Objectivist Institute to suggest that she may have protested a bit too much.

- *The Communist Manifesto* – Karl Marx, Friedrich Engels. Indispensable in understanding the appeal of socialism both in terms of class analysis and emotive appeal.

Lastly, for those interested in the grand narrative of the rise and fall of civilizations and their struggle to rise once more we have two recommendations, one fictional, one historical:

- *The Foundation Trilogy* – Isaac Asimov. Future history informed by the patterns of the past, and what happens when something comes along that breaks the mold.

- *The Decline and Fall of the Roman Empire* – Edward Gibbon. A truly magisterial work, it is the story of how the modern world came to be after Rome fell and Constantinople struggled to survive. Six volumes, twelve hundred years of history – there really isn't anything quite like it.

This isn't a laundry list – each of these has a direct hook into the immense intellectual currents that swirl underneath the surface of *Atlas Shrugged*. It would be an easy task to triple its length; far more difficult to cut it.

Works Cited in this Volume:

The Driver – Garet Garrett , 1922

Ayn Rand: The Russian Radical – Chris Matthew Sciabarra, 1995

Beyond Good and Evil – Friedrich Nietzsche, 1886

"Interview with the Vamp" Reason Magazine, August/September 1995

The Journals of Ayn Rand – Leonard Piekoff, 1999

The Revolution Betrayed – Leon Trotsky, 1936

Notebooks, Summer 1886 - Fall 1887 – Friedrich Nietzsche

The Myth of Sisyphus – Albert Camus, 1942

Introduction to the 35th anniversary edition of *Atlas Shrugged* – Leonard Peikoff, 1992

On Power – Bertrand de Jouvenel, 1993

My Favorite Intermissions – Victor Borge, 1971

The Poison of Subjectivism – C. S. Lewis, 1932

And last but very much not least, Dr. David Kelley for his invaluable outline of John Galt's speech, available for perusal on the Objectivist Center website (www.objectivistcenter.org)

CPSIA information can be obtained
at www.ICGtesting.com
Printed in the USA
LVOW04s0242080116
469670LV00019B/1238/P

9 781482 654493